Groucho and W. C. Fields
Huckster Comedians

The antiheroic side of two hucksters: W. C. Fields is victimized by his wooden nemesis, Charlie McCarthy, while Groucho Marx is pursued by his forever derailing brothers, Chico and Harpo.

Studies in Popular Culture
M. Thomas Inge, General Editor

Groucho and W. C. Fields

Huckster Comedians

Wes D. Gehring

University Press of Mississippi
Jackson

Library of Congress Cataloging-in-Publication Data

Gehring, Wes. D.
    Groucho and W. C. Fields : Huckster comedians / Wes D. Gehring.
      p.   cm. – (Studies in popular culture)
    Includes bibliographical references and index.
    ISBN 0-87805-724-2 (cloth). – ISBN 0-87805-725-0 (pbk.)
    1. Marx, Groucho, 1891–1977—Criticism and interpretation.
    2. Fields, W. C., 1879–1946—Criticism and interpretation.
    I. Title. II. Series: Studies in popular culture (Jackson, Miss.)
    PN2287.M53G44 1994
    791.43'028'092273—dc20   94-18366
                                                      CIP

British Library Cataloging-in-Publication data available

TO
HUMORIST
Viv Sade
AND
SCHOLAR AND MENTOR
Tom Inge

CONTENTS

"We're making motion picture history here."
—Egbert Sousé (W. C. Fields), as a substitute
film director in *The Bank Dick* (1940)

PREFACE AND
ACKNOWLEDGMENTS

The key objective of this study is to compare and contrast the flimflam comic shtick and antiheroic humor of W. C. Fields and Groucho Marx during the golden age of American sound film comedy, the period sandwiched between the 1929 stock-market crash and the country's 1941 entry into World War II. The study also explores possible con artist and antihero roots for the two comedians in various popular culture sources, and the lives of the men themselves.

There is, of course, no single correct "reading" of artists Fields and Marx. Each critiquing author or film viewer brings his or her special perspective to a master work and learns from the work, ideally, as much about himself or herself as about the comic art. While it should never be forgotten that comedy analysis is another way of celebrating laughter, I hope that this critical study underscores anew the cultural significance of Fields and Marx.

In many ways this book began with a 1950s childhood watching these comedians' films on television. It reached another level when I did analytical biographies of Fields and the Marx brothers, and of some of their comedy contemporaries, including Charlie Chaplin, Laurel and Hardy, Robert Benchley, and director Leo McCarey. Consequently, the work in hand is a natural progression of my interest in and study of these comic artists. Much of it would have been impossible, however, without several important archives and their invariably helpful staffs, including the New York Public Library system, which houses the Billy Rose Theater Collection; the Library of Congress (particularly the Manuscript Division, the Motion Picture, Broadcasting and Recorded Sound Division, and the Library Reading Room); the Margaret Herrick Library at the Academy of Motion Picture Arts and Sciences (Beverly Hills); the American Film Institute (Beverly Hills); the UCLA Theatre Arts Library within its University Research Library (Los Angeles); the University of Iowa's Special Collections Library and its main library (Iowa City); and Ball State University's Bracken Library (Muncie, Indiana).

All stills, except Figure 1 and the frontispiece caricatures, were provided by the Lester Glassner collection. The exceptions are from the author's archives. The Charles Bruno drawings of Fields and Charlie McCarthy originally accompanied the November 1937 *Screen Book* magazine article "W. C. Fields Wins by a NOSE!" The Marx Brothers caricature first appeared with the February 1936 *Photoplay* piece "Those Mad Marx Hares."

Since the germination period for this book has covered many years, there is hardly space for all the individual thank-yous. But a few people stand out. My longtime editor, M. Thomas Inge, helped make this and several of my other books possible. My department chairperson, "Dr. Joe" Misiewicz, assisted with both release time and facilitating university financial help. Teaching colleague Gary Meunier provided helpful suggestions. Janet Warrner, my typist and general troubleshooter, was forever available and helpful. And Kathy Huggler provided further copy editing.

Friends and family were ever supportive, with daughters Sarah and Emily always available for Fields and Marx screenings.

**Groucho and W. C. Fields
Huckster Comedians**

"Remember, folks, cast a vote for Fields and watch for the silver lining. Cast several votes for Fields and watch for the police."
  —W. C. Fields (*Fields For President*)

"If you write about yourself, the slightest deviation makes you realize instantly there may be honor among thieves, but you are just a dirty liar."
  —Groucho Marx (*Groucho and Me*)

CHAPTER 1   Introduction

In the 1930s, depression America went off the gold standard, but gold resurfaced in the decade's film comedy, from W. C. Fields—truth with a potato nose—to the leader of America's own particular brand of Marxism—Groucho. In W. C. country, the national bird was the "little chickadee" and the national anthem "Godfrey Daniel." Groucho country was more a socialism of silliness.

Although W. C. Fields and Groucho Marx are seldom bracketed together outside their common 1930s film comedian status, a four-part comparison significantly extends the analytical boundaries of what we already know about them and the period.

Their dominant entertainment personas are classic variations on American hucksters of decidedly different eras. The tough times of the 1930s encouraged the comedy popularity of harder, older, and more cynical comedians like W. C. and Groucho. This worldly slant was in direct contrast to the previous decade and its favored film comedians. Both the 1920s and its movie clowns were generally youthful and optimistic, a phenomenon best exemplified by the Jazz Age's top comedy box-office draw—Harold Lloyd's bespectacled go-getter character.

In contrast, Fields's comedy characterization was often in the tradition of the late-nineteenth-century carnival show sharpie (approximating the era of America's last depression, the 1890s). His huckster was a second cousin to both the slick Yankee peddler and the inspired comic charlatans who had populated the humor of the Old Southwest earlier in the nineteenth century (see Chapter 2). Fields robustly embraced the Southwest's tall tale and any or all earthy humor this might entail, as in his recurring *Mississippi* (1935) yarn about his days as an Indian fighter, when he took down his old Bowie knife and "cut a path through a wall of living flesh."

Fields as huckster had surfaced full-blown in the 1923 Broadway hit *Poppy*. He went on to essay frequent variations of this methodically flamboyant figure (Professor Eustace McGargle) throughout his career. Famous for a drawling verbal slapstick dripping with the comically overstated language of the nineteenth-century romantic novel, he physically complemented this with a graceful visual slapstick born of his early juggling days. And, as film historian Gerald Mast has suggested, Fields often used his grandiose language just as he used his grandiose huckster clothing to disguise his crooked intentions (266). Fields was capable of the fully outrageous con, such as selling a "talking dog" at the opening of the sound-film adaptation of *Poppy* (1935). But his typical scams remained in the world of everyday reality, from the shell game featured so prominently in *Sally of the Sawdust* (1925), the silent-film version of *Poppy*, to hoodwinking his landlady out of rent money in *The Old Fashioned Way* (1934).

Groucho, in contrast, was the updated twentieth-century huckster. And the stakes were now much higher, whether the mustachioed one was president of a college (*Horse Feathers*, 1932) or a country (*Duck Soup*, 1933). Indeed, Groucho's comic paranoia about the intentions of his *Duck Soup* enemies has direct satirical ties to the later black-humor insanity of *Dr. Strangelove*'s (1964) General Jack Ripper (Sterling Hayden), who believes fluoridated water is a Soviet plot to assist in the takeover of America. And General Jack's views result in a slapstick Apocalypse, certainly in keeping with the comic irreverence of the nihilistic Groucho and his brothers.

Befitting faster times, Groucho's shyster had a saturation comedy tongue that spewed out words and assorted puns at the speed of comic sound. In a Groucho world, the message was that nothing was as it seems, and this was especially true of his language. And as if to compensate for this Groucho verbal monopoly, one brother, Harpo, spoke not a word. The joy of the pun is the suggestion that nothing is going unsaid. Like Groucho's direct address, to be examined in Chapter 4, his puns stop time and remind the audience that things are not as they seem.

Another pivotal comparison that draws Fields and Marx together focuses on a figure of frustration. Though the two are most identified with the con artist, both also showed an antiheroic side. It was most obvious with Fields, who periodically played whole films in this character, notwithstanding an occasional bit of larceny coming through. For instance, when Fields's celebrated antiheroic husband in *It's a Gift* (1934) is forced by his wife to share a sandwich with their brat of a son, the comedian bends the meat onto his side before dividing the bread.

While Groucho did not fluctuate between huckster and antiheroic roles as did Fields, the otherwise dominating Groucho invariably played antihero to his brothers. Thus, by studying the comedy duos within the Marx team (especially Groucho and Chico), one sees the normally comic "King Leer" in continuous comic defeat. Prime examples would include Chico's inability to stop at merely pump-priming bids in *The Cocoanuts* (1929), ruining Groucho's Florida land auction, and the tootsie-fruitsie ice cream scene in *A Day at the Races* (1937), where Chico sells Groucho a "library" of unnecessary betting books. The most other-worldly illustration, however, appropriately draws upon eccentric Harpo. In *Duck Soup*'s (1933) classic mirror scene, Harpo, comically disguised as Groucho in his nightgown and cap, magically passes as his brother's reflection. It is funny and somehow fitting that the invincible huckster Groucho should be vulnerable only to his brothers—like a "superman" comedian who is just one of the boys among the Kryptonite crowd. Groucho is the ultimate example of how one can just never get too self-important among family. For this reason, M-G-M's mid-1930s attempt to tone down the team, making Groucho and Harpo particularly susceptible to the outsider, was a misreading of their comedy personas (see Chapter 3).

Though not a primary focus of this book, another antiheroic characteristic is also periodically evident in the films of W. C. and Groucho: comic absurdity bordering on the surreal. (In fact, during the thirties, the antiheroic style was known as "lunatic" comedy.) The Marx brothers are better known as creators of absurdity— beating a world gone mad at its own game—and Groucho's victimization by his brothers is also frequently nonsensical. For example, in *Animal Crackers* (1930) Chico wants to question people in the house next door. When Groucho replies, "Suppose there isn't any house next door," Chico calmly answers, "Well, then, of course we got to build one." With Harpo, it is more a product of his bizarre otherworldly nature, from his *Duck Soup* tattoo that comes alive and startles Groucho (and the film audience) to the innumerable surprises he pulls from his magic pockets.

Though Fields is not as readily linked to the surreal as are the Marxes, surrealism is an occasional presence in his work. Examples include the cello that *gives birth* to illegitimate little bass fiddles in *The Barber Shop* (1933) and the movie-within-a-movie plot in *Never Give a Sucker an Even Break* (1941), which allows a parachuteless Fields to dive out of an airborne plane to retrieve a bottle of liquor!

W. C. and Groucho are also linked in terms of their ability to utilize variations on the huckster/antihero base (as well as elements of the traditional American crackerbarrel figure) to succeed in such other media as print, radio, and television. In Marx's case, success in other media even allowed him to develop a new persona, a phenomenon I explored in the article "Television's Other Groucho" (Gehring, 267–82). Naturally, the comedian's *You Bet Your Life* quizmaster had comedy components viewers had seen before, especially (with the program's long run) the antiheroic, self-deprecating humor associated with his age—as when, for example, he told a guest who worked as a blood analyst, "Don't look at me unless you analyze Geritol." Still, his TV character was a consciously toned down, more realistic persona that fit a "cooler" medium relying on relatively more audience involvement, à la Marshall McLuhan's famous distinction. An overly demonstrative performer, such as the movie Groucho, suited the "hot" motion-picture medium, with its high-definition, information-laden image, but would not have worn as well on television.

A final shared tie between Fields and Marx (and the foundation upon which the preceding three comparisons are built) is a shared late-nineteenth-century upbringing that paralleled both the heyday of the P. T. Barnum huckster and the birth of the modern comic antihero. Though I am not aware of the analogy having previously been made, it seems more than fitting that American humor's golden age of the con artist (what I discuss in Chapter 2 as the "individualization of manifest destiny") is immediately followed by the mainstream emergence of the ultimate figure of frustration—the comic antihero. Thus, one has moved from the manipulator king to the most manipulated character in seemingly less time than it takes to lose in the old shell game.

Fields and Marx were not only of this transition period, their often-deprived early years (crowded immigrant urban backdrops) had them simultaneously wearing huckster/antihero hats. For people born into underdog settings, using a con was part getting ahead and part simple survival. Both W. C. and Groucho assimilated these lessons at a tender age (see Chapter 3).

The analysis of these W. C.-Groucho parallels adds to our understanding of two remarkable American comedians and the eras within which they worked and may serve as a springboard toward granting them greater recognition as innovative comedy figures (particularly Fields's antiheroic work and Marx's darkly modern con artist). It is past time to concede these two artists the "literary" status an earlier age bestowed upon the traditional print author.

My favorite analogous argument is film theorist André Bazin's interrelating of Chaplin's screen alter ego Charlie with epic characters of literature: "For hundreds of millions of people on this planet he [Charlie] is like a Ulysses or Roland in other civilizations" (144). A character of this type transcends any one story or collection of stories, whether they are printed or cinematic. Such a character has withstood the test of time, and the works in which he or she is showcased are "read" and "reread" through the years. The essence of this is supported by the writings of *Cahiers du Cinéma* theorist Alexandre Astrue, especially his celebrated essay "The Birth of a New Avant-Garde: La Caméra-Stylo." The metaphor of "caméra-stylo" (camera-pen) implies that film is meant to go beyond the movie "image for its own sake . . . to become a means of writing just as flexible and subtle as a written language" (18). Thus, the extra filmic significance an epic character brings to cinema frees the medium from the immediate frame-by-frame demands of the story. Without trying to be sacrilegious about what constitutes traditional literature, the comic art of W. C. Fields and Groucho Marx is more familiar to the general public than is most written literature, and it has been for some time.

"It is good to be shifty in a new country."
—Johnson J. Hooper,
Simon Suggs' Adventures

"In America there are two classes of
travel—first class and with children."
—Robert Benchley, Pluck and Luck

CHAPTER 2 **Background of the American Comic Con Artist and the Antihero**

Con artist, confidence man, grifter, huckster, diddler . . . whatever the name, the type has been around as long as there have been people. In his comic 1844 essay on the phenomenon, "Diddling: Considered as One of the Exact Sciences," Edgar Allan Poe observes, "To diddle is his [Man's] destiny. . . .This is his aim—his object— his end. Perhaps the first diddler was Adam" (367, 369). Although most associated with the horror genre, Poe was both a student of the diddle and an active practitioner. For instance, his essay "The Balloon Hoax," about a fictitious three-day crossing of the Atlantic, was originally published as fact in the *New York Sun* newspaper. But Poe was just as apt to play diddler detective. In "Maelzel's Chess-Player," he offers a huckster's explanation as to how this "mechanical" figure seated at a box (a popular period attraction) could play chess: by hiding a small chess player inside.

Poe is an excellent starting point for discussing the con man. His "Diddling" essay provides amusing insight on the subject, and personal-slant companion pieces by other authors of this huckster genre are hard to find. Of course, as befits the topic, one should not accept everything at face value. For instance, even the essay's full title, "Diddling: Considered as One of the Exact Sciences," is a Poe in-joke on the reader, as his hoax pieces always play on a period public being more susceptible to a con if everything seems terribly *scientific.*

Poe's work appears early in what might be called *the* huckster time and place: nineteenth-century America. Literary historian Susan Kuhlmann nicely describes the era's con artist as the "individualization of manifest destiny . . . the belief that a free man may be whatever he claims he is, may have whatever his skills can win" (6). Kuhlmann goes on to suggest that the characteristics of those who "opened" our country—resourcefulness, adaptability, nomadic tendencies, and a desire to get ahead—also describe the con man. While most cultures, past and present, have no doubt had confidence men, there is recognition even outside this country of nineteenth-century America's special affinity for the genre.

Indeed, in 1855 French commentator Charles Baudelaire linked this country's fascination with and fondness for the con man with the fact that "Americans love so much to be fooled" (Matterson, xviii). That might seem a strange claim to the contemporary reader, but literary historian Stephen Matterson bolsters the position by citing the great period success and popularity of America's greatest real-life huckster—P. T. Barnum. Barnum's autobiography, *Struggles and Triumphs*, which first appeared in 1855 and was revised and updated throughout the showman's long life, is generally considered the most widely read book in America (after the Bible) during the second half of the nineteenth century. His biography represents a blueprint for success based on an affectionate kidding of the public. And while the reader might note examples of the public responding favorably to a Barnum diddle, as when twenty-four thousand people turned out for a "Grand Buffalo Hunt" that actually featured only a very modest herd of yearling buffaloes (126), the real thrust of his book and conning career, as huckster historian Gary Lindberg suggests, finds the public "paying to be entertained" (187).

One might liken the Barnum attraction, such as his famous exhibition of an alleged mermaid, to an elaborate practical joke, something his autobiography frequently notes the showman had also long enjoyed doing in private. In fact, early in the book Barnum gives great significance to an elaborate practical joke his grandfather played upon him. This gentleman, for whom Phineas Taylor Barnum was fittingly named, had gifted his grandson early with property—one "Ivy Island." As time passed, much was made of the child's wealth by friends and family. Eventually, while still a youngster, Barnum visited his island, which turned out to be worthless property near a swamp. Though this "gift" might seem cruel to some, the conning conspiracy necessary to bring it off seems to have fascinated the young Barnum, possibly because the conspirators continued in character for a time, even after the hoax was exposed. For example, his mother "hoped [the land's] richness had fully equaled my anticipations" (Barnum 55).

Further emphasizing the timeliness of Poe's 1840s huckster-writing and Barnum's 1850s self-promotion is the date of July 7, 1849, which might be fixed as the single day when the huckster phenomenon best caught the American public interest (Kuhlman, 4–5). On this day, one William Thompson was arrested in New York City for his own special brand of diddling. The *New York Herald's* July 8, 1849, account stated the "genteel-appearing" Thompson would stop a "stranger in the street" and engage in conversation ("Arrest of the Confidence Man," 227). Eventually he would ask, " 'Have you confidence in me to trust me with your watch until tomorrow?' " The *Herald* then noted that when responding to Thompson's "novel request," the stranger often assumed Thompson "to be some old acquaintance, not at the moment recollected," and "supposing it to be a joke," would comply with the proposal.

From the Thompson case and its media attention the phrase "confidence man" entered the language (Lindberg, 6). A period defense of American vulnerability (even among New Yorkers) to the con artist soon surfaced, one on which Thompson was no doubt "banking." That is, as an August 18, 1849 article in *Literary World* stated, for a swindler to be so successful "shows that all virtue and humanity of nature is not entirely extinct in the nineteenth century" (Duyckinck 228). The tendency for the American public to be easily hoodwinked compliments the *trusting* nature of the people.

A supplementary reason Poe is an interesting point of departure for discussing the American huckster can be found in examples from his pivotal "Diddling" essay, which includes a repertoire of huckster stories that work on several levels. There is the pure celebration inherent in Poe's sharing of classic cons. As literary critic Daniel

Hoffman notes, "Poe tells his diddling yarns with obvious relish, the joy, in fact, of the diddler himself" (181). Like a parody artist having affectionate fun with a favored target genre, Poe's enthusiasm for the task at hand entertainingly belies his alleged "Exact Sciences" approach. Poe's selections also provide a historical survey of what were then already accepted popular-culture diddler tales. Lastly, as suggested by the venerated axiom "everything old is new again," Poe's historical survey also seems to act as a source for future huckster talks. For instance, the first example on Poe's list involves diddling a church camp-meeting. Just a few years after Poe's essay appeared, Southwest humorist Johnson J. Hooper penned his classic 1849 con artist story, "Simon Suggs Attends a Camp-Meeting," with predictably profitable results (which will be addressed shortly).

Another argument for Poe as huckster-starting-point is the analogy that the modern American artist, especially the writer, often indulges in a variety of hoaxes. This is made possible by the premise that a "work of fiction is a kind of contract between reader and author (Matterson, xvii). The reader places confidence in what the storyteller relates. Yet Poe was a pioneer in manipulating that confidence—a pioneer in suckering the too-accepting reader into truths he or she might not otherwise have examined, had it not been for some conning "fiction."

Such confidence-men artists also have the "nasty habit of revealing the worm in the American Eden apple; he's mostly got a worm, or a snake, eating away at his own conflicted heart" (Murphy 75). That is, it is payback time for these artists, who often feel hoodwinked themselves by some aspect of the forever-elusive American dream. And the worm eating at Poe might be called another American artistic precedent—scorn "directed against a nation which refuses to support the profession of letters because [it is] too exclusively intent upon the making of money" (Hoffman, 182).

The metaphorical worm eating away at the artist's heart might also be exemplified by keying upon one of this study's focus comedians: W. C. Fields. He suffered from a persecution complex that was not without some basis in fact—after all, he (like Groucho) had been cheated out of pay in vaudeville's lower echelons, and had seen his material cut savagely (as when Ziegfeld demanded more time for his show girls and when Hollywood producers excised the very scenes that particularly bewitched W. C., such as the one about the dying trapeze mother). Thus, Fields saw his eventual critical and commercial success along the lines of the title for his 1939 film, *You Can't Cheat an Honest Man*. Such a personalized reading of this old huckster precept adds a poignant real-life wrinkle that is as much quiet moxie as creative scam. *He had survived*. And we inadvertently celebrate that survival as we laugh with his screen huckster.

A final reason for the attractiveness of Poe when discussing the American diddler is the high-profile mysteriousness of the man himself; his own manipulative persona overshadowed even his writing. Besides his inventive claims of a noble heritage, or his patented eccentric behavior, "Poe seems willing not only to burlesque his own serious themes but to capitalize on the suspicion that he is a trickster" (Lindberg 62). Thus, it is fitting that Poe surfaces as a character in what is argumentatively still the most ambitious novel ever dedicated to the huckster genre—Herman Melville's long-neglected *The Confidence-Man*.

Melville's 1857 book, inspired in part by the aforementioned real case of William Thompson (and by the world of P. T. Barnum), features a shipboard Confidence Man transforming himself into eight different figures. The brief appearance of the Poe-inspired character occurs when the Cosmopolitan (the final disguise of the Confidence Man) is debating the philosophy of fellow passenger Mark Winsome (representing Emerson) (230). Critic Harrison Hayford convincingly suggests that the unnamed figure who interrupts them symbolizes the late-in-life Poe attempting to raise money for a projected literary review (344–53).

One level of the subtle ironic humor represented in the scene is that Winsome refuses to buy a literary pamphlet from the Poe figure, fearing he is a huckster, and warns the Cosmopolitan of this concern: "I take him for a cunning vagabond, who picks up a vagabond living by adroitly playing the madman" (231). But the individual whom Winsome is warning is, of course, actually the Confidence Man himself, a figure many critics have equated with the devil.

A second darker layer to the scene would be to interpret it as representing the concern Melville scholar Hennig Cohen "reads" throughout the book: "how to live in a world in which nothing is what it appears to be, in which the only thing knowable is that nothing can be known, and the only thing believable is that nothing can be believed" (Melville, Introduction, x). Certainly this darker level is suggested in the novel by Melville's troubling description of the alleged Poe figure as a desperate character, part "inspired-looking man," part "crazy beggar" (230). There is no definite reason for the portrayal, but critic Hershel Parker offers a provocative yet feasible answer: "If this attitude seems to display inhumanity toward poor Poe, one must suppose that Melville was well enough aware of similarities to himself in the picture" (Hayford 353). One might dovetail this explanation back to the earlier characterization (Murphy 75) of the huckster artist suffering through a private angst over the false illusions of life—and ultimately, in the case of Poe and Melville, over having their literary greatness go unappreciated by the public.

Beyond the shifty nature one associates with Melville's Confidence Man, the character represents the ability to survive through change—which very much speaks to the nineteenth-century American experience. Melville suggests that life is a costume party where all the disguised guests should be prepared to play the fool. To do any less (sans costume and a sense of humor) makes one a burden both to oneself and to the party. Moreover, to not join the masquerade suggests an eventual inability to survive. Thus the huckster's ongoing adaptation is synonymous with "Yankee ingenuity," one of the celebrated components of the American experience. But to play the *devil*'s advocate—and what better place than with the sometimes Lucifer-like Confidence Man—a more troubling interpretation of the costume-party metaphor might suggest that behind one's many masks there is no real identity. And what is success if the individual is lost?

The dark side of the huckster artist will be expanded upon later in the text. For now, it is enough to say that Poe represents, as defined through this section, a kind of diddler poster boy for a genre much closer to mainstream Americana than most Americans would acknowledge.

The huckster is as old as time. But his mainstream American emergence might best be tied to two schools of humor—the New England Yankee and the sly frontier character of the Old Southwest, both of which would fall under the comic umbrella of the capable cracker-barrel figure. Pioneer humor historian Walter Blair dates the heyday of both camps from 1830 to 1867, labeling author Seba Smith's Yankee Jack Downing as representing an approximate starting point for American humor (*Native American Humor*, 38, 39, 62).

The Yankee is rich, however, in American antecedents, be it the real figure of Benjamin Franklin (1706–90) or the character of Jonathan in Royal Tyler's comedy play *The Contrast* (1787), "the first full portrait of the New-England-man. The earliest attempt at characterizing the real American" (Tandy 2).

However, even more influential were the farmers' almanacs of the time, such as the *Old Farmer's Almanac* of R. B. Thomas (1766–1846), started in 1793, which was "perhaps the most popular publication of its kind in the early years of the century. Thomas . . . hit upon the idea of putting advice [shades of Benjamin Franklin's Poor Richard] to rural readers . . . into the form of salty [comic] speeches presumably made by actual farmers" (Blair 19).

Early comic historian Constance Rourke argued that uniqueness for America and the character of the Yankee came through the guise of Smith's Jack Downing: "The Yankee emerged in a new role, as oracle" (23). Prior to this the Yankee had been thinly drawn, more the butt of the joke than its originator. Of equal importance, the long-legged patriot Downing became the model for the United States's unofficial logo, Uncle Sam.

Though it might seem that Yankee antecedents—whether Tyler's play or Thomas's almanac—are not given the significance of Smith's Downing, early comedy historians are unified in their "reading" of Jack Downing. For example, pioneering humor scholar Jennette Tandy declares that with Smith's character the "lowly Yankee first took an important place in American political and social satire" (2).

The bottom line on this character, about which there is no debate (and which frequently tied him directly to the huckster), was his cagey capability. He could take care of himself, à la "Yankee ingenuity," all of which eventually became synonymous with the American archetype—Uncle Sam.

Historian Blair called this capability "horse sense," even entitling a study *Horse Sense in American Humor* (1942). The character had "learned everything from experience. When he gets into a new situation, he whittles his problem down to its essentials, sees how it compares with situations in his past and how it differs from them, and then he thinks out what he should do—figures out the right answer" (vii).

A key insight of huckster historian Lindberg's research is most applicable at this point: "Industriousness and cunning complement each other; they are not alternatives" (97). Put another way, there have always been two angles to the American success (or self-made man) story—perseverance *and anything* is fair if it succeeds, a most fitting philosophy for the comedy worlds of Groucho Marx and W. C.

Fields. Other comedians have also worked these waters, but none had a persona so tied to fraudulent funniness. Through the years, however, Americans have tended to emphasize perseverance. It was not that nineteenth-century citizens were unaware of slippery ethics aiding one's success—indeed, Charles Darwin's "survival of the fittest" research seemed to legitimize it—but who wants to publicize, let alone recommend, the less admirable path to success?—unless one is playing the comic. It is for this reason that Barnum's autobiography accents the "Yankee stick-to-it-iveness" of his character over the huckster side of his personality (324).

Along the same lines, Franklin's how-to-succeed-oriented *Autobiography* (which was not published until early in the nineteenth century) forever locked him to the practical "a penny saved is a penny earned" Poor Richard image, despite a real Franklin of a much more colorfully complex nature. For instance, Franklin claimed, presumably tongue-in-cheek, that he invented bifocals in order to watch both the woman in his arms and the door for her husband. Be that as it may, a close reading of his *Autobiography* still reveals the occasional huckster tendency, just sanitized by way of the good cause—such as young Franklin's way out of an abusive apprenticeship to his brother, or the politically wise elder Franklin raising money for a hospital. In the latter case he observed, like the proud Yankee he was, "I do not remember any of my political maneuvers. . . . I more easily excused myself for having made use of cunning" (114).

An important nineteenth-century slant on the period popularity of the huckster is also lost in today's more democratic times. That is, a pivotal villain of the time, both real and imagined, was the aristocracy. (Fields and Marx carried this tradition on later in their comic attacks upon America's wealthy high society. This is just one more way of celebrating the country's love affair with the underdog.) Unlike the aristocrat, whose success could be accounted for by the unfair advantage of a birthright, the Yankee succeeded on his own. If his means were sometimes questionable, had he not entered a real-world competition where the aristocracy had always had unjust advantages? Consequently, the Yankee was merely playing catch-up. One might quote that old definition of a con artist: "someone with merely an overripe imagination."

This catch-up had two levels. It was strongly attached to an emerging patriotic image of the United States as a young democratic country on the fast track among a family of old nations slowed by the dead weight of aristocracy. For example, American popular culture historian John G. Cawelti observed, "Jack Downing became an embodiment of a young America on the make" (66). This is in keeping with the earlier reference to the "individualization of manifest destiny" (Kuhlman 6).

The 1830s emergence of a sly Yankee also has much to do with the appearance of the concept of America's common man and the rise of anything approaching Jeffersonian democracy in the country's history. The year 1828 had seen the election of Andrew Jackson as president. Often considered the first "people's president," he conducted a one-man battle against any infringement (in his opinion) upon this man's rights by the federal government. This is best exemplified in his successful campaign to close the national bank—an event Seba Smith makes good use of in the Jack Downing "letters."

Two important developments during this period also helped to secure and to mold the national significance of the sly common man. The 1830s saw the rise of the inexpensive (penny) mass newspaper, a medium that launched Downing and other Yankee figures. Cheap newspapers also gave the common man access to what, in the past, had been privileged information—the affairs of the nation. At this time such activities were of special interest to the common people, who felt they had a spokesman in the presidency—Jackson.

As if in anticipation of the news possibilities of this mass media event, the 1830s saw the first serious internal threat to the continuing existence of the United States, South Carolina's threat of secession in 1832. President Jackson's strong hand in thwarting any such attempt was a boost to national identity. Humorists (especially Downing-creator Smith) dealing with such an issue were therefore of special interest to a national audience. Fittingly, Smith had recently "promoted" Downing to the role of friend and advisor to the president—no doubt playing upon the importance of Jackson's key unofficial real life advisers, the punningly named "kitchen cabinet." Thus, Downing's strong words of encouragement to the president, seconding the Union position, represent a cornerstone of what the Yankee figure came to represent—a patriotic common man interested in getting ahead.

Strangely enough, the most pivotal early (1830s) Yankee figure after Downing was Sam Slick, the product of Canadian author Thomas Chandler Haliburton. But as Cawelti notes, Slick had

"American ancestors and almost immediately became American property" (69). For instance, Barnum's autobiography chronicles a Yankee impersonator doing "Sam Slick, junior" (123), while Blair's later watershed history and anthology, *Native American Humor* (1937), includes a section on Haliburton's Slick (229–36).

The huckster importance of Haliburton's Yankee contribution is obvious, beginning with the name Sam Slick. He represents the ultimate peddler, the salesmen's salesman. Drawing upon the long tradition even then of the shrewd New England peddler, clock-selling Slick's rustic words of sly wisdom made him very popular well into the 1860s. Being of the people had its distinct business advantage—this Yankee understood what motivated sales. Combine this with smooth talking and one had the key to Slick's successful clock-selling—an appeal to "soft sawder" (flattery) and "human nature." Slick gains people's confidence with compliments and then tempts human nature with the mere request that he be allowed to leave a clock for a short time, because he is allegedly late to some prior commitment:

> We can do without any article of luxury we've never had, but when once obtained, it's not in human natur' to surrender it voluntarily. Of fifteen thousand [clocks] sold by myself and partners in this province, twelve thousand were left in this manner, and only ten clocks were ever returned. . . .We trust to soft sawder to git them into the house, and to human natur' that they never come out of it. (Haliburton, 29)

Fittingly, Slick spells Yankee common sense as *cents*. It is merely good business: "If a man seems bent on cheating himself, I like to be neighborly and help him do it" (Waters, xvii). Note the inspired tongue-in-cheek use of the term *neighborly*, which comically counters the populist (people helping each other) tendencies one normally associates with both the word and the Yankee world.

A harsher variation on Slick being "neighborly" is the observation of Barnum (who very much saw himself as a real-life Yankee) that "when people expect to get 'something for nothing' they are sure to be cheated, and generally deserve to be" (112). W. C. Fields would later title a film *You Can't Cheat an Honest Man* (1939). This footnote to Barnum is a cornerstone of Fields's comedy. Earlier in Barnum's autobiography he indirectly posits a reason for being sly that becomes more timely with each passing year: self-defense. "Sharp trades, tricks, dishonesty, and deception," he notes, "are by no means confined to the city" (56); rural customers trading for merchandise at the country store where he was working constantly misrepresented the quantity and/or quality of what they were bartering.

Celebrating the huckster often comes down to America's fixation on winning. Indeed, one might equate the earlier "Slick" analogy with any number of still-common sales-pitch compliments based in a con, such as "He [or she] could sell ice to the Eskimos." Significantly, Melville's parade of hucksters in one figure, the title character of his pivotal *The Confidence-Man*, is sometimes equated with a Yankee peddler.

Unlike most Yankees, Slick is not much taken with politics, finding the private sector more profitable. But this does not keep him from comic insights on the often-diddling nature of the politician: "Politics makes a man as crooked as a pack does a peddler. Not that they are so evil either, but it teaches a man to stoop in the long run" (Tandy 41).

One should add, however, that Yankee bending of the law was often also done for the general good. Mark Twain's Hank Morgan, the title character of his novel *A Connecticut Yankee in King Arthur's Court* (1889), excelled in this area. Morgan had been the ultimate "Yankee of the Yankees" before he mysteriously awakened in medieval England (20). Assuming the title "THE BOSS," in the spirit of a benevolent machine politician, he attempts to introduce progress to the Middle Ages. Besides bringing a modern comic touch to the spirit of Yankee common sense (he reduces court magician Merlin to doing the weather), Twain's Morgan largely returns to an early Yankee slant: a comedy attack on the aristocracy.

The second major comedy-camp contributor to the nineteenth-century emergence of the American confidence man was Southwestern humor. Contemporaneous to the Yankee (1830–1867), the Southwesterner is more amorally earthy than the New Englander, with little interest in politics. And while the Yankee peddler normally operates his con in a legitimate business (Slick's clock peddling), the Southwesterner is more apt to be simply dishonest, as in the Simon Suggs motto that opens this chapter: "It is good to be shifty in a new country." In the aforementioned "Simon Suggs Attends a Camp-Meeting," Simon pretends to be saved and then calmly makes off with a collection plate earmarked for a Suggs church. Along similar lines, Suggs's creator Johnson J. Hooper begins his

Simon Suggs' Adventures (1867) with his character exiting home just after cheating his "hardshell" Baptist-preacher father out of a pony and putting a "thimble full of gunpowder" in his mother's pipe.

As Suggs's surprise for his mother illustrates, Southwestern humor is often based on physical discomfort, which is also a given in the films of W. C. Fields—such as sitting on knitting needles in *The Old-Fashioned Way* (1934). Literary historian and critic F. O. Matthiessen presents a strong case for George W. Harris's Sut Lovingood being the ultimate example of this—he "delights to put lizards in a parson's pants, or to turn loose a hornet's nest at a prayer meeting" (642). As the Yankee made sport of the aristocracy, Southwestern humor (and Lovingood in particular) comically attacked any semblance of hypocrisy—a trait this comedy school often associated with religion and the law.

Unlike the Yankee, the Southwestern figure can also be the huckster victim. For example, Mark Twain (who owes his greatest humor debt to this comedy camp) helped establish his writing career with "The Notorious Jumping Frog of Calaveras County." This 1865 tale chronicles Jim Farley's luck at frog betting, until someone fills Dan'l Webster, his prize jumping frog, full of quail shot up to his chin. (While both Groucho and W. C. would sometimes play the huckster *victim*, it was especially true of the one with the bulbous nose, as when Fields inadvertently kissed a goat in *My Little Chickadee*, 1940).

In T. B. Thorpe's "Big Bear of Arkansas" the central character is conned by no less than a tall-tale variety of "bar" (bear). Besides this rather unusual example of hoodwinking, there are two additional reasons why the 1841 essay is especially pertinent to the confidence-game subject at hand. Southwestern humor is peppered with tall tales, either loosely based on real people such as Davy Crockett and keelboatman Mike Fink or one hundred percent pure imagination. And the tall tale is just another variety of the con. As Thorpe's hunter spins his yarn to an eclectic riverboat crowd in "The Big Bear of Arkansas," there is a sense of audience enjoyment without necessarily believing word one. The listeners are voluntarily suspending their sense of disbelief to be entertained. This is the kind of thing Barnum meant about people paying to be entertained via the diddle. Barnum's exhibits, such as his alleged mermaid, were nothing more than tall tales seemingly come to life. The payment to Thorpe's hunter (and this would hold true of any epic storyteller) would include both the heady attention of an admiring audience and the favors (such as food and drink) they would bestow upon him. (Fields's films, especially the period pieces, frequently find him spinning tall tales, such as his ongoing whoppers about fighting Indians in *Mississippi*, 1935.)

An additional case for the huckster uniqueness of this Thorpe essay is the setting that it shares with Melville's later, all-important *The Confidence-Man*. Both works open on a Mississippi riverboat bound for New Orleans, with the promise of a colorful passenger list. Though this is a connection one might make between many works of the period, Thorpe's piece (while decidedly more upbeat than Melville's) has a world-of-the-con-artist aura about it distinctly prescient of the later novel. And despite the modest length of Thorpe's essay, it includes additional bits and pieces that further prefigure Melville's book. For instance, the Arkansas "b'ar" hunter suggests at one point that his unbelievably manipulative bear opponent is really the devil, another identity (besides that of Yankee) sometimes applied to the title character of Melville's novel.

In discussing the vulnerable-to-the-con Southwestern figure, one cannot ignore this humor school's greatest graduate, Mark Twain. His masterpiece, *Huckleberry Finn* (1884), is essentially about the young title character discovering the lies of life—a metaphorical confidence game that embraces all of society. For example, Huck finds an America that celebrates democracy yet still maintains slavery, a country that preaches Christianity and yet condones racial violence and hate. However one describes this dishonesty, Twain's work often anticipates the collective victimization and/or guilt (for being part of a game-playing society) that will become an increasingly mainstream focus of twentieth-century con-related art.

In terms of a more traditional, though still vulnerable, nineteenth-century huckster, Twain's Colonel Sellers, from the 1873 novel *The Gilded Age* (coauthored with Charles Dudley Warner), is of special interest to this study. Sellers is a likable wannabe huckster floundering in the greedy and crooked politics of post–Civil War America. While the book gave a shady period of history its name, the popular Sellers gained even greater recognition when the work was adapted by Twain for the stage.

The storyline represents an interesting time-capsule look at a huckster era so appropriately named "Gilded." And Sellers manages to be both funny and poignant as he attempts to literally cash in on the western land-speculation deals that fueled so much period corruption, especially among the politicians and government officials of Washington, D.C. The open secret of many successful land speculations was often tied to property accessibility via Congressional bills addressing factors like building canals or deepening and straightening rivers. Fittingly, one is able to see Sellers assist in putting together a property package and then lobby Congress for legislative assistance.

Like so many hucksters before and since, Sellers is verbally slick: "The Colonel's tongue was a magician's wand that turned dried apples into figs and water into wine as easily as it could change a hovel into a palace and present poverty into imminent future riches" (Twain and Warner, 71–72).

There is often the sense in diddling literature that the ultimate goal is not riches but rather the playing of the game. This would seem to apply to Sellers, especially since he never does make the big score. In fact, he sometimes seems so wrapped up in his tapestry of words that the following *Gilded Age* description fits Sellers better than the character for which it was meant: "a very entertaining fellow, having his imagination to help his memory, and telling his stories as if he believed them—as perhaps he did" (168). Such a huckster is hard to dislike, especially since his verbal ramblings are occasionally peppered with comic common sense, such as Sellers's populist approach to the monetary gold standard—"Talk about basing the currency on gold; you might as well base it on port. Gold is only one product" (306–07). When one reads the novel it is difficult not to think of W. C. Fields as the likable Sellers, especially comically "overselling" the shakedown-artist dialogue of Twain and Warner.

Regardless of how much one thinks the huckster's audience is aware of his tricks, American pioneers historically were very vulnerable to such flowery language. As critic Susan Kuhlmann observes, "the frontiersman's longing for expanded emotional and intellectual life . . . [made him] the willing victim of the storyteller" (50).

Sellers still manages to be a sympathetic character because his diddler dreams are of the everyperson variety—the get-rich plan or scam with which most people have flirted, be it the 1870s or the 1990s. Indeed, *The Gilded Age*'s subtitle, "A Tale of Today," remains timely. And the fact that Sellers never does succeed makes him all the more of an everyman figure. The land-speculation fever of *The Gilded Age* eventually draws in the most unlikely of characters, just as it did in real life. Again, this demonstrates the commonness of the temptation.

Twain's evenhandedness when dealing with wannabe hucksters like Sellers is no doubt tied to his own ambivalence toward get-rich schemes. The humorist had grown up in a family where land speculation was part of the norm—forever hoping the extensive holdings of his father, who died when the author was a boy, would one day represent a fortune. It never happened. (This Twain background was the inspiration for the land speculation aspect of the novel's plot.)

Much later (late 1880s) Twain was bankrupted by what was to be the revolutionary typesetting machine of James W. Paige. This complex machine proved too mechanically temperamental to ever make the fortune it promised; instead, it cost Twain, its chief financial backer, his personal fortune (Kaplin 281–86). Consequently, despite the humorist's knowing satire of a get-rich era, he was susceptible to the same temptation, and his characters are all the more sympathetic for it.

With this sort of background, it is fitting that Twain (like Poe and other modern American artists) assumes a sometime-huckster position in his writing, a manipulating of the reader's confidence in Twain the storyteller. His *Gilded Age* examples are all the more comic because he baldly places them in direct address, what for the stage or screen would be called the "fourth wall," the invisible line that separates actor and audience. For instance, late in *The Gilded Age* is the entertaining maneuvering: "We beg the reader's pardon. This [just-completed description of the novel's heroine's melodramatic situation] is not history, which has just been written. It is really what would have occurred if this were a novel [which it is]. . . .But this is history and not fiction" (Twain and Warner 400–401). Direct address is a frequent later tool of Groucho Marx, such as his frequent put-downs of his brothers, after Chico has been inflicting his bad puns on him, or Harpo has managed to hoodwink the normally dominant Groucho.

There is an additional diddler in Twain fiction to be noted. Probably the most famous, and certainly the character that first came to mind as this project initially germinated in my mind, is Tom Sawyer. It would be difficult to find a more celebrated con in American literature than this boy's selling of chances at whitewashing his

Aunt Polly's fence, something he was assigned as punishment. When I paid a 1970s visit to Twain's boyhood home in Hannibal, Missouri (the setting that inspired the novel), a facsimile of the fence had already reached American shrine status—despite its con-artist foundation or *because* of it?

Tom and the fence are a microcosm of diddler basics. At its most fundamental, the whitewashing is an actualization of what a con is—covering something up. While Tom enjoys his new-found wealth from selling painting chances—including many prizes of an earthy, Southwestern-humor nature, such as "a dead rat and a string to swing it with" (Twain, 25)—the ongoing impetus is the con itself. It is simply one more example of the game-playing fun Tom pursues throughout the book.

In fact, just as one symbolically connects whitewashing and the con, the con *game* metaphor begs to be tied to Tom's favorite fun activity: playing *pirates*. And, like so many all-American diddlers, Tom manages to be sympathetic. Reasons for this might range from allowances granted any nostalgic look back at childhood to a modest case of revenge, since Tom's victims initially "came to jeer." But the broadest motive in terms of hucksterism is escaping work—particularly manual labor.

For a nation allegedly built on the work ethic, avoiding physical employment has often been surprisingly visible in the country's humor and its ties to hucksterism. Certainly, Southwestern humor makes no bones about where it stands. George Washington Harris's character Sut Lovingood observes: "Men wer made a-purpus jis' tu eat, drink, an' fur stayin awake in the yearly part ove the nites" (Blair, *Native American Humor*, 375).

The world of the Yankee is more sly on the topic. Lip service is often paid to work, but his diddling component seems to separate the Yankee from the crowd. For instance, a good part of the impetus for Jack Downing's journey to the Capitol is his belief that a political job would be easier than farming. And self-styled real Yankee P. T. Barnum is quite bald about the subject: "As I grew older, my settled aversion to manual labor, farm or otherwise, was manifest in various ways, which were set down to the general score of laziness" (55). Humorist Kin Hubbard nicely summed it up years later, when he had his crackerbarrel-Hoosier figure Abe Martin observe: "More people die from overwork than all th' loafin' put t'gether" (127).

Like the huckster, the antihero—a figure of perennial frustration, forever trying to create order in an irrational world—is as old as time. Still, the character often is considered a phenomenon of the twentieth century since this is when he came to center stage in American humor. Harbingers of this development might begin with the writing of Charles Darwin (1809–1882) and Sigmund Freud (1856–1939). Comparison of their importance in terms of the decentralization of the individual in the grand scheme of things could be made to Copernicus's then-heretical discovery back in the sixteenth century that God's earth and creations merely orbited the sun, and not vice versa.

Darwin's shocking claims for Man's haphazard evolution from lesser beasts rather derailed the comfortable noble claim of being made in His image. The nineteenth-century huckster might have found legitimacy in a study that heralded the "survival of the fittest," but Darwinism's long-term effects reduced mankind's sense of uniqueness to something less than heroic. Darwin's writing on evolution still qualifies as probably the most radical change in image mankind has ever had to address. Serious doubt was cast on the literal truth of Christianity for the first time. As with later theories of Freud, Darwin's work might fundamentally be labeled naturalism, in that it leads one away from the supernatural. Coupled with the oppression of the nineteenth-century Industrial Age, belief in a God-centered rationalism was rapidly failing. Here was fertile ground indeed for the comic antihero.

While Darwin took away claims to some heavenly heritage, Freud's pioneering work in psychoanalysis effectively called into question the possibility of even being in control of one's own mind. Freud's influence on twentieth-century "literature" was immense. He was the first guide to the dark powers of the unconscious—a cinema of the brain forever serving up unexpected shocks, or the milder slips of the tongue now labeled with his name. Add to this Freud's emphasis on the taboo subject of sexuality and one has a veritable smorgasbord of subjects for the modern humorist. His work also made neuroses and personal obsessions acceptable material for the comic arts. Early pivotal antiheroic humorists like Robert Benchley, James Thurber, and S. J. Perelman found this a particularly rich area to explore.

Still, in nineteenth-centruy American humor the antihero generally played a secondary role (when he appeared at all) to the more capable crackerbarrel types, such as the New England Yankee or the generally crafty Southwestern figure. For example, in Haliburton's Sam Slick tale "Taming a Shrew," the hero stops at the home of henpecked friend John Porter. That night, under cover of darkness, skilled ventriloquist Slick enters the house posing as Porter, bent on elevating his friend's domestic position. Shockingly to the contemporary reader, Slick whips the wife into respect for the man she thinks is her husband. The female-dominated Porter has much in common with future antiheroic husbands, especially those in the world of James Thurber and W. C. Fields. But the difference here is that while Thurber and Fields's henpecked focus character has no defense (beyond fantasy), supporting-character Porter has story-star Slick to change things. Interestingly, the physical violence visited upon Mrs. Porter is often reversed in the later antihero world, where milquetoast husband after husband cowers before the wife who dominates him and who is frequently made all the more comically threatening by wielding a tree-trunk-sized rolling pin.

It should be added, moreover, that sometimes the seemingly vulnerable character of the crackerbarrel world, such as Twain's Huck Finn, still manages to get across basic axioms of wisdom. Humor historian Norris Yates has labeled such figures as examples of the "wise fool":

> the humorous writers frequently made the country-store philosopher expound unwelcome truths behind a protective mask of character deficiency or linguistic, logical or factual error. . . .Thus Huck Finn notices that the hogs have the run of a certain country church, and he says, "Most folks don't go to church only when they've got to; but a hog is different" (22).

Generally, secondary characters like John Porter or "wise fools" such as Huck Finn mark the typical nineteenth-century predecessors for the later antihero. These ancestors of antiheroic figures of frustration existed in a comedy world still considered to be rational, Darwin and Freud notwithstanding. The dominant comedy type continued to be the capable, reasoning crackerbarrel philosopher. Yates implied just that when he noted "one important difference between [crackerbarrel figures] and the Little Man [comic antihero] is that the latter is not certain of his identity" (257).

The full blossoming of the antiheroic figure is usually credited to the mid-1920s-founded *New Yorker* magazine and to the writings of

Benchley, Thurber, Perelman, and Clarence Day (Blair, *Native American Humor*, 167). (The magazine's city title baldly underscores another key to antiheroic humor—it is in and about the city.) But precursors existed in such other media as newspaper comic strips, the movies, and vaudeville.

Four early strips that anticipate the antiheroic world are Rudolph Dirk's "Katzenjammer Kids" (1897); Bud Fisher's "Mutt and Jeff" (1907); George Herriman's "Krazy Kat" (1913); and George McManus's "Bringing Up Father" (1913). In the antiheroic tradition, each strip showcases a great deal of frustration, often in the most physical manner. Certain violent acts are repeated so often they can be considered trademarks of each strip, like Ignatz Mouse braining Krazy Kat with another brick, or Mutt giving Jeff one more black eye. Fittingly in a 1963 interview on Hy Gardner's television show Groucho likened the earlier real-life antics of the Marx brothers to the adventures of the Katzenjammer Kids.

Anticipating the antiheroic world, these signature scenes of comic violence often have a female catalyst, such as the Katzenjammers' Mama beating the kids and the Captain with her ever-ready rolling pin and frying pan; or "Bringing Up Father"'s title character Jiggs finding himself the permanent target of wife Maggie's vases and rolling pins. (Though Mutt and Ignatz are both males, these strips too play upon the concept of feuding "couple.") As will be expanded upon in Chapter 5, American immigrant families had a strong tendency to be matriarchal, as was the case in the childhood homes of W. C. Fields and Groucho Marx. And while the mothers of these comedians were amusing characters themselves, early portrayals of women in antiheroic humor, such as the aforementioned pioneering comic strips, were often less than kind. "This denial of female jocularity was probably tied to the dominant comic tradition's function as a release of male anxieties and fears; a laughing and joking woman posed a potential new threat to male authority" (Jenkins 256). This menace to masculinity was one humor cross Fields and Marx comedy contemporary Mae West had to confront in the 1930s. But as this book will demonstrate, depicting women as devoid of humor was strictly business as usual for W. C. and Groucho.

Frustration in these strips does not, however, limit itself to a "female" antagonist. Sometimes it foreshadows the irrational world of the antihero. Herriman's "Krazy Kat" is an obvious example, with a title to underline the point. That is, the strip features a docile cat who loves a brick-toting mouse (Ignatz) who is often arrested by a cat-loving police dog (Offissa Pupp).

This bizarre situation, moreover, goes one step further—"back to the days of Cleopatra," as pioneer popular-culture critic Gilbert Seldes explains, when

> a mouse fell in love with Krazy, the beautiful daughter of Kleopatra Kat. . . .Advised . . . to write his love, he carved a declaration on a brick and, tossing the "missive" . . . he had nearly killed the Kat. . . .It has become the Romeoian custom to crease his lady's bean with a brick laden with tender sentiments. (237)

Each time Krazy gets beaned, he sees hearts and arrows, while Ignatz feels confident that he has knocked the cat silly, one more time. Neither animal, then, really knows what is going on. Such is the stuff of the antiheroic world.

"Krazy Kat" is the most obvious cartoon foreshadowing of the antiheroic irrational world (in part because it is generally considered the most imaginative American strip ever done). However, the often-comparable theater-of-the-absurd tendencies of "Mutt and Jeff" should not be neglected. Predating "Krazy Kat" by several years, Mutt first meets Jeff when the latter is in a mental institution—believing himself to be heavyweight fighter Jim Jeffries (thus, the name Jeff). Even more reminiscent of "Krazy Kat" is the fact that the frustrations caused by Jeff routinely result in Mutt smacking him with a brick to the noggin.

The pertinence of "Mutt and Jeff" to this study is not limited to an antiheroic, crazy-comedy connection. This might be called a pivotal crossover strip, combining elements of both the antihero and the huckster. That is, Mutt is a wannabe confidence man whose schemes are constantly derailed by classic nincompoop Jeff. This anticipates Groucho's frequent huckster frustrations at the hands of the sometimes idiotic Chico. Comic-strip historian and archivist Bill Blackbeard goes so far as to suggest that the "vulgar vitality and lowbrow fun" of the early "Mutt and Jeff" episodes (then known as "A. Mutt") are in line with the equally amoral escapades of slippery Sut Lovingood (xiii).

While Augustus Mutt is much more the antihero than Lovingood, the huckster link is well taken and will be discussed later when the huckster/antihero crossover tendencies of Groucho Marx and W. C.

Fields are examined at length. However, maybe the most fascinating slant to "Mutt & Jeff" is that creator Bud Fisher, in the best tradition of huckster-oriented artists through the ages, performed his own con in creating the strip, making it a crude spoof of the then-current notion of newspaper comics.

Like newspaper cartoon strips, movies came on the scene in the 1890s. And, America's first major film comedian, John Bunny (1863–1915), is an antiheroic precursor of major significance, anticipating the henpecked Jiggs of "Bringing Up Father." A funny fatso, Bunny's tall, skinny wife (normally played by Flora Finch) is a comic clash both in size and temperament, more dominating mother than spouse.

A Cure for Pokeritis (1912), one of his few surviving films, is an excellent capsulization of a basic Bunny dilemma: sneaking out of the house to drink and play poker with the boys. As will be the case with Jiggs, both are comedy fifth columnists, working behind married lines (their own). All of this very much anticipates the antiheroic W. C. Fields. Their cowardly conflict against the pretense of culture and society is symbolized by their dominating spouses. But unlike John Porter, there is no Sam Slick to come to the rescue.

The antiheroic world is also anticipated in the early films of pioneering comedy director and producer Mack Sennett (1880–1960). At his most creative, during what has come to be called his Keystone period (1912–1915), Sennett was best at cinematically canning chaos. Originally a journeyman performer in everything from circuses to vaudeville, he later described what he enjoyed about burlesque comics in terms that could be applied just as aptly to his film work: "They made fun of themselves and the human race. They reduced convention, dogma, stuffed shirts, and authority to nonsense, and then blossomed into pandemonium" (Sennett and Ship, 28–29).

Fittingly, Sennett's hallmark creation was the Keystone Kops, out-of-control surreal policemen who reduced classic authority figures (policemen) to so much meaninglessness. As Bunny anticipated Jiggs, Sennett's Keystone Kops would foreshadow the absurdity of Krazy Kat, right down to the funny spelling and the alliterative joke of double *k*'s for their pivotal characters.

Sennett's greatest gift to antiheroic film comedy was making slapstick totally cinematic for the first time. His company was also an important early "laboratory" for the careers of such comedy giants as Charlie Chaplin, Harry Langdon, and director Frank Capra. Sennett had intuitively tapped into the twentieth century's most fundamental contribution to humor—the world's ever-accelerating comic absurdity.

Some might also count Charlie Chaplin's (1889–1977) classic tramp character (1914) as an antiheroic forerunner. Such inclusion is, however, problematic. On one level, his anti-establishment tendencies and everyman vulnerability (especially in romance) place him in the antiheroic camp. However, his inspired mime and general physical dexterity, as well as his ability to best hulking heavies and pursuing police—with rarely a henpecking wife in sight—ultimately make him a much more capable character than a Jiggs, John Bunny, or W. C. Fields. This foot-in-each-camp conflict was the catalyst for my 1983 book, *Charlie Chaplin: A Bio-Bibliography*. In the final analysis, he probably has more in common with the nineteenth-century comedy character, often being reminiscent of the "wise fool." That is, Charlie and the capable crackerbarrel philosopher often carried on the tradition of the court fools and jesters by revealing "unwelcome truths behind a protective mask of character deficiency" (Yates, 22). Whether addressing yesterday's kings and queens or today's cinema audience, the wise fool forever remains an invaluable servant of the truth. And as comedy historian Sandra Billington suggests, the fool might now be seen as a symbol of any popular entertainer, since both "survived through wit and tricks" (123). Regardless, the pathos Chaplin occasionally brought to his "little fellow" (the comedian's own description of the character), such as the lost love of *The Tramp* and *The Bank* (both 1915 films), set a new artistic level for a typically antiheroic situation.

Ironically, the much later posture of the "little fellow," such as in the last tramp film (*Modern Times*, 1936), finds him much more vulnerable to the system than the rough-and-tumble feisty character who had exploded onto the scene in the 1910s. By the 1930s, society's relationship to the individual (as symbolized by the tramp) had moved from an indifferent nuisance to a calculated threat to the individual. Thus, in *Modern Times* the tramp has a nervous breakdown while working on a factory conveyor belt, where he metaphorically becomes a mechanical nut tightener, just like the machines around him; the individual was no longer safe in society.

The danger of dealing with Chaplin on any level (such as antihero) is becoming lost in his significance to film comedy history. He remains *the* standard against which all cinema clowns are measured. Moreover, he still represents the ultimate gauge for filmmakers, comic and otherwise. Because Chaplin wore all the production hats; he wrote, directed, scored, and produced his own films. Many comedians, from Harry Langdon to Jerry Lewis, have attempted to duplicate this accomplishment and failed.

Regardless of how one pigeonholes his persona (capable or antiheroic), Chaplin's perennial-outsider tramp would have appealed to many of the early-twentieth-century urban (often immigrant) have-nots, as would the minimal language demands of silent film. Such frustrations helped fuel the need for a new antiheroic humor. Like much of his audience (Chaplin himself was an immigrant), the "little fellow" often seems new to the city. This is best demonstrated in the funny/sad *The Immigrant* (1917), which poignantly juxtaposes the promise of America (via a Statue of Liberty shot) with shipboard officials callously herding the new arrivals into a line.

The medium of vaudeville (which had employed Chaplin prior to his film debut) had its own contribution to make in the development of the antihero. Entertainment historian Albert F. McLean, Jr., observes in *Vaudeville as Ritual* that again and again after 1900 critics implied that a "new humor" had developed in this country—"a new humor with which vaudeville had much to do" (106–07).

The primary manner in which the new vaudeville comedy seemed to anticipate the antiheroic was in its focus on frustration via the industrialized urban setting. America's industrial growth was fed by tens of millions of immigrants anxious for success, very few of whom, as shown in a watershed muckraking novel like Upton Sinclair's *The Jungle* (1906), actually ever succeeded. Consequently, McLean suggests that urban-based frustrations created a demand for this new humor, an "antidote for larger doses of the Myth of Success" (109).

Though vaudeville historians might seem more cognizant of this immigrant connection, it was certainly present in all media of then-period American comedy. A prime example is the fractured English of the Germanic "Katzenjammer Kids" newspaper comic strip, which is set somewhere in the jungles of East Africa, "perhaps the former German East African colony, if not Polynesia" (Gerger, 19). Not surprisingly, given the setting, period stereotypes of African natives were used. But cartoon historian Arthur Asa Berger credits this strip with still giving these characters a certain amount of "dignity and authority" (43).

Along different ethnic lines, "Bringing Up Father" is about a second-generation Irish family, a nationality factor that is more obvious when considering the strip's author's name (McManus) or its popular title among fans—"Jiggs & Maggie." (Along personal lines, my second-generation Irish maternal grandfather was a great fan of "Bringing Up Father," which premiered during his childhood.) Regardless, strip authority Bill Blackbeard credits this cartoon with having a broad second-generation-American reader sense of identification, which ranged from European Jews to the Chinese (ix). Even more significant in terms of immigrants and antiheroes is Blackbeard's statement concerning the dominance of second-generation American families by women:

> Almost always in such economically ascending family units it was the woman who most ardently and efficiently embraced the rules and shibboleths of central American culture, while the men, still largely engrossed in the business of making the new money, wanted to relax in their infrequent leisure much as they always had, with cheap liquor, gambling, sports, and the company of their culturally disinterested fellows. (ix)

Blackbeard is not alone in noting this immigrant power shift from father to mother. For instance, author Joseph McBride makes a similar observation in his 1992 biography of the immigrant Frank Capra, *The Catastrophe of Success*. Certainly, broad generalizations need always be handled carefully, but this shift of power nicely mirrors the world of the antihero, where the wife is more mother than spouse to her childlike husband. McManus's strip's title, "Bringing Up Father," demonstrates this married parent/child dichotomy perfectly.

What is significant about this observation concerning immigrant life and McManus's humor is its linkage with a prototypical example of the antiheroic world. It is a natural, though hitherto neglected, insight that merits a study all its own. Still, the basic antiheroic slant to the immigrant experience—to survive is to be forever wary of becoming an entry-level victim of some con based on confusion over customs and language—should be remembered.

The cultural shift in power, from father to mother, in the immigrant community might also be briefly examined in reference to Freud. According to the pioneering psychoanalyst there was a natural attraction between the male child and his mother. But if there was little counterbalancing by the father (either through absence or domination by the wife/mother), there could be a tendency toward anger by the child. And for Freud, as well as many comedy theorists, wit represents a key form of aggression. In discussing this issue as it applies to Fields and Marx, practicing psychologist and academician Gary Meunier said that he felt the biting humor of both comedians could be "read," in part, along these Freudian lines. (Of course, Groucho's aggressive tendencies were also fed by his early inabilities to receive the attention he wanted from his mother.)

As an American comedy aside, this period ethnic factor could surface even in the traditional setting of the crackerbarrel humorist—best demonstrated by the great turn-of-the-century popularity of humorist Finley Peter Dunne's Irish bartender Mr. Dooley. And one must always remember that the inspiration of American immigration's influence on antiheroic humor was often created out of less than amusing, occasionally shocking, human obstacles.

It should not be surprising that vaudeville's early humor relied on dialect and ethnic stereotypes. For the contemporary viewer, the early vaudeville days of the Marx brothers (of German-Jewish heritage) reflect the continued pervasiveness of dialect humor well into the twentieth century. Groucho would, for a time, use a German dialect, while Harpo would briefly essay an Irish one. Chico also developed his Italian accent during this period, continuing it, of course, throughout the brothers' later film career.

As these new comics were slowly weaning themselves from the more obvious gimmicks, such as blackface and dialects, a rather apropos characteristic was descending upon them—apropos, that is, for comics dealing in urban frustration. Vaudeville historian Douglas Gilbert defines it as "a combination of outrageous distortion, noisy satire, and mad humor, adding up to an insanely imaginative entertainment—'nut' acts in the argot of the profession" (251). One is again reminded of the Marx brothers, who honed their crazy comedy in the lowest levels of vaudeville.

The nut act, however, of the new vaudeville comedy was Joe Cook. Little known now, this antiheroic pioneer (who began in blackface) has seemingly slipped through the cracks of time. But his status at the forefront of vaudeville's crazy-comedy movement has an added significance here. He was a special favorite of Benchley, the most instrumental of the pantheon of four *New Yorker* writers, in the first full articulation of the antihero. In fact, fellow pantheon member Thurber observed, "One of the greatest fears of the humorous writer is that he has spent three weeks writing something done faster and better by Benchley in 1919" (Bernstein, 227).

The importance of Cook's post-blackface nonsense tendencies to kindred spirit Benchley was brought home to me while researching a biography of the latter comedian, *"Mr. B" or, Comforting Thoughts About the Bison*. In reading through Benchley's tongue-in-cheek *Life* criticism (the old humor magazine, not the later pictorial) it quickly became obvious that the humorist known as the keeper of the "dementia praecox" process (crazy-comedy tendencies) had a thing about Cook:

> Anything involving Joe Cook robs us of whatever critical faculties we may possess . . . [His act] is still the same epoch-marking repudiation of all standards of sanity which have held civilization cowed for so many centuries (seven, I think it is, or possibly eight). ("A Few Words About Joe Cook," 20)

Benchley was especially taken with Cook's imitation of three "Hi-wayans" (Hawaiians), a nonsense yarn he would tell on a center-stage chair, with his trusty mandolin (an instrument of which Benchley was also a long-time fan) on his lap. The routine was an outlandish explanation as to why Cook could—but would not—imitate a fourth "Hi-wayan." (His comic shorthand imitation of three "Hi-wayans"—a whistle, a mandolin plinking, and marking time with his foot—opened the act.) Cook would methodically relate several chance investments (worth an ever-escalating fortune), with the yarn-topping question as to why should someone worth $350,000 bother to imitate four "Hi-wayans"?

Another Cook routine prescient of Benchley, one which struck a direct comic blow at the industrial mechanization that was so much a part of the catalyst for this "new humor," focused upon an elaborate mechanical contrivance. This stage-filling machine, with its many bizarre-looking gears, merely performed the simple task of activating a slapstick that bonked a sleeping man, who would then strike a gong. This was how the hired man (once a common summer fixture on the American farm) was called to supper! The special Benchley connection here, besides the patented absurdity of the situation, is found in the fact that Cook's routine included a comic mini-lecture on the parts of the machine. Much of

Benchley's humor, in both his essays and his award-winning short film subjects, is also dependent on the humorist's assumption of an incompetent professorial pose, where he talks on various given topics, all of which are indirectly yet royally lambasted as he struggles through his quasi-lecture. (Period newspaper cartoonist and vaudevillian Rube Goldberg is now the name most associated with contraptions intended to do the simple with the maximum amount of mechanical strangeness.)

An important part of vaudeville's contribution to this "new humor" was developing a monologue of sidewalk conversation tendencies, which was likely to be sprinkled with comic observations and then build to a single comedy pay-off line. And as was suggested earlier, the humor often addressed the depersonalization of the urban setting. This orientation is effectively exhibited in a segment (reprinted verbatim, punctuation errors and all) from a routine (circa 1900) by then-prominent comic James Thornton:

> While coming to the theatre tonight, I got on a [street] car, the car was full, so was I; every seat was taken, so was my watch, the man alongside of me had a mouth full of sailor's delight [chewing tobacco]. He was endeavoring to expectorate on the ceiling, not having the necessary five hundred [dollar fine] for doing it on the floor, the unexpected expectoration of the expectorator . . . hit the [streetcar] conductor a wallop in the eye. (McLean 122–23)

This sidewalk conversation style need not, however, have the period shock effect of Thornton's "expectoration" in someone's eye. Joe Cook's favorite monologue, and one of the most amusing surviving vaudevillian yarns, focuses on the national pastime, baseball, with the comedian's own special absurd twist. For instance, "The score was tied—five to three—in favor of us. We needed six runs to win. . . .I was playing second base and right field, as I was too good for one position" (Gilbert, 257). One could confuse this with the later standard patter of Groucho, such as his *Animal Crackers* line, "If you take cranberries and stew them like applesauce, they taste much more like prunes than rhubarb does."

Another important nut comedian of vaudeville, and an additional favorite of Benchley the critic, was Ed Wynn. His ability to move from straight comedy to pathos gave him more in common with Chaplin's "little fellow" than any other character in this chapter, an analogy with which Benchley was in agreement ("The Personal Service of Mr. Ed Wynn," 842–43). Benchley's *Life* critique of Wynn (a column from which he also dated the beginning of his criticism career) describes a stage character with many now-classic antiheroic traits:

> Ed Wynn never quite attains what he sets out after. His waistcoat is always buttoned just one or two buttons too high. His clothes, while perhaps suitable for other occasions, are never quite right for the particular event in which he is taking part. . . .His language . . . is always just a shade too refined or rather badly assembled, so that the general effect is one of undeniable failure. (842–43)

Cross-fertilization among various media—newspaper comic strips, the movies, and vaudeville—frequently took place. For instance, Chaplin's screen character was so popular that within a year "Chaplinitis" had enveloped the world. This craze touched off marketing schemes that are still with us. There were Charlie Chaplin lapel pins, spoons, statues, paper dolls, squirt rings, and whatever else his likeness could be reproduced upon. The "little fellow" soon began appearing in his own regular newspaper cartoon strip, while both film and vaudeville began featuring tramp imitators.

Another overnight marketing success was McManus's "Bringing Up Father," with likenesses of Jiggs and Maggie selling an eclectic assortment of products, as well as surfacing in numerous stage and screen adaptations. While other antiheroic-oriented period hits existed, these two examples represent polar extremes of the buffeted male, from Jiggs's wife-dominated male to Charlie's lonely independence.

The 1920s represented a significant decade for the comic antihero. He was hardly a new figure in American humor, as the preceding examination has shown. Yet this period saw him take on an increased visibility, particularly because of *The New Yorker* magazine. Credit for this antiheroic blossoming, as *the* American humor historian Walter Blair observes in his pivotal *Native American Humor*, is usually given to this publication, "the magazine which was more responsible than any other medium for the rise of a new type of humor" (165).

This is not to suggest, however, that other period humor magazines, in an era particularly rich with such publications, did not showcase similar comedy pieces. Sometimes these even both predate *The New Yorker* and include material from what would become its "pantheon four" contributors. Thus, one might note *Life, Judge,* and *College Humor* (which drew largely from the then-pervasive college humor journals) as other important period comedy publications. I place *Life* first because of pivotal Benchley's 1920s involvement there.

Still, *The New Yorker* was different. Its birth was a *conscious* celebration of this new urban humor. It was a magazine, as its prospectus declared, "not edited for the old lady in Dubuque." Moreover, as humor historian Norris Yates has observed, this magazine

> was to give the highly literate but nimble [antiheroic] humorists their most important outlet of publication and to carry respect for competence in general and for stylistic smartness without brashness in particular to an extreme that amounted almost to fetishism concerning the word and the precise phrase. (228)

Of the four *New Yorker* writers, Benchley and Thurber best exemplify the full arrival of the comic antihero and were most productive during the 1920s and 1930s. Day's writing, such as his *Life With Father* (1935, about his turn-of-the-century eccentric father), more closely represents the transition from Yankee to antihero; Perelman anticipates comedy pushed to the extremes of absurdity in the post–World War II period.

Benchley and Thurber provide two classic variations on the antihero. Benchley's comically inspired ability to expand at length (in an entertainingly professorial style) on everyday trivia and frustration remains a good part of his ongoing appeal, which has direct ties to Groucho's popularity, such as Groucho's commentary on the origin of hooks in *Monkey Business* (1931) and his efforts to teach science in *Horse Feathers* (1932). I expand on the Groucho connection later. Benchley gives comic voice to the little questions and irritations with which we all quietly (and sometimes not so quietly) suffer. And by topping it off with a Benchley-produced smile of recognition, he gifts us with a minor victory we might not otherwise have known.

Examples abound, such as "Rapping the Wrapper!" (the inherent traumas of opening a roll of mints) (*Benchley—or Else!* 69); "Do Insects Think?" (a decidedly antiheroic concern) (*The Benchley Roundup*, 44–45); "Back in Line" (where he reveals that "six-tenths of the population of the United States spend their entire lives standing in line in a post office") (*No Poems or Around the World Back-*

wards and Sideways, 188); and the valuable lessons of "How to Break 90 in Croquet": "Taking an easy grip on the handle with both hands in the manner of a flute player, only more virile, you bend over the ball, with the feet about two feet apart and both pointing in the same direction" (*From Bed to Worse and Other Comforting Thoughts About the Bison*, 27).

Going beyond the comic universality of Benchley's everyday topics, humor theorist Hamlin Hill suggests another level of significance. As if directly addressing Benchley's comedy, Hill posits that the antihero deals with the frightening outside world by not dealing with it at all, focusing, instead, "microscopically upon the individual unit . . . that interior reality—or hysteria. . . . In consequence, modern humor deals significantly with frustrating trivia" (174).

Of course, it must be added that Benchley's trivia often did more than flirt with the absurd. Indeed, until Benchley entertainingly ceded the "dementia praecox" process (crazy tendencies, best demonstrated here by language reduced to comic nonsense) over to S. J. Perelman (see Benchley's introduction in Perelman's 1937 *Strictly for Hunger*), he was the genre's leading practitioner. Benchley's wonderfully demented foreword to *Inside Benchley* (1942) is a classic example of the phenomenon: "While thumbing through some old snow which had accumulated in the attic last winter, I came, quite by accident, upon ten (10) or so volumes of prose works which I had dashed off during my career as a journalist (1915—7:45 p.m.)."

In researching my Benchley biography, I had the opportunity to study his unpublished diaries. I was especially taken with his asterisked addition to his June 5, 1913, entry: "One year later—on rereading this, it seems that the author [Benchley] was slightly confused here" (Diary Box 5). Besides presenting an amusing extension of the nebulous, Benchley coins an excellent description of his later comic persona: "slightly confused here." The phrase also nicely anticipates the famous future portrayal of Thurber's antiheroic alter ego as having "a sheer grasp of confusion."

Another variation on the antihero, after the Benchley focus on trivia/frustration (often over an inanimate object) deals with domination by the wife—a Thurber specialty. His childlike male is most effectively shown in the eight stories comprising the "Mr. and Mrs. Monroe" section of his *The Owl in the Attic* (1931), especially in "Mr. Monroe and the Moving Men." In this story, once the wife leaves, the husband is helpless—despite the fact that before she had left "little Mrs. Monroe had led her husband from room to room, pointing out what was to go into storage and what was to be sent to the summer place" (25–26).

While the Monroes represent an excellent Thurber case study of men and women, the humorist reveals the secret to women's domination in the essay "Destructive Forces in Life" (12). Near the story's beginning he pens a drawing of an unhappy man and smiling woman, titling it "A Mentally Disciplined Husband with Mentally Undisciplined Wife." This domestic mugshot leads to the sad story of another frustrated male. Thurber's gender-war message is, "The undisciplined mind [of the woman] . . . is far better adapted to the confused world in which we live today than the streamlined mind [of the man]" (18). Just as medical science derives vaccines from the viruses that cause disease, it seems the best safeguard in an irrational world is to behave irrationally.

Even when a battle of the sexes is not taking place, Thurber remains entertainingly consistent on his theory of the undisciplined woman's mind, to which he attributed the eccentricities of his capable yet half-baked maternal grandmother, who believed that "electricity was dripping [from empty sockets] all over the house" ("The Car We Had to Push," 41). Though providing humorous insights on gender differences is not Benchley's norm, his autobiographical essay "Three Men in the Dog House" comically revolves around his dominatingly eccentric mother's belief that when one saw three or more men traveling by buggy, they were drunk. One might reason with her, but she remained forever convinced that they were "up to no good" (232–33).

This, then has been a brief survey of the antihero in American humor. The section provides a sense of America's colorful background in this area. It will, of course, also represent an antiheroic measuring stick (just as the huckster section was a gauge) for the W. C. Fields/Groucho Marx pages that follow.

"[My family] were poor but dishonest."
—W. C. Fields

"Although it is generally known, I think it's about time to announce that I was born at a very early age."
—Groucho Marx

CHAPTER 3 **W. C. Fields and Groucho Marx**
An Analytical Dual Biography

W. C. Fields once said of the Marx brothers' vaudeville act: "[I] never saw so much nepotism [a brother act, written by an uncle, managed by the mother] or such hilarious laughter in one act in my life. In Columbus I told the manager I broke my wrist [he had a juggling routine] and quit" (R. Fields, *W. C. Fields By Himself*, 481). While no record seems to have been left of Groucho Marx's views on W. C. Fields's vaudeville act, Groucho's biographer son (more nepotism!) said in *Life with Groucho* that his father considered Fields "one of the all-time great comedians" as well as "one of the few people who's ever been able to make Father laugh out loud" (A. Marx, *Life with Groucho*, 173).

As if taking no chances about being upstaged at birth, Fields (born William Claude Dukenfield) arrived over ten years prior to Groucho (Julius) Marx's October 2, 1890, birth. For the sake of familiarity and simplicity, the two will be referred to by their stage names throughout this work.

While there is no question about the accuracy of Groucho's birth date, there has always been some uncertainty as to Fields's, though January 29, 1880, has found the widest acceptance. This disparity might also be applied to their early years; much more is known about Groucho's childhood. Groucho and others have written extensively about *Minnie's Boys*, to use the title of a Broadway play about the brothers' early vaudeville team and their stage mother, Minnie Marx. Moreover, Groucho had those famous and information-generating siblings Chico (Leonard, born 1887); Harpo (Adolph, 1888); and Zeppo (Herbert, 1901) Marx. (Brother Gummo—Milton, 1893—left the team early and is not as well known.) Indeed, Harpo's inspired autobiography, *Harpo Speaks!*, is arguably the best single source on the early Marx brothers years.

Fields, though a proud author (a comic essayist, whose one book, *W. C. Fields for President*, 1940, was a collection of short pieces loosely based around a tongue-in-cheek campaign), was nowhere as autobiographically prolific as Groucho. And no Fields sibling, of which there were four, ever came forward to write the early family story. Late in life his sister Adel assisted Fields's grandson Ronald J. Fields in compiling the book *W. C. Fields By Himself: His Intended Autobiography* (1973), a collection of the humorist's writings, from correspondence to script ideas. But though often a fascinating volume, it is still largely an anthology of Fields's adult years.

The grandson's book is most provocative in its opening revisionist pages, when it contests Fields's longstanding claim of early estrangement between himself and his family. For the record, and drawing from the Fields-approved, three-part period biography (1935) in *The New Yorker*, one might recount this putative "resignation from family" in the following manner (Johnston, "Profiles: I," 23): A small shovel had been left in the yard by eleven-year-old Fields. As if anticipating his son's future forté in physical comedy, James Dukenfield stepped on it, causing the handle to strike him in the shin. The young Fields found this extremely funny, which did nothing for an already shaky relationship. Thus, his father promptly bounced the shovel off the boy's head. Acting more out of revenge than comic theory's "rule of three" in the progression of the humorous event, Fields came up with the ultimate *topper*: from the hayloft he dropped a box on his father's head.

Fields won the battle but lost the home, or so the story goes, and decided it best to run away. The boy's next few years, consequently,

have sometimes been described as Huck Finn-like (Johnston, 23).
But with freedom came deprivations, such as sleeping in the hidea-
way of the "Orland Social Club" (the gang he was in), which was not
much more than a hole in the ground with a leaky plank roof.

The revisionist compilation by his grandson documents an eventual reconciliation between Fields and family. But as I noted in my
1984 biography of the comedian, the book offers little conflicting
evidence related to the boy's solo hard times (Gehring, *W. C. Fields:
A Bio-Bibliography*, 5). Incongruously, the grandson's volume even
contains a Fields letter to an old "Orland Social Club" friend, refer-
ring specifically to these vagabond days and signed "your old tramp
friend" (R. Fields, 450). The truth, no doubt, lies somewhere between the two camps.

Groucho never made an extended exit from his childhood home.
Indeed, because his mother so favored his older brothers Chico and
Harpo, he tried to attract her favor by being the model child. Still,
there were six early parallels between Groucho and W. C., involving
immigrant backgrounds, parental relationships, strong motherly influence on their comedy personas, the general hardships of their
childhoods, and an early fascination with performing. (Huckster
tendencies often tied these categories together.)

Besides the obvious insights to be found in such comparisons, it is
important to remember that in our culture "the personal life of a
comedian or clown is often considered to be something special"
(Pollio and Edgerly, 215). The blanketing comfort a comedian brings
to a public's myriad of individual problems has generated a timeless
fascination with a clown's background that goes beyond the merely
analytical, as if we were to be privy to the magic of a comic Merlin's
spell.

The most obvious parallel between W. C. and Groucho was that
both were born into immigrant families. James Dukenfield had
come to Philadelphia from London before the American Civil War,
in which he was both wounded and decorated. Groucho's father
Simon, who shortened his name from Marrix to Marx in America,
arrived in New York from the French province of Alsace, which had
been annexed by Germany after the Franco-Prussian War of 1871.
Because of this background he eventually went by the nickname
"Frenchie." Groucho's mother, Minnie Schoenberg, was originally
from Dornum, Germany. Only Fields's mother, Kate Felton, was a

native-born American, although she was from Philadelphia's Germantown District.

As if drawing directly from the previous chapter's reference to immigrant families traditionally being dominated by the woman, such was the case in these two households. For example, Kate Dukenfield was forever badgering her husband about his Cockney accent, something that W. C. would soon learn from her.

Minnie Marx dominated her family on an even broader scale, especially in her show-business drive as it related to a team called the Marx brothers. For example, she had the clan move from New York City to Chicago to help their vaudeville bookings. As the family's later critic/personality mentor Alexander Woollcott phrased it, "She had *invented* them. They were just comics she imagined for her own amusement" (54).

Until other people, as in paying customers, became as imaginative as Minnie about her boys' talent, she often played the huckster. For instance, during the group's early touring in small-time vaudeville (when the team included Groucho, Gummo, and Harpo), they were billed as a juvenile act, despite the members being teen-aged and older. Minnie capitalized on this by always obtaining half-price train fares, claiming each of the boys was thirteen. Eventually the act physically outgrew the ruse, though Minnie refused to admit it. When a conductor eventually reported to her that one "kid" of hers "is in the dining car smoking a cigar and another one is in the washroom shaving," Minnie (acting the wise fool) sadly shook her head and said, "They grow so fast." (G. Marx, *The Groucho Phile*, 18).

Minnie's stage-door-mother tendencies had increased clout with Groucho, given the show-business success of her younger brother Al Shean (changed from Schoenberg). At the beginning of the 1890s Shean had both organized and starred in the influential vaudeville comedy and musical act the Manhattan Comedy Four (which naturally sends one thinking of the later Four Marx brothers, especially since Uncle Al's comedy writing for his nephews helped elevate them to big-time entertainment). Today Shean is best known as part of the later vaudeville team of Gallagher and Shean (whose signature musical refrain was "Absolutely, Mr. Gallagher?" "Positively, Mr. Shean"), one of America's favorite comedy teams early in the twentieth century.

It was as if the coincidence of Groucho's birth (1890) paralleling the start of Uncle Al's vaudeville fame meant something extra to this nephew. Certainly the monthly visits of Shean would have represented a unique experience for any deprived child from a poor family, whether it was a Marx brothers family or otherwise.

Maybe the beguiling factor for Groucho, which differentiated him from his brothers, was that the entertainment-bitten mother he so idolized had obviously placed her brother Al on a comparably high level. Since Groucho was forever trying to please his mother anyway, some of Groucho's fascination with entertainment and Shean might have been an attempt at a closer relationship with Minnie.

But there were many other factors. For instance, young Groucho was self-conscious about his appearance and shy around girls. Uncle Al, in Groucho's own words, was a "handsome dog" (which period photography documents), whose sexual conquests were legend in the family and something he enjoyed elaborating on during each visit.

And there was the little factor of a party happening each time the funny and famous uncle visited. Shean's arrival generated a storm of Minnie-directed activity, as her boys were sent to buy Shean's favorite food and drink. Groucho's regular assignment was to purchase Kümmel cheese; Harpo normally bought the huckleberry cake; and Chico (being the oldest) picked up the beer.

Another plus for the boys was the financial side to their uncle's visits; as he prepared to leave he gave each one a silver coin. (Memories of the amount later varied, from Harpo recalling a top amount of a quarter, to Groucho placing the figure at a dollar.) Regardless, any amount for poor children would have been a major windfall.

Still, Groucho was the only one of the boys initially intrigued by show business. Harpo remembered it was always Groucho who begged Uncle Al to perform. The future mustachioed one also recollected seeing Shean perform in various vaudeville theaters around New York, something otherwise little commented on in biographical material concerning his brothers.

As related to this book, maybe the most pertinent attraction of Shean to the young Groucho was the hucksterism of a real showman. Minnie had no family corner on that characteristic. Writing in *Groucho and Me* over half a century later, the comedian remained mesmerized by the flashy conquering-hero visits of Uncle Al. Shean would arrive in frock coat and a silk hat, brandishing a gold-headed cane. As if he represented slumming royalty, a crowd of youngsters would begin to form, anxious for his traditional tossing out of nickels upon his exit. On stage or in real life, Shean was a tough act to follow.

Al, who was pulling down the then-astronomical salary of $150 per week, inspired some huckster thinking on Minnie's part. According to Groucho, Shean's "success convinced my mother that the theatre was a soft and lucrative racket" (*Groucho and Me*, 41).

Shean's hit status also inspired one of the most amusing attempted diddles in entertainment history. Al's brother Henry, deciding he should try show business too, devised a fake ventriloquism act. Henry's mock dummy would be his young and undersized nephew Gummo, encased in papier-mâché. Unfortunately, Uncle Henry was hard of hearing and Gummo stuttered, and since timing is a bit of everything in comedy, the act died rather quickly.

The ventriloquism slant had an earlier family connection. Groucho's maternal grandfather Lafe (Louis) Schoenberg, the father of Henry, Minnie, Al, and five other children, had been a touring magician and ventriloquist in Europe. And while there is no record of Lafe having hidden any of his children in a papier-mâché dummy, he had more than a little of the huckster in his otherwise mediocre act. For instance, he shocked audiences with his challenge to sever anyone's head and then reattach it. Here was an inspired con, until someone called his bluff (Lafe had not thought anyone would chance it), and he was run out of town by spectators who at least like to see their cons attempted.

With this kind of family background, Minnie did what was necessary for vaudeville survival and eventual success, from maximizing her managerial efficiency with a family act to using Frenchie's one great skill—cooking—to bribe prospective vaudeville bookers. Author Hector Arce's authorized biography *Groucho* likened Minnie's public persona to that of Barnum. Her wheeler-dealer skills were best showcased during the Chicago period, when she rechristened herself with the non-Jewish name Minnie Palmer, after a popular vaudeville star of the same name. She felt it would both help avoid anti-Semitism and add prestige, obviously aware of the possible windfalls through name confusion. The ploy was so effective that years later (1928) one of the first film articles on the Marx brothers included a lengthy notation on Mother Minnie but with actress Palmer's background (Wilson, 48). In fact, when Jack Benny was interviewed for the 1973 *The Marx Brothers Scrapbook* (he had a close vaudeville relationship with them), he still referred to their mother as Minnie *Palmer* (G. Marx and Anobile, 44). For someone based in Chicago, as the Marx family then was, Minnie's choice of names also borrowed from the grandeur of the city's renowned Palmer House (Arce, 97).

In later years Chico's daughter suggested that Minnie even encouraged her sons' anti-marriage womanizing ways because she "didn't want to share [control-wise] her boys with another woman" (M. Marx, 22). All this is not to detract from Minnie's many positive traits, from her fun-loving gregariousness to her open-door policy toward her friends and family. An early Marx brothers biographer termed their flat a "bus station," where "the door was never locked, there was a pot of coffee forever simmering on the stove, and the neighbors wandered in and out at random" (Crichton, 2, 4).

Still, while enjoying comic put-downs, Minnie was tough and could make the hard decision. Gummo once observed that when the United States entered World War I (1917) his mother "realized that somebody in the family would have to go. . . .You couldn't expect the young one [Zeppo] to go. Chico [by now in the act] was married. Groucho and Harpo were important to the act. Mom said, 'We can do without you [Gummo]'" (G. Marx and Anobile, 21).

Not surprisingly, another early parallel between W. C. and Groucho was that their later comedy personas drew more than a little from their mothers. For Fields, Kate Dukenfield's apparently congenial address followed by the cutting aside is the cornerstone of the humorist's comedy. An example of Kate's wit would be the following comment to a neighbor, "How do, Mrs. Barton, you're just too sweet in that tailored suit. You musta been to Paris. (Aside to family: 'She's been looting a farm somewhere. There's not a clothesline in town that she could steal rags like that off of.')" In truth, years later (1924), after she had seen her very successful son on Broadway, W. C. asked Kate's opinion of his work. Her simple reply was, "I didn't know you had such a good memory" (Taylor, 10). (Fields's methodical verbal pacing and the long-drawn-out vowel sounds were also said to be characteristic of his mother's speech.)

Fields's propensity for the tall tale quite possibly also has links to his mother. Although no such comments by Kate from the comedian's childhood survive, except for her colorfully elaborate asides, W. C. has credited her (something he rarely did for anyone) with being able to top him in this department. To illustrate this, an adult

Fields remembers telling Kate about his entertainment-related travels, a particular passion of Fields. He claimed that while visiting a particular aborigine tribe "they invited me to dinner—a very excellent repast, starting off with whale."

"Goodness!" replied Kate Dukenfield. "I should think that would make a meal itself" (Taylor, 10).

Fittingly, though not fortunately for his mother, turn-of-the-century pictures of Kate look a lot like the portly, prominent-nosed comedian late in his career. Add to this a family memory of Mrs. Dukenfield's voice being gravelly (another Fields trademark), and one has a number of mother-son comedy connections. Possibly with this in mind, the comedian would later indirectly footnote his mother's influence in the film short subject *The Barber Shop* (1933). Showcasing many Fields asides on the sidewalk (the original location of Kate's cracks) in front of the barber shop, the comedian called his movie town Felton City, after his mother's maiden name.

Just as Fields and his mother excelled at the cynical aside, Groucho's biting putdowns seem a direct outgrowth of his mother's verbal style. Since Minnie ruled the family and husband Frenchie, it is possible that a young Groucho would assume the normal relationship between men and women to be one of verbal attack. But because Groucho was initially the family member most vulnerable to his mother's barbs, one might suggest, as does Groucho biographer and friend Hector Arce, that the comedian eventually assumed the mantle of verbal attacker out of self-defense (39). Certainly, this must have been a factor in Groucho's later decidedly misogynistic comedy, especially his famous film cracks at the expense of stuffy, matronly socialite Margaret Dumont. For example, in *Cocoanuts* (1929), he told her, "I'll meet you tonight under the moon. Oh, I can see you now—you and the moon. You wear a neck-tie so I'll know you."

Appropriately, numerous recent "interviews with comedy writers and comedians have shown that professional humorists typically had strong and consistent models of joking and clowning in one or both parents" (McGee, 190). The oral-history text most often cited is the William F. Fry and Melanie Allen collection—*Make 'Em Laugh: Life Studies of Comedy Writers*, with the Norman Lear and Bob Henry interviews being the most provocative. Also, the comedians studied were invariably closest to their mothers, *even* if she had not been overly protective in the pre-school years. Indeed, studies have now shown that elementary-age children with a marked sense of humor—which W. C. and Groucho demonstrated—are more likely to have had "a lack of prior maternal babying and protectiveness" (McGee, 192).

An added parallel is that as an obvious corollary to the strong mother figures of both Fields and Groucho, their fathers were much less respected. W. C. later described his parents' union as "a marriage of convenience, as my father had a blister on his big toe and couldn't travel very far to find a girl" (Monti, 39). James Dukenfield peddled fruit and vegetables from a horse-drawn cart in the streets of Philadelphia. Just as W. C. enjoyed mocking his father's Cockney accent at home, in the streets he relished parodying his father's food-hawking voice. (The comedian's later nasal drawl is sometimes considered an outgrowth of this street spoofing, Mrs. Dukenfield's deliberate gravelly voice notwithstanding.)

From childhood on, Fields had a lifelong interest in words, especially funny-sounding ones. This, too, spelled trouble for the father. The boy savored announcing such produce as "pomegranates, rutabagas, calabashes"—whether Mr. Dukenfield had them for sale or not (Ford, 65). Fields's early interest in juggling created further father-son tension; the boy practiced with the produce, invariably bruising it.

As if all this were not enough for the antiheroic father/husband Mr. Dukenfield, the young Fields hated the Claude portion of his given name and was forever after James to legally change it to Whitey (a childhood nickname based on the comedian's blond hair). It was not unusual for the exasperated father to hit him. Much later, a tongue-in-cheek Fields would observe that he had received so many cuffs on the head with the back of James's hand that he "often wondered what the other side of the hand looked like" (Monti, 39). Despite this comic reframing, it is not hard to understand the boy's runaway tendencies, even if he later possibly exaggerated the duration of his leave-taking—exaggeration that is probably another example of Fields flirting with the tall tale off-screen, much as he did in the movies.

Variations of these father-son interactions do reappear in Fields's later films. For example, in *It's a Gift* (1934, arguably his best movie), he runs a grocery store, with one routine revolving around a customer's attempt to buy ten pounds of kumquats (a funny alliterative use of the double *k* sound, comically compounded by having the word spelled out incorrectly—with a *k*). Naturally, the sketch is frequently punctuated with the word *kumquat*. And just as Mr. Dukenfield seems to have been constantly bothered by his son, Fields's screen persona is perpetually annoyed by mischievous little boys. *It's a Gift* features the comedian's perennial film child nemesis Baby LeRoy, who in this outing turned on the spigot to the store's molasses keg, forcing proprietor W. C. to put out a sign saying "CLOSED ON ACCOUNT OF MOLASSES."

But the screen comedian was not always so diplomatic. In *The Old Fashioned Way* (1934) a boardinghouse child (LeRoy) dips Fields's watch into a jar of molasses during dinner. When no one is watching, W. C. nearly punts thc kid out of the room. (Of course, this section begs to also include a Fields signature statement: "I love children . . . parboiled.") With dark comedy finesse (and a touch of the surreal) he could draw humor from something that was less than funny in childhood.

There would be more future film huckster examples. When the young Fields accompanied his father on fruit-and-vegetable-hawking rounds, W. C. experienced firsthand the haggling that would go on between James and tough-bargaining Philadelphia housewives. The con-artist philosophy was further instilled in the comedian by his childhood jobs, both for his father and others. With a produce-wagon horse to feed, one of W. C.'s chores was to obtain hay. It was the boy's assignment to follow the hay wagons that area farmers brought to the city market each Friday and collect any stray bits. Unfortunately, one could not always depend on much hay falling off the wagons. Consequently, as if anticipating some sort of Orwellian "doublethink," English-born James Dukenfield told his son, "Of course, you must not steal, but if you can grab a few hands full from the [passing] wagons it will be all right" (Tulley, 60).

In addition, a huckster history lesson from his father would later result in the title of Fields's first feature-length starring film role— *It's the Old Army Game* (1926). The phrase refers to the nineteenth-century sleight-of-hand con game in which a pea is hidden under one of three walnut shells faster than most betting eyes can detect. The comedian's father and Yankee soldier veteran told him that after the Civil War (heyday years for Barnum) traveling hucksters and circus drifters referred to their shell games as "It's the old army game. A boy can play as well as a man." The hook of mentioning that a boy could play was an attempt to lull the adult sucker into something allegedly quite easy.

1. Fields at the old shell game in *Sally of the Sawdust* (1925).

Fields was never quite sure if his father had been a shell-game con artist—or a victim—only that he seemed to know a lot about it. Given Mr. Dukenfield's aforementioned tip on the acquisition of hay, I would venture to bet he was the one hiding the pea.

Interestingly enough, hucksterish Fields's first title preference for his 1926 movie was *Never Give a Sucker an Even Break*; Paramount thought it a bit harsh. The fact that Paramount was reluctant to use the title is significant, since it was the most nurturing of the major studios towards comedians in the pre–World War II period. The comedian kept trying to use the film title until 1941, when Universal finally consented. Even so, Fields had managed to make the expression the meat of the printed moral at the close of *It's the Old Army Game*.

When his father farmed him out into the job market at age nine to earn money for the family, Fields's huckster education continued. Like P. T. Barnum's early general-store experiences, Fields's job as a cigar-store clerk was a story of gamesmanship. The establishment allegedly sold three types of cigars, priced at three, ten, and twenty cents. But in truth the store only had the cheapest variety. If a customer ordered one of the more expensive brands, he was given the three-center and charged the higher price!

Groucho's father Frenchie was less respected and more antiheroic than James Dukenfield. Mr. Marx was a tailor but it was a job description applied loosely at best. Groucho observed, "his record as the most inept tailor that Yorkville [New York's Upper East Side, in Manhattan] ever produced has never been approached. This could even include parts of Brooklyn and the Bronx" (G. Marx, *Groucho and Me*, 15). Unfortunately, this tailor was also colorblind and did not believe in using a tape measure. Half his finished work went unaccepted by customers, and of course he had very little repeat business. Family finances were meager, with "Misfit Sam's" (his nickname among customers) income as a tailor "hovering between eighteen dollars a week and nothing" (*Groucho and Me*, 15, 23).

Even Frenchie, therefore, was forced into a traveling-huckster scenario. "Misfit Sam" found himself roaming farther and farther outside the neighborhood as his reputation spread. When Groucho or another son accompanied him, the boys could, however, learn the art of haggling firsthand, as was the case with Fields traveling with his father.

And just as there was a sneaky factor involved in W. C. helping his father obtain the hay, Frenchie's family assistant was the "Defect Concealer." That is, besides his door-to-door pitch for tailoring jobs, Frenchie tried to peddle flawed material remnants from old jobs. The underage "Defect Concealer" had to be manipulatively skillful, since the fabric had to be held up in such a manner that the potential customer did not see the holes or tears.

As one researches Frenchie's position in this zany household, there is a Germanic twist that heightens his antiheroic image. He had left his homeland to avoid German subjugation, yet he had married a dominating German woman in America. Then his bride brought her German parents to their new household, and other relatives of Minnie Schoenberg soon joined them. As one Groucho biographer observed, Frenchie had left his French province to avoid German domination but had now "let down his guard and was irrevocably subjugated by [another] German horde" (Arce, 26). Even his nickname originated in German derision; his sons sarcastically coined it as a comment on their father's loss of all things French.

Frenchie probably would have felt just as much at home in a

cartoon-strip episode of "The Katzenjammer Kids," with Minnie playing Mama. And like the adult antiheroes of that strip (the Captain and the Inspector), Frenchie could not put anything past his domineering mother-figure. For instance, Minnie once caught him in bed with one of her perennially visiting relatives. Though this did not result in the most pleasant of time for Frenchie (there is no record of Minnie's weapon of choice being a frying pan or a rolling pin), his mother-figure eventually forgave him and drove the young woman from the tiny apartment.

While in no way condoning Frenchie's action, there is a comic slant to it that further accents his antiheroic nature. Who but a comic prisoner of some immigrant farce (that does describe his plight) would attempt such an indiscretion in a minuscule household bursting with his wife's relatives?! It sounds more like something out of Marx brothers *film*, either the stateroom scene in *A Night at the Opera* (1936), where people are so packed in they just come rolling out when the door is opened, or Groucho's attempt to

2. Packed in like sardines—the stateroom scene of *A Night at the Opera* (1936).

get romantic with someone in *A Day at the Races* (1937), in which Chico and Harpo hover about and above as the most incompetent of wallpaper hangers. Of course, the cynic might hypothesize that Frenchie was merely getting revenge by doing something stereotypically French (being romantic) in a decidedly German household.

A further connection between W. C. and Groucho involved the hardships of their childhoods. Despite the revisionist claims of Fields's family, there seems little doubt there was a father-son conflict that made the boy familiar (at least periodically) with a street existence.

To illustrate, in Fields's last years his mistress Carlotta Monti remembers him saying, "I don't want any funeral. Just cremate me. I had enough of the cold ground in my youth" (Monti, 229). There are also periodic references in Fields literature to how early street deprivations later made him forever thankful for simple pleasures: "To this day [Fields at fifty-five, in 1935], when I climb in between clean sheets, I *smile*. When I get into bed and stretch out—god damn, that's a sensation" (Johnston, "Profiles: I," 24).

Young W. C. periodically was in trouble for stealing. Early accounts, such as the aforementioned Fields-authorized biography, claim he had to cheat and steal to live (23). Regardless of motive, even his family acknowledged the youngster's pleasure in petty crime.

The most common tale of Fields's five-finger-discount tendencies concerns robbing a Chinese laundry (with a baker business theft tied into some accounts). Fields would have a crime assistant at the nearest trolley-car track with his back toward an approaching train. By waiting until the last possible second before jumping clear, the youngster (note even then that Fields avoided the dangerous role) created a noisy distraction (from the train's clanging bell and squeaking brakes). With this *sound* cover easily drowning out the small safety-bell door sounds of most nearby businesses, W. C. was then free to saunter in and steal whatever he pleased. Depending on which story version one hears, the payoff ranged from the cash-register contents to money *and* lemon meringue pies.

The boy's free-spirited larcenous ways placed him not only at odds with family, business owners, and the law, but also up against other dangers. Many up-and-coming young toughs attempted to obtain one-step reputations by beating up Philadelphia's version of Huckleberry Finn (his main defense was periodically playing the fool—pretending to be generally addled in the head). Moreover, his skills as a pool hustler also put him in periodic danger of physical abuse from the suckers who had mistakenly assumed they were going to be the ones taking the money.

In contrast to Fields the budding juvenile delinquent (acting out for attention?), Groucho attempted to obtain favor by being the perfect child. But this approach was not successful, either. As Chico observed, Groucho "was always trying to be the good son, while I was busy being the bad one—and yet Minnie [their mother] always forgave me and loved me and was never that way with Groucho" (M. Marx, 172).

Part of Groucho's less-than-favored position with his mother might have been based in appearance. Older brothers Chico and Harpo had decidedly Germanic looks with light hair and fair complexions. Also Germanic in appearance, Minnie thought of herself as more German than Jewish, and as her older boys' light hair darkened with age, she kept it light with peroxide. Groucho's prominent nose, dark, coarse hair, and dark complexion favored the family's Jewish heritage. In addition, Groucho had a cast in his left eye that kept both eyes from tracking in unison.

Beyond the question of adequate affection for Groucho at home, there was the ongoing problem of a tight income, given Frenchie's mediocre tailoring skills. Thus, late-night moves to avoid paying overdue rent were not uncommon. Even with this periodic cleaning of the slate, any Marx family possession that might happen to be valuable was still in danger from a live-in delinquent: Chico. Groucho later observed, "there were times when the pawnshop on Third Avenue contained more of the Marx family's possessions than the Marx flat did" (*Groucho and Me*, 22).

Chico needed the money for what was becoming an obsession— all forms of gambling. Today the psychiatric community knows it to be a compulsive behavioral disorder. Then, it simply meant Groucho and family had to either hide favored items or quickly liquidate such possessions themselves. Chico's compulsion could also add further eccentricity to the house, such as Harpo taking the hands off his watch to safeguard it. Ironically, even Chico's card playing could further negatively color Groucho's relationship with his card-playing parents. The future mustachioed one neither liked cards nor demonstrated any skill along these lines, and Frenchie told him that "until you learn to be a good pinochle player you will never be a real man" (*Groucho and Me*, 24).

Like the young Fields, Groucho and his brothers grew up on the streets in tough neighborhoods. While the Marx boys also were involved in their fair share of petty crime, they were more likely than Fields to avoid fights. To a degree, this was possibly in their upbringing. Frenchie, an immigrant who came to America in part to avoid the German military draft, could not physically punish his children—though by taking the offender to another room he could fake a good beating. On the other hand, the Civil War–decorated James Dukenfield had no trouble physically disciplining his children.

Moving beyond W. C.'s con of playing dumb in a dangerous street situation, the Marxes fell back on several different huckster techniques. These ranged from the most bold of diddles (assuming the ethnic dialect of the gang whose space had been violated) to carrying some expendable trinkets with which to bribe one's way out of trouble. Groucho hit upon the most foolproof safety valve—just do not leave the neighborhood!

This simple defense tactic was really based in another Groucho trait that often made his youth difficult. The youngster loved to curl up with a pile of library books—rather an alien characteristic in his family and among young peers. He often was the odd boy out. Indeed, it added to the estrangement with his mother, who nicknamed him "der dunkeler" (the dark one) because he was somehow suspect for reading. Ironically, this label also reinforced the fact that he looked more Jewishly dark than Chico and Harpo, the sons Minnie most favored.

Like Fields's back-of-the-hand joke concerning being struck by his father, Groucho tended to deflect pain with humor. Consequently, probably the best look at the dark side of his youth came from the straight-talking autobiography of Harpo, the brother with whom he was always closest:

> When I was a kid there really was no future. Struggling through one twenty-four-hour span was rough enough without brooding about the next one. You could laugh about the Past, because you'd been lucky enough to survive it. But mainly there was only a Present to worry about. (H. Marx, 27)

Because of this poignant sense of "no future," it seems fitting that the young Groucho loved reading the forever-hopeful Horatio Alger stories. Conversely, given the later pointed cynicism of his humor, the Groucho-Horatio connection might now make one smile.

But huckster historian Gary Lindberg has sketched out the relevance between the Alger world and any tendency to parody it. Lindberg uses Mark Twain's whitewashing scheme in *Tom Sawyer* as his focus, in which Tom goes from being the poorest of poor boys in the morning to the owner of all the other boys' riches in the afternoon. Lindberg observes that Tom's turnabout "is not so much spoofing the ethic of Franklin and Horatio Alger as indicating how the ethic converges with the popular admiration for conning enterprises and with the tolerance for playfully relaxed principles among 'boys'" (188). The bottom line in each case is success and the freedom it brings.

Lindberg later adds: "To notice Tom's lack of inwardness is to be reminded that the autobiographies of Franklin and Barnum, like the lives of Alger's characters, are also peculiarly free of psychological complication" (192). This break with painful feelings allows a character like Tom (or Groucho's later screen persona) the security of almost any action *not* being interpreted as cruel.

An amusingly telling example of a premeditated Groucho con that avoided conflict outside the family was his bread scam. It was his job to buy the family's daily loaf of bread, which cost a nickel for a fresh loaf. But the young businessman found he could purchase day-old bread for the more reasonable price of four cents a loaf, and thus was born a modest source of income.

Without belaboring the early hard times of W. C. and Groucho, it is fitting at this point to expand upon a previous observation concerning our culture's fascination with the clown's background. Clowns comically comfort us in our short lives with their resilience—both physically and spiritually (Welsford, 314–15). Moreover, society seems most fascinated with the clown biography that reveals tragic roots—the adaptability to provoke laughter despite personal sadness. Thus, W. C.'s and Groucho's successes, despite difficult early years, are the stuff of comic legend—humor's version of the phoenix. It also provides an added legitimacy to their forays into antiheroic humor, despite their more pronounced images as hucksters.

In all the sub-genres of comedy, the clown variety is the most predictable—which is why so many people enjoy clowns. Their comedy shtick is familiar, and one savors the entertainment comfort of a known persona. Variations from the norm are still within certain boundaries. Story is forever secondary to the clown's antics, whether it be Groucho's sexual innuendo, or W. C. Fields's wife-dominated male. Of course, variations on classic routines such as Fields's golf and pool sketches, invite comparison with earlier renditions. This guarantees "that the comic performer remains imperfectly integrated into any particular character role" (Jenkins, 145).

A final early tie between W. C. and Groucho was their fascination with being performers. The catalyst for Fields was seeing the Burns brothers' juggling act at a Philadelphia vaudeville house, with dates for this momentous event ranging between 1888 and 1895.

Suffice it to say, a young W. C. was mesmerized by the art of juggling *and* (an often neglected point) by comedy. (As if setting an important precedent for his new career, Fields had snuck into this vaudeville theater.) The Burns act was grounded in comic subterfuge, by which one of the tennis balls being juggled was periodically seen to be on the verge of getting away, only to be caught with some miraculous comic movement.

Fields's huckster tendencies would continue to serve him well throughout his entertainment days. Thus, W. C. *borrowed* the Burns brothers' act, after he spent two years of conscientious practicing. (He was, no doubt, an early believer in the sincerest form of flattery being . . . theft.) In time he would improve upon the act's humor and subterfuge by adding more conscious errors, though the seemingly accidental ease with which he invariably solved each mistake, such as a dropped ball, further revealed his gift for juggling. He intuitively knew that the best comedy is either spontaneous or made to seem that way.

By the turn of the century Fields was a vaudeville headliner, both in this country and abroad. Providentially, he was asked at this time to write two essays for Percy Thomas Tibble's prestigious but now very rare British reference volume, *The Magician's Handbook: A Complete Encyclopedia of the Magic Art for Professional and Amateur Entertainers.*

Fields's essays, which are entertainingly written in and of themselves, explain the mechanics of two comic juggling tricks—"A New Hat and Cigar Effect" and "The Great Cigar-Box Trick." The showstopper, as well as the trick requiring the most subterfuge (fittingly for Fields) was the cigar-box routine. This involved throwing five boxes into the air (in his earlier act borrowed from the Burns brothers, he juggled five tennis balls). W. C. then "catches the whole five balanced upon each other's end, making quite a tall pile as they steady down" (125). However, just as the applause reaches its zenith, the balance of the boxes is "accidently" destroyed and they fall . . . almost . . . before it becomes obvious to the audience that the boxes are attached by a cord.

As if drawing directly from Barnum's thesis that people enjoy being fooled (see Chapter 2), Fields wrote that this cigar-box con "secures a laugh so hearty as to nearly shake the foundation of the theatre when the audience sees how they have been sold" (125). Impressively, the juggling comedian added that viewer appreciation for this diddle would even surpass the impressive initial audience response when they thought the routine was one of "miraculous dexterity." Thus, playing the huckster with a surprise topper could double one's laughter quotient.

Despite Fields's amusingly breezy style in these essays, as in his later writing, he still meticulously explains the mechanics of each routine as well as the fine tuning involved in milking it for laughs. The deliberate comedy style described anticipates the screen heritage Fields would eventually give the world, though he does not talk general comedy theory in Tibble's book.

Two entertainment stops along Fields's way up demonstrate both the type of dues he paid as a performer and the persistence of his huckster tendencies. The first stop was an early teenage booking as a juggler and part-time drowning victim at Fortescue's Pier in Atlantic City. There was no admission charge for Fields's comic juggling and the other acts. The Pier made its money strictly from selling beer and sandwiches. Consequently, when business was down, Fields would swim out and pretend to be drowning. The dramatic rescue and resuscitation would always attract a crowd. Concession barkers would successfully descend on the mob, and management would be happy. The increasingly waterlogged young man often did his drowning act several times daily.

The later alcoholic Fields would sometimes kiddingly credit this unorthodox marketing technique as the source of his longtime dislike of water (though his famous, or infamous, X-rated explanation is more succinct: "I never drink water because fish f____ in it." This statement was apparently uttered on numerous occasions by the comedian. Bob Hope, on a late 1960s visit to *The Tonight Show*, credited Fields with recycling it during a break in the production of

The Big Broadcast of 1938, a film in which they both starred.) Regardless, while one cannot deny the comic logic by which a part-time drowning career would lessen one's interest in water, it is surprising that he and his biographers never addressed the black-comedy learning experience it must have been for the young Fields to see how hungry and thirsty an all-American crowd could become after contemplating a near-tragedy. Certainly this was the kind of life experience that contributed to his darkly comic world view as an adult, not to mention a further justification for hucksterism (if there had ever been any doubt) based on a less-than-positive image of the human species.

The other early entertainment position of special interest found Fields juggling at the Globe Museum in New York, an inexpensive entertainment establishment whose eccentric acts (including a bearded lady, a fire eater, and a headless woman) were reminiscent of Barnum's once precedent-setting, New York–based American Museum with its attractions such as the "Fejee Mermaid." Fields considered his countless daily shows in a small stall at the Globe invaluable practice, crediting them with the takeoff to his career that soon followed this experience (Mullett, 145). But once again it was a setting where entertainment was strongly equated with hucksterism, especially as Fields spent much of his free time during this period with these "performers."

Fields's early Globe Museum connection might also have contributed to his Barnum-like fascination with using legitimate human oddities, especially dwarf-sized individuals, as part of his comedy. Barnum's autobiography is laced with the successful utilization of such cases, from his General Tom Thumb and little Commodore Nutt, to the "woman in miniature," Lavinia Warren. Barnum would call such examples a "perfect treasure" for the showman. Likewise, Fields would later pursue a similar hiring practice, though for more comically perverse reasons. For instance, according to his first biographer, Robert Lewis Taylor, the comedian invariably hired the most physically "grotesque" characters, preferably dwarfed, to play the caddy stooge in his classic golf routine.

This tendency in Fields should not be confused with a dwarf prank the comedian played on Florenz Ziegfeld (with whom he constantly argued during W. C.'s years in the *Follies*). The superstitious Ziegfeld considered dwarves bad luck, and when Fields found this out he hired the dwarf William "Shorty" Blanche as his personal man Friday. Eventually, Shorty was included in the act, but Fields's inclination toward physically odd characters predated this, matching his lifelong dark sense of humor. At its most basic, it possibly reflects the Victorian era's fascination with the grotesque, on which Barnum so effectively capitalized. Indeed, Barnum found the greatest fascination for the bizarre in Europe, and Fields, too, toured the Continent extensively.

There is a Barnum-related irony that bears noting at this point. Like the showman, part of Fields's interest in entertainment was based in a dislike of physical labor—a tendency that had greatly concerned both their fathers. The paradox for young W. C., however, involved the strenuous workload he then assumed to master juggling. Combining a philosophy of "If I can lift it I can juggle it" with sixteen-hour practice days, his training was both laborious and at times painful, as he tried to catch and balance any manner of things on his face and feet.

Still, the bugaboo traditional labor job that kept Fields's juggling craft looking ever more attractive was a short-lived early-morning ice-delivery position. Whenever he felt like taking a day off from juggling practice, W. C. threatened himself with, "Screw back to Philadelphia and get on that ice wagon" (Johnston, "Profiles: II," 24). In a 1926 interview for an article appropriately titled "He Hated Alarm-Clocks," the comedian also underscored the importance of learning a trade that did not involve getting up early (Hanemann, 39).

Like Fields, Groucho's early inspiration for a career in entertainment came out of vaudeville—the aforementioned show-business success of Minnie's younger brother Al Shean. But despite this prominent entertainment connection, the vaudeville rise of Groucho and company would be slow. Indeed, Groucho's 1905 beginning in show business found him victimized. This aborted start was as a fifteen-year-old boy singer in the Leroy Trio. It was hardly a wow act, and the naive teenager, who "knew as much about the world as the average retarded eight-year-old" (G. Marx, *Groucho and Me*, 55) soon found himself stranded in the wilds of Colorado. Not only had his partners disbanded the act without telling him, but they also had relieved Groucho of his money as he slept.

As with the early career of Fields, this would not be the only time Groucho would find himself stranded. History would repeat itself in Dallas and again in Chicago. Though not yet tagged with the nickname Groucho, he was building an impressive portfolio of reasons for having it.

The initial show-business version of the Marx brothers did not occur until 1907. Composed only of Groucho, Gummo, and singer Mabel O'Donnell, the group was christened by Minnie as The Three Nightingales. This was either a con, or as Groucho later speculated, reflected the possibility that his mother had never heard a nightingale. Mabel was soon replaced (her voice always veered off key) by a young singer named Lou Levy. In 1908 the modestly successful group became a foursome with the addition of Harpo. About 1910 Minnie moved their home base from New York to Chicago because the latter city was more of a booking haven for small-time vaudeville.

In Chicago the Four Nightingales became The Six Mascots, a short-lived singing and dancing act that was beginning to add a modicum of humor to its material. The troupe included Groucho, Gummo, Harpo, bass singer Freddie Hutchins, and two girl singers. However, when the girls left the group early, Minnie attempted a con that even she could not pull off: Mother Marx and her sister Hannah replaced the girls. These two maturely stout "ingenues" quickly ended both the run of this particular Marx act and any lingering onstage aspirations of Minnie.

But later the same year (1910) the brothers organized and began touring with a show called *Funn in Hi Skule*. The troupe would come to be called the "3 Marx Bros. & Co.," with a 4 replacing the 3 after the 1912 addition of Chico. It was with this sketch that a rough early facsimile of what is now known as Marx-brothers humor started to emerge.

Their use of Peasie Weasie material, a then-popular style of comic song (based upon word plays such as puns) in vaudeville and burlesque, would foreshadow the later nonstop verbal slapstick of the team's mature work. Groucho's German Herr Teacher (Mr. Green, though still with an accent) was a mustachioed older-man persona that anticipated the essentially dirty-old-man character that he would play in the future. The sketch's cartoon-like satire of education is a primitive first cousin to what the Marx Brother's later films do best—bringing anarchic comedy to frequently rigid institutional settings.

Though already well established as a performer in the first decade of the twentieth century, W. C. Fields's glory years as an artist begin in the 1910s. The culmination of his overseas entertaining occurred

October 11, 1913, when he gave a command performance at Buckingham Palace before King Edward VII. There is a certain irony, of course, in this distinction, since the young Fields (and his mother) had enjoyed baiting the elder Fields about his English accent.

The comic juggler was the only American performer so honored on this occasion. Appearing with him was the now-legendary French stage tragedienne Sarah Bernhardt, who sporadically lent dignity (if little else) to early silent cinema—a medium W. C. would soon try.

The following year, 1914, after Fields's lengthy success in big-time vaudeville, a major career move came when he was signed for New York's famed *Ziegfeld Follies*. Starting in 1915, he would be in seven consecutive editions of the *Follies*, a record for Ziegfeld performers. Now Fields would be able to showcase his talents among the greatest comedians of the day: Will Rogers, Ed Wynn, Fanny Brice, Bert Williams, and Eddie Cantor. While he still juggled, Fields had also developed through the years a number of other routines that he utilized in the *Follies*.

The most famous of these sketches, his pool routine, would be recorded on film in 1915 as the one-reel (ten-minute) *Pool Shark*. Inspired by his pool-hustling youth, the stage routine added its own con—an elaborate, specially made trick pool table—which complemented his juggling. But because the table was both difficult to move and in use twice daily for Manhattan's *Follies*, it was not available to the Long Island studio where the film was shot. Thus, the con's use of a trick table gave way to trick photography, with the recorded routine not being an authentic reproduction of the stage sketch.

Fields's one-reel film *His Lordship's Dilemma* was made immediately after *Pool Sharks* and showcased a golf routine, another of his stage sketches. The movie is now lost, so just how much of the act made the transition to the screen is unclear. But since his golf-club props were decidedly more mobile than the cumbersome pool table, this second film short probably pictured the golf bit more accurately than *Pool Sharks* did its act.

Although the comedian would not make another film for a decade, these two shorts are important in his pivotal work of the 1910s. Besides reflecting his first foray into this medium, they set two important film precedents. In future movies, Fields would continue to recycle variations of his stage material, often playing real-life huckster by commanding large writing fees for essentially recycled (though invariably entertaining) material. Not surprisingly, there would be several more film appearances of these early mainstay routines of pool and golf.

In addition, *Pool Sharks* and *His Lordship's Dilemma* feature more Fields signature material: both display his enjoyment of the bottle, or what the former film calls "angel milk." And *Pool Sharks* also includes the eventually obligatory comic battle with a little boy.

Another pivotal Fields development during the 1910s, in addition to the film and *Follies* connections, was his writing. Becoming more serious about his comic compositions, he began to copyright them. Doing research on the comedian in the early 1980s, I happened upon his seemingly forgotten copyrighted sketches at the Library of Congress (Gehring, "W. C. Fields: Copyrighted Sketches," 65–75). Between 1918 and 1930, W. C. registered twenty-three separate comedy documents on sixteen subjects (some sketches were copyrighted more than once when changes were made).

This least known of his then-professional activities now looms as a fascinating look at the evolution of his antiheroic humor. Indeed, this documentation of Fields's victimized-male persona—his time usurped by dominating women, machines, and the urban setting in general—places the comedian's work in the vanguard of this character's development.

One of the earliest of these sketches, "The Mountain Sweep Stakes" (1919), shows Fields to be a much more avid period-film fan than has been previously suggested. The plot is a parody of the standard melodrama, anticipating the comedian's spoof of the play-within-a-play *The Drunkard* in his later movie *The Old-Fashioned Way* (1934). But "The Mountain Sweep Stakes" is peopled with a cross-section of 1910s film stars, from pioneer cowboy William S. Hart and vamp Theda Bara to Hollywood's first cinema couple, Mary Pickford and Douglas Fairbanks, Sr. These stars and several others are amusingly integrated into the story, with Fields demonstrating an excellent understanding of his star characters.

The greatest "Mountain Sweep Stakes" revelation—spell it *bombshell*—is the hero of the piece: Charlie Chaplin's Tramp figure. Historically, the comedian with the potato nose was better known for his later less-than-charitable thoughts of Chaplin. For instance, Fields's last mistress recalled, "To his [comedy] contemporaries he was fairly charitable, with the one notable exception of Charlie Chaplin. He referred to him as a 'goddamned ballet dancer.'

It had to be pure jealousy" (Monti, 74). This sense of envy is comically caught in another later W. C. pronouncement, his assessment for friends of a revival of Chaplin's *Easy Street*: "He's the world's greatest ballet dancer, and if I ever meet the son of a bitch I'll murder him!" (Chaplin, 143).

Yet in "The Mountain Sweep Stakes," Fields makes the Chaplin character the winner—literally and metaphorically. The Tramp captures the big mortgage-saving car race (on foot!) and is allowed to maintain more of his screen uniqueness. For example, unlike the other silent-film stars parodied in the sketch, the Tramp maintains the universality of his silence. He does not fall comic victim to lines like "Dug [Fairbanks] is my sweet Patootie."

Fields also pays Chaplin a hucksterish compliment by including a scene in his 1919 "The Mountain Sweep Stakes" (and thus copyrighting it) that had already appeared two years earlier in another Tramp film, *The Adventurer*. The Fields scene in question has ice cream being delivered to the Bara and Chaplin characters, with the latter spilling some into his own trousers. But while he tries to shake it down his pant leg without distracting Bara, the ice cream drops through both his pants and the floor grating underneath, ending up on the back of a diner below.

As luck would have it, Fields himself, in an obscure 1920s interview, acknowledges the source of the scene, though not as a theft in connection with his sketch: "I think the funniest scene I almost ever saw was in one of Chaplin's old pictures. He is eating some ice-cream and it falls down his trousers. You remember that one [*The Adventurer*]" (Redway, 33).

Though Fields was a gifted, innovative comedian, such "borrowing" was not unusual. He himself observed, with con-man honesty, "Thou shalt not steal—only from other comedians" (Monti, 69). There is a famous story from the 1910s where Fields picks a backstage fight with a comic contemporary who was allegedly using some W. C. material. But after they were pulled apart, with sketch origins compared, it was found that Fields had forgotten he had actually lifted the comedy items from the other performer years before!

While Fields had attained entertainment prominence early in the 1910s, Groucho and his brothers were still struggling in vaudeville's lower levels. But just as Fields's comic writing skills (occasionally peppered with borrowed material) had led to his rise, a new Marx brothers sketch during this period gave Groucho and company added significance. *Home Again* was written and staged for them by their Uncle Al Shean in 1914, the same year Fields signed with Ziegfeld. It is a show in two parts. *Home Again* opens at the New York pier of the Cunard Lines, where Groucho and family, including Gummo as his son, have returned from Europe; it concludes at a party at Groucho's villa on the Hudson. The latter segment was an improved variation on an earlier Marx brothers comedy sketch.

As with Fields, the Marx brothers films would later steal from themselves, with high-society parties and ocean liners often serving as settings for future films. Their "anything goes" humor is especially perfect in a decadent party, where one expects the unusual and enjoys effronteries to elitists. Moreover, they bring "welcome insanity [to] the deadly affair that is supposed to be fun and never is" (Adamson, 153).

Home Again was a major critical and commercial success. After a New York opening at the Royal Theatre (following several trial months on the road), *Variety* described it as "the best tab[loid] New York has ever seen . . . an act big time could depend upon for a future" (16). The routine soon opened to more praise at the celebrated Palace Theatre, the dream play-date of every vaudeville act. The time was 1915, paralleling Fields's opening year in the *Follies*.

Groucho's *Home Again* character is the wealthy, elderly Henry Schroeder, thus continuing his stage persona of an old German comedian. But international politics soon would necessitate a change. The early World War I German sinking of the British passenger ship *Lusitania* (in May 1915), with many Americans aboard, suddenly made everything German suspect, and Groucho's stage persona immediately lost its Teutonic tendencies.

As if to give special significance to the period, as well as their approaching celebrity, the Marxes would also receive their famous nicknames at this time. They were inspired by cartoonist Charles Mager's phenomenally popular parody strip *Sherlock, the Monk* (1910), which spoofed Sir Arthur Conan Doyle's Sherlock Holmes and was populated with characters whose dominant idiosyncrasies were reflected in their names, all of which ended with the letter *o*. Nicknamed by a fellow vaudevillian, the tags stuck. Cynical Julius became Groucho; harp-playing Adolph converted to Harpo; girl (chick)-chasing Leonard changed to Chicko (a typesetter later accidentally dropped the *k* and the new spelling was retained), and the gumshoe-attired Milton became Gummo. (Herbert, not yet with the team, acquired the nickname Zeppo at a later date.)

That Groucho and company should have a comic-strip connection at this time is most appropriate. As suggested in the previous chapter, one cannot fully understand period humor developments without examining the era's cartoon strips. This is especially true of Groucho and his brothers; their celebration of absurdity seems right at home among what were frequently antiheroic newspaper funnies.

There is no evidence that the brothers drew anything beyond their nicknames from the strip, though Groucho seems to have closely followed it for years. Still, the basic premise of *Sherlocko*, balancing parody with the satirical undercutting of any number of established authority figures, would soon be the norm of the Marxes.

In an age before the national audiences of radio and television constantly necessitated new material, the Marxes were able to tour for years in Uncle Al's *Home Again*. It also represented a safety valve in times of trouble. For instance, in the fall of 1918 the Marxes mounted a musical comedy they hoped would carry them to Broadway. Called *The Street Cinderella*, it was unable to find an audience, largely because of the severe Spanish influenza epidemic then afflicting the country. Because of the disease, which would eventually kill tens of thousands, health officials restricted the Grand Rapids, Michigan, opening of *Cinderella* to an audience where every other seat and every other row had to be empty. With many patrons also protecting themselves by handkerchief veils, the environment was not the most conducive for a musical-comedy success. The tour never made it out of Michigan, and Groucho and company returned to *Home Again* via the facsimile production *'N Everything*.

Arguably, the single most important career openings for both W. C. and Groucho took place on Broadway less than nine months apart. The date for Fields was September 3, 1923; the play was a period musical comedy called *Poppy*. It made, or actually remade, his career and presented him with a new character (a full-blown huckster) and feature-film opportunities. Professor Eustace McGargle was a small-time 1870s con man who attempted to utilize his daughter in a definitely big-time swindle—passing her off as the heir to a fortune. Film historian William K. Everson observed: "McGargle had not been written with Fields in mind, but he well could have been" (27).

Fields would recreate the role twice for film (*Sally of the Sawdust*,

1925, and *Poppy*, 1936), and would frequently play variations of McGargle for the rest of his career. Today, of course, Fields is most closely identified with the carnival huckster, always on the lookout for suckers. But as this chapter will soon examine, it is unfortunate to suggest, as so many authors have, that Fields seldom strayed from this trickster character in his future work (Everson, 27; Taylor, 182; Yanni, 25).

Groucho and his brothers opened on Broadway on May 19, 1924, in *I'll Say She Is!* The storyline was about a rich girl looking for thrills from a love match. Eventually she is allowed to imagine herself as Napoleon's wife Josephine. The Napoleon scene was the revue's key sketch, and it was co-written by Groucho. It revolved around Napoleon's (Groucho) frequent returns from the war front to thwart the sexual advances of his advisers Gaston (Harpo), Francois (Chico), and Alphonse (Zeppo) upon Josephine, who was more than happy to meet the advisers halfway. Thus, a suspicious, tracking Groucho observes, "They say a man's home is his castle. Mine must be the Pennsylvania Station. Come out, come out, wherever you are" (G. Marx, *The Groucho Phile*, 45).

The sketch also features such celebrated and later recycled Marx brothers lines as "Beyond the Alps lies more Alps, and the Lord 'Alps those that 'Alps themselves" and "'Why, that's bigamy.' 'Yes, and it's bigamy, too.'" Appropriately, and probably not accidentally for a group that so thrived upon puns, Groucho's leading lady Josephine had a stage name—Lotta Miles—based upon her then well-known modeling association with the Springfield Tire Company.

The most germane thing about *I'll Say She Is!* to this book is that during this dream sequence Groucho plays a hucksterish powerful character (Napoleon) constantly brought to comic antiheroic lows (loss of love) by his brothers—a part, as previously examined, that his childhood prepared him to play. It also anticipates the best of their later films, such as *Duck Soup* (1933), where Groucho plays another conniving ruler, President Rufus T. Firefly of Freedonia, forever frustrated by his underling brothers.

The success of both *Poppy* and *I'll Say She Is!* was built on the most shaky of foundations. Fields was used to performing short routines that were long on juggling and contained little, if any, dialogue. The thought of memorizing a play's worth of dialogue terrified him: "I can't remember my lines in a twenty-minute sketch;

how the hell can I remember the dialogue in an entire play?"
(R. Fields, *A Life on Film*, 18–19). But *Poppy* producer Philip Good-
man signed Fields and then played nursemaid throughout rehearsals
as the comedian kept quitting because of his inability to remember
dialogue. And just as the comedian played a huckster, his performance was based in hucksterism—he was encouraged to ad lib if he
forgot lines. Plus, for pivotal dialogue, prompters were stationed at
both ends of the stage.

Impressively, the performance was seamless. Critic and humorist
Robert Benchley even observed that "*Poppy* . . . brings W. C. Fields
out of pantomime into a long intricate speaking-role that he handles
with all the ease and skill that he has in the past bestowed on
billiard balls and [juggling] cigar boxes" ("Overture," 18).

Unlike Fields's personal challenge to remember lines, Groucho
and company's success with *I'll Say She Is!* was over an entirely
different sort of obstacle—they had been blacklisted by the all-
powerful E. F. Albee of the cadillac vaudeville circuit Keith-Albee, to
whom the Marxes were under contract. (The team's summer 1922
English tour had been undertaken without his approval.) Being
blacklisted is hardly the most conventional route to Broadway, but it
proved to be the Marxes' catalyst. Starting with a bargain-basement
Philadelphia production in the summer of 1923, *I'll Say She Is!* went
on the road and the Marxes worked it into the spring 1924 New York
hit that changed their careers.

The Broadway triumphs of W. C. and Groucho generated a number of 1920s opportunities for the comedians. Fields would divide
his time between movies (see the Filmography) and stage work,
while the Marxes followed *I'll Say She Is!* with more Broadway hits:
The Cocoanuts (1925–28) and *Animal Crackers* (1928–30; both sets
of dates include tours). Each production would later be made into a
film.

While Groucho and company were thus giving the public more of
what they tapped into from *I'll Say She Is!*, W. C. had still another
experience of career-expanding magnitude—J. P. McEvoy's stage
production *The Comic Supplement*. *Poppy* had served up a nearly
complete comedy character (McGargle), which Fields, once over his
fear of memorizing lines, wisely recognized as a perfect vehicle for
many of his undirected entertainment tendencies. *The Comic Supplement* then became the finishing degree for the comedian's already proven antiheroic inclinations.

Paradoxically, this important revue closed on the road, although its best routines (and Fields's) reached Broadway in the 1925 spring and summer editions of the *Ziegfeld Follies*. Thus, little is written about *The Comic Supplement*, in terms of literature on either Fields or the theater in general. Yet it is the basis for the comedian's excellent silent film *It's the Old Army Game* (1926), which was remade as his greatest movie *It's a Gift* (1934). *The Comic Supplement* origins for these films are frequently obscured by filmographies that merely credit *It's the Old Army Game* to an unnamed play of McEvoy and Fields or just to Fields. And sometimes there are references to a story by Charles Bogle—which was one of many writing pseudonyms the hucksterish Fields enjoyed using.

Besides these Fields-McEvoy connections, the latter's 1923 hit antiheroic play *The Potters* was the basis of Fields's equally successful 1927 film of the same name (often considered his best silent film). McEvoy also provided dialogue for the comedian's underrated film *You're Telling Me* (1934).

A closer look at the evolution of *The Comic Supplement* suggests, however, uncanny parallels in the comedy thinking of McEvoy and Fields. McEvoy's 1924 copyrighted version of the production contains the foundation for two sketches now considered classic Fields—"The Drug Store" and "The House by the Side of the Road" (the stately, lawn-destroying picnic). My research shows that when the rare original 1924 script is compared to an equally scarce January 1925 dress-rehearsal copy, the revision shows the unquestioned influence of Fields (McEvoy).

Most obviously, the revised revue had a pool routine that included Fields's standard cue-through-the-table finale. His celebrated "Sleeping Porch" sketch (examined later in this book), which he would copyright the following month, first appears in this rewritten *Comic Supplement*. The picnic scene, while strong in the original, is now bolstered by such Fieldsian antics as opening a can with a hatchet and talking with a full mouth (both of which survive in the later film renditions). Regardless of how credit is divided, there is no denying that a McEvoy story or premise seemed to bring out the best in Fields.

As the title *Comic Supplement* suggests, the production was a multifaceted tribute to the era's famous newspaper comic strips. Stage lighting makes the performers often look like cartoon characters. A dancing chorus turns their backs on the audience and reveals a cartoon line-up that includes Mutt & Jeff, Barney Google, and Jiggs. Within this live-action strip, a put-upon husband/father reads comic strips that are about a put-upon husband/father. Not surprisingly, in an interview later that year (1925), Fields stated he would like to play roles of the "American husband"—the "pathetic" figure of the "newspaper cartoons" (Waterbury, 102). Once again, the cartoon strips demonstrate their antiheroic significance in a watershed period of American humor.

As a real-life backdrop, the comedian had a certain affinity with the frustrated husband so often featured in the comics and the Fields-McEvoy collaborations. In 1900 he had married Harriet Hughes, a chorus girl from one of the acts opening with him. For a time she had traveled with him as an assistant, but pregnancy necessitated her retirement, and William Claude Fields, Jr. was born in 1904. Harriet attempted to get the comedian to quit show business, feeling the nomadic life of an entertainer was not fit for a family.

During the rest of his life Fields would support his wife and son with a weekly check, but their relationship quickly became a permanent separation. A cross-section of Fields letters to his estranged wife over the years would seem to represent a graduate degree in the area of battling husbands and wives:

> Your low cunning and scheming will some day cause you no end of grief. [1915]
> You have been a lazy, bad-tempered, arguing troubling [sic] making female all your life. . . . I haven't one good thought or memory of you, and the very thought of an interview with you fills me with rage. [1920]
> I have worked exactly 17 weeks this year—I have worked my brain and worried the whole year. . . . You know I was dropped from the movies. . . . For Christs be satisfied—I have enough trouble trying to find a new job. [1928]
> I am in receipt of your complaint No. 68427. . . . I hope to Christ the next cold I get knocks me off and then you will know what real hardship is. [1933]
> (R. Fields, *W. C. Fields by Himself*, 58, 65, 76, 445)

There is little information about Fields's life with early mistress and former *Follies* dancer Bessie Poole, which produced another son named William—William Rexford Fields Morris (born 1917). New York friends mistakenly believed (more game-playing by Fields) that W. C. and Bessie had once been married and then amicably divorced, with special arrangements being made for the son (more weekly payments?). Fields's history of dysfunctional family relationships, starting with his own childhood, no doubt contributed to both his antiheroic written humor and his fascination with the similar writing of others.

Of Fields's copyrighted sketches that predate *The Comic Supplement* and all things McEvoy, his routine "Off to the Country" (there were three early 1920s variations) is probably his best antiheroic family showcase. The sketch is full of missed trains, troublesome children, a bothersome wife, a surly ticket taker, a sneaky revenue officer, and loads of visual humor, thanks to Fields's ever-present assortment of props. The Flivertons never do get their holiday; instead, Papa is arrested for violation of the Volstead Act—he had a bottle of brandy.

The surname Fliverton appears frequently in the copyrighted sketches, underscoring the antiheroic nature of the writing. That is, Fliverton is unquestionably a reference to the most antiheroic of machines, the Model-T Ford, then frequently called a flivver. Moreover, one of the copyrighted sketches in which the Flivertons appear is called "The Family Ford" (in three variations).

The Model-T Ford was so associated with comic frustration that countless period jokes circulated on the subject. (Example: The farmer wanted to be buried in his Model T, because he had never been in a hole yet it hadn't been able to get him out of.) Later in the 1920s the antiheroic comedy careers of Laurel and Hardy would be strongly associated with this car. Consequently Fields's choice of the family name Fliverton was more than a little fitting.

The automobile, moreover, later became a metaphor for the "uncontrollable machines" of the modern world (Seidman, 150). This is best exemplified in Fields by the out-of-control car rides that close both *The Bank Dick* (1940) and *Never Give a Sucker an Even Break* (1941). (The closest parallel for Groucho would be the *Duck Soup* (1933) motorcycle sidecar, which magically takes off on its own—leaving the mustachioed one behind on a powerless cycle.

In mid-1921 Benchley would say that Fields's copyrighted sketches in general and the Flivertons' adventures in "Off to the Country" in particular are "enough to give [Fields] the Pulitzer Prize for next year. It is a comforting thought that each year there will always be Mr. Fields with something of his own that can be relied upon" ("The Follies," 18).

As an antiheroic postscript to Fields's real-life 1920s interactions with women, much as he was taken with the stereotypically beautiful chorus girl, he often played the loner. Fields was overly sensitive about an eczema problem that inflamed his nose and hands. He was self-conscious enough about it to push himself to relearn juggling wearing gloves.

But the insecurity went beyond eczema. A friend from the period, Louise Brooks, the enigmatic actress and icon of the helmet haircut and riveting stare, wrote in her 1971 *Sight and Sound* essay, "The Other Face of W. C. Fields": "After several devastating experiences with beautiful girls, he had decided to restrict himself to girlfriends who were less attractive, and whom he would not find adrift with saxophone players." Thus, the often misogynistic comic art of Fields had a complex core: a long-festering marriage, broken relationships, personal insecurities, and, of course, the dominating mother.

Antiheroic frustrations related to family would not surface in Groucho's 1920s stage or screen work, though, as will be briefly discussed below, they eventually become an occasional topic of his writing. And the roots for such material begin during this decade. In 1920 Groucho married Ruth Johnson, a dancer featured with Zeppo in the *Home Again* troupe. In 1921 son Arthur Marx was born to Groucho and Ruth, with daughter Miriam arriving in 1927. As with most families, comic repercussions soon followed the arrival of the children. For instance, Arthur's birth was immediately granted special status in Groucho folklore as the cause of the comedian's greasepaint mustache. The proud father was said to have stretched one hospital visit too long and returned to the theater with only time to apply the most cursory of stage mustaches. This greasepaint throw-back to an earlier, more primitive make-up tradition (as opposed to the more realistic facsimile he had been applying with glue) was accepted by the audience, though management initially had doubts, and Groucho permanently switched to the less time-consuming process.

Earlier it was mentioned that Fields's comedy of frustration merited pioneer status in the evolution of the antihero. But as noted in Chapter 2, the world of antiheroic humor was and is also known for outrageous comic distortion, emphasizing the absurd nature of the modern world. Groucho and company considered themselves followers of this "lunatic" slant (Seton, 734).

But their initial Broadway triumph in *I'll Say She Is!*, which was in part a zany anthology of their "Greatest Hits" from years of vaudeville, also places them in the vanguard of the antiheroic movement. Their 1920s ascension to leading roles as Broadway's resident crazies, on- and off-stage, makes them natural participants in this comedy evolution. As comedy historian Gerald Weales has suggested in his justification for crediting the Marx brothers' involvement: "It is more useful to think in terms of a shared intellectual and social climate [1920s New York, the center for the ultimate literary articulation of the movement] in which lunacy, verbal and physical, could flourish" (58).

For purists still distracted by the presence of Marx brothers playwrights and screenwriters, it should be kept in mind that while the team did not control their later film productions in the unquestioned total-auteur manner of a Chaplin, they were, like W. C. Fields, largely undirectable. Moreover, Groucho was often involved, though uncredited, with the writing, and later emerged as an author himself. Even the team's (especially Groucho's) future involvement with a pivotal antiheroic "lunatic" writer like S. J. Perelman (on *Monkey Business*, 1931, and *Horse Feathers*, 1932), involved considerable influence exerted by the Marxes, not at all the simple attribution to Perelman that represents traditional assumptions about authorial credit (Ward, 660).

Both W. C. and Groucho would go west in 1931. They would do their best films for Paramount Studio, only a year apart—Groucho and company in *Duck Soup* (1933) and Fields in *It's a Gift* (1934). Both men were pivotal movie comedians in sound film's golden age (the 1930s). And while they appeared in films after 1941, a case can be made for that year as representing a symbolic close to both their movie careers.

After *Never Give a Sucker an Even Break* (1941), Fields's poor health limited him to brief guest sketches in multiple-star, many-segmented features. Groucho and his brothers retired the team with *The Big Store* (also 1941). They would briefly regroup later, and Groucho would go on to the occasional solo film role. But after 1941 his career focus was overwhelmingly radio and, eventually, television.

The West Coast moves of Fields and Groucho represented a major new thrust to their careers and their lives. Unlike many of their East Coast friends and colleagues, who were also drawn to California by sound film's need for new talent, Fields and Marx embraced Hollywood as a new home. In contrast, the members of New York's famed Algonquin Round Table, of which Groucho had been a sometimes member, were routinely disparaging of what they saw as the lowbrow mentality of both the film community and its celluloid product, which patently misused the writer. So why go there? Hollywood's easy money caused eastern talent to swallow their artistic principles.

The anti-Hollywood stance might best be represented by Algonquin member Robert Benchley, the celebrated humorist and critic who found additional fame as an actor and sometime writer in films of the period (and who, as we have seen in Chapter 2, was among the pioneering antiheroic writers). A friend of both Fields and Marx and a great admirer of their work, Benchley rigidly divided his time between comedy jobs on both coasts. However, he was forever unhappy about spending any time in the film capital.

Benchley's position on the subject is most entertainingly addressed in his 1934 tongue-in-cheek article "How Do You Like Hollywood?," in which he comically chronicled his seven working trips to the West (49–50). Though the essay is amusing, the bottom line was that he consistently found the place boring and his efforts wasted. Most bittersweet is the piece's recurring title gag. Benchley was constantly being asked, "How do you like Hollywood?" And he would reply, "Fine! But this isn't my first trip, you know!" Still, he would find the question asked again his next trip. Though superficially amusing, it subliminally suggests Benchley's real feelings and fears about the place. It was as if he really had not been there before. His work there was immediately lost down some popular-culture abyss. One might also interpret Benchley's comment as damning Hollywood for having neither context nor history, that it is always reinventing itself on many levels.

Fields and Marx did, of course, have ongoing battles with the filmmaking powers that be. And initially, at least privately, Groucho could sound like the Algonquin bunch. For instance, in a 1931 letter to a midwestern friend, shortly after his arrival in California, Groucho described film party gossip as "all the claptrap that goes to make a Hollywood conversation one of the dullest on earth" ("1931, April?"). Fittingly, the letter was written while Groucho and his family were renting a bungalow at the Garden of Allah Hotel, the preferred West Coast haven for East Coast writers and performers.

During this stay, before Groucho could find a suitable house, the Marxes' Allah neighbors included Algonquin friends Benchley and Dorothy Parker.

California and film work looked increasingly good to Fields and Marx for several reasons. The Depression and sound movies, which took both audiences and stellar performers from the stage, made Broadway successes increasingly difficult. For example, in late 1930 Fields opened on Broadway in *Ballyhoo*, a satire on real-life huckster-promoter C. C. Pyle's failed 1920s across-the-continent foot race, "Bunion Derby." *Ballyhoo*'s loose plotline allowed Fields to pack the production with his best material (from his juggling cigar-box routine to his pool act) by making him "the harassed manager of a bankrupt transcontinental walking race, fleeing creditors, and fleecing poker partners by the blandest sort of chicanery with the cards" (Arkinson, 24). It was W. C. Fields as huckster.

Ballyhoo reviews generally praised Fields (especially Heywood Broun's critique in *The Nation*) (25) but found the overall production mediocre. Still, in the earlier *Poppy*, Fields's con man had energized what some critics had otherwise seen as a so-so book. *Ballyhoo* closed in February 1931 after a short, troubled run.

The Groucho and company hit movie *Animal Crackers* (1930, the East Coast film adaptation of their stage hit) demonstrates Broadway's precarious position from another slant. Just as today some filmviewers avoid high theater prices by waiting for the production to appear on videotape, early in the Depression many audience members delayed seeing a popular but expensive stage show until it was adapted to film, at relatively lower ticket prices.

. No less a publication than *Variety*, then as now the entertainment-industry bible, dispensed with its standard review of *Animal Crackers* to ask the provocative question: "Why [see] *Animal Crackers* on the stage at $5.50, when even the ruralites know they will see it later on the screen at 50 or 75¢?" The piece went on to say: "In this Paramount picture they [Groucho and brothers] are just the same [as on stage]."

Career timing also made a West Coast move attractive; both Fields and Marx were ready for change. W. C. was over fifty and Groucho was past forty. Their lives had been consumed since late childhood with either hectic vaudeville touring or the more prestigious yet still daily grind of Broadway.

Fields had actually been bitten by the film bug earlier, as he attempted to launch a movie career in the second half of the 1920s, but stage boredom was still a key factor: "I used to get sick of doing the same thing [on stage] night after night, year after year. I don't want to go back to the stage—not for a long time, anyway" (Hanneman, 98). Unfortunately, though his film work occasionally garnered good reviews, his silent films were generally neither commercial nor critical hits. Consequently, his initial West Coast residency lasted just one year, as he bounced back to the New York stage in 1928 via Earl Carroll's *Vanities*. Fields's 1931 trip west was a new and more committed attempt to conquer the movies, with the early 1931 stage failure of *Ballyhoo* probably symbolizing his burnt bridges.

Groucho and his brothers had found early sound-film success with the New York–based movie adaptations of their stage hits *The Cocoanuts* (1929) and *Animal Crackers* (1930). But the promise of new material, written expressly for the screen, was attractive. In an earthy period letter to a friend, Groucho wrote that returning to the production of *The Cocoanuts* (for its film adaptation) represented all "the thrill of a warmed-over potroast, and giving in to a dame that you were through with many years ago" ("1930?").

The West Coast film world was inviting to Fields and Marx in that it represented a unique position on the entertainment ladder. To W. C., the ambitious performer, movies provided the largest audience possible—something he found very exciting. Though film deprived a performer of immediate audience feedback, consummate artist Fields had started (during silents) attending multiple commercial screenings of his work to measure viewer response. And if the comedian's past relationship with his work was any gauge (such as copyrighting his sketches, sometimes numerous times for modest variations), he would have been equally pleased to permanently record his material on film.

Moviedom's unique status for Groucho and his brothers was the payment of top dollar in the entertainment world. This is not meant as a crass statement, since rare is the person who is not drawn to financial security. Moreover, it spoke directly to Groucho, both because of an extremely deprived childhood, as well as the then-recent loss of his personal fortune in the 1929 Wall Street stock market crash.

Obviously, the money angle would have been attractive to Fields, too, since he also had had challenging early years, though he had weathered the crash (despite rumors to the contrary). Fittingly,

Fields and Marx were extremely frugal with their money throughout their lives.

A more traditional case for the allure of California for these comedians was the pleasantness of its climate in those pre-smog days. Unlike previous anti–West Coast cracks, such as the film capital's alleged cultural provincialism, a nice climate hardly seems subject to debate. But many East Coast talents connected the film industry's easy money, which supposedly distracted them from more significant projects, with an overly pleasant climate that diverted one from any work.

For instance, in a period letter from Hollywood, Robert Benchley would write his family: "I wish I were back [in New York] where it is good and cold. I still hate this dump [Hollywood] as much as ever. . . . And the climate just knocks me for a loop. I doze all the time and have no pep at all" ("Dec. 7, 1928"). Vestiges of such total anti-Hollywood, pro–New York elitism live on today in the life and work of Woody Allen.

In contrast to any anti-climate bias, Fields and Marx were happy to escape the East Coast cold. W. C. was a major fan of warm-weather automobile trips and roadside picnics. Indeed, his 1931 trip west was by car. His last mistress, whom he met early in his California years, has written movingly of the comedian's love of sightseeing along the geographically diverse but always temperate settings close to their film-capital home. When "motoring" by majestic scenery, writes Carlotta Monti, "a heavy silence hung over him . . . he was actually awed by the wonders of nature, although he wouldn't admit it. 'I remain silent so that I can hear the flowers grow' was his excuse" (102).

Years before the death of Groucho's mother Minnie in 1929, he and his brothers had wanted to relocate their parents to a warmer climate. When their 1931 westward move took place, their father Frenchie went along, paralleling the earlier package deal where Minnie's parents had lived in Groucho's childhood home.

Within a year of this migration Groucho confessed in a letter to a midwestern friend: "I fought this off [buying a house] as long as I could, but . . . here I am, just another [California] yokel. From now on you can expect nothing in my letters but climate [a satirically self-deprecating crack on the nonstop period praise of the weather by new "immigrants" to the West Coast]" ("1932?").

Marx also enjoyed doing garden and yard work in this perennially lush climate. One of the most inspired real-life Groucho stories, with a fittingly bawdy punch line, is tied to this interest. During World War II Beverly Hills residents had a shortage of grounds-keepers, since their usual Japanese laborers were in the infamous internment camps. Thus, when a Beverly Hills matron saw an unrecognizable Groucho (sans greasepaint mustache and eyebrows and in dirty old clothes) doing yard work, she immediately stopped her car and approached the comedian, asking what the lady who lived there paid him. Groucho quickly terminated her negotiation by answering that no money exchanged hands; the lady let him sleep with her.

Interestingly enough, both Fields and Groucho enjoyed the chance to play tennis year-round in temperate California. Though this might seem something of a stretch for the stocky Fields, his juggling background gave him a hucksterish trick-shot edge, especially with respect to putting different spins on the ball. He was also good at deciding controversial baseline shots in his favor based on his ability to find crushed ants in-bounds—alleged victims of Fields's shot. Of course, such larcenous behavior was less overt than in the days of his youth, when he acquired his juggling balls by hanging out near tennis courts and stealing any wayward balls. Part of tennis's attractiveness to Fields might, however, be based on the fact he could now play a sport that had been so beyond his economic station as a child.

Whereas W. C. kept his mind on the sport at hand by the perennial side bet (which forever inspired his creative cheating, e.g., the deceased ants), it was difficult for Groucho to take any sport seriously. But like Fields he had played tennis, even back east, in recent years, weather permitting. Rapidly becoming *the* sport of 1930s Hollywood, tennis drew Groucho because it was something he could do with his family. Such interest would contribute to son Arthur's great success as a nationally ranked amateur player late in the decade.

If there was anything hucksterish about Groucho's tennis game, it was his use of comedy. Breaking up an opponent with laughter was the technique he found most effective in defeating his first wife, whose playing skills were superior to his. Appropriately, it was a strategy he might have drawn from the writing of friend Benchley, whose comedy essays he greatly admired. Regardless, this make-'em-laugh approach to tennis is reminiscent of Benchley's "How to Play Tennis" (*"From Bed to Worse,"* 1934), in which the humorist comically documents using just this approach as a child. Groucho would also apply his distracting comedy to whomever he was playing golf with, once he had decided this was one more game in which he would not break ninety.

Fields was a bigger fan and better golfer than Marx. What had started as a spoof of the game in his vaudeville golf routine grew to a fascination à la the later fixation of Bob Hope. (Appropriately, when the two comedians jointly starred in *The Big Broadcast of 1938*, Hope was impressed with Fields's ability to work some golf material into his screen action.)

Regardless, Fields got into an early 1930s golf habit that nicely showcases both his love of southern California's natural beauty and his own sneaky tightness. He had rented a home on the scenic and exclusive Toluca Lake, just across from the Lakeside Country Club. With no long-term studio contract, he played golf daily. *But* he avoided paying greens fees by rowing across the lake and starting his round of eighteen holes in the middle of the course. After playing, he would quietly and ever so cheaply exit as he came . . . by rowboat.

Despite the parallels that drew them to 1931 California, Fields and Marx had radically different positions with regard to the film industry. Groucho and his brothers came to Hollywood and parent studio Paramount as conquering heroes. Their two East Coast–produced films had been phenomenal critical and commercial hits. In contrast, Fields came west without even a contract.

Both comedians took in the Hollywood party scene, which was not typical behavior for either of them. Groucho's modest sampling was out of curiosity; W. C. was scrambling for work—playing the dusk-to-dawn life of the party to generate attention. Things did not change quickly. Groucho and company's first Hollywood film, *Monkey Business* (1931), was another hit. Fields managed to snare a supporting role in the Warner Brothers movie *Her Majesty Love* (1931), but while his reviews were good, the film failed at the box office.

In 1932 things began to look up for Fields both professionally and privately. He received second billing to Jack Oakie in the zany *Million Dollar Legs*, a critically well-received film satirizing both depression-age government and the Olympics, which were being held that summer in Los Angeles. This was also the year in which the comedian began making a series of film short subjects for his longtime drinking and golfing friend, movie-comedy pioneer Mack Sennett.

Like Groucho's brother Chico, whose card-playing connections helped the team's career, W. C.'s interest in the links gave Fields's screen career the jump start it needed. The comedian's old studio from silent days, Paramount, produced *Million Dollar Legs* and was the parent company through which Sennett released his films. The studio seems to have used these short subjects (see the Filmography) as a test that contributed to signing the comedian to a long-term contract in 1933.

The year 1932 was also when Fields met his last mistress, Carlotta Monti. The insecurity of his past romantic relationships was probably reflected in their May-December ages. The twenty-four-year-old Monti was nearly thirty years Fields's junior. A minor contract player he met during a publicity stills shoot, she would play lover, companion, and nurse to him in the often stormy remaining fourteen years of his life.

Much later her perceptive autobiography *W. C. Fields & Me* (with Cy Rice, 1971) was reminiscent of Lita Grey Chaplin's underrated *My Life with Chaplin: An Intimate Memoir* (1966). Both offered unique insight on already long-established personalities, but unlike Chaplin's second wife (who had gone through a messy divorce from the comedian), Monti had no score to even. Carlotta, whom *Newsweek*'s review of her book would label "His Last Chickadee," also includes an excellent section dealing with Fields on comedy (Cooper, 92–92b).

In an early 1932 letter to his estranged wife, Fields details health and financial problems. But in mid-year correspondence to her he observes that "prospects are more effulgent than when I last wrote" (R. Fields, *W. C. Fields By Himself*, 144). This is a very upbeat prognosis to communicate to someone constantly on his case for more financial support. Maybe he was merely pleased that the letter (now lost) to which he was then responding nagged more about rumors of his excessive drinking than the need for money. Fields's support of his estranged wife and son was adequate, given the times, especially since his son was now approaching thirty. But it was not commensurate to that of a film comedian.

While things were looking up for Fields in 1932, the careers of Groucho and his brothers were going over the proverbial top. Their fourth successive commercial and critical film hit, *Horse Feathers*, landed the team on the cover of *Time* magazine (August 15, 1932), though the recognition was as much a hosanna for their nonstop body of film successes as for this feature.

The film had been delayed in production when Chico was injured in a serious automobile accident April 9, 1932. Groucho, spending his free time at the hospital, wrote to a friend later that month: "All in all [the incident] is a general nuisance, but then so is Chico" ("1932, April"). This was more than a comic tongue-in-cheek aside; Chico's lifelong addiction to gambling would make financial caretakers out of younger brothers Groucho and Harpo. It also further contributed to Groucho's tightness with a dollar. Thus, his California housing arrangements were invariably more modest than those of his free-spending brothers.

Like W. C.'s hucksterish golf tendencies (via the rowboat), Groucho also used cons to economize. He enjoyed swimming with his children Arthur and Miriam (ages ten and four the year of the move west) and had maneuvering for free water privileges down to an art form. Ploys ranged from open-door—or more correctly, open-pool—status with neighbors (Who is going to turn down Groucho and children?) to housesitting at Chico's beach residence. As the Marx brothers' sometime scriptwriter S. J. Perelman later observed, Groucho's "passionate avocation" was "the collecting and cross-fertilization of various kinds of money" (132–33).

The only down side to 1932 was Groucho and Chico's short-lived radio program *Flywheel, Shyster, and Flywheel*, which began late in the year. As the title implies (doubly), Groucho was an opportunistic lawyer, with Chico as the office process server. Ironically for such a huckster-oriented hero, the program was not a hit. But the review from the influential *Variety* suggested the problem was not with the con but rather with material too adult for youngsters ("Refineries," 34).

W. C.'s Hollywood fortunes continued on the upswing in 1933, but Groucho's took a dive. Coupled with the movie pump-priming success of Fields's short subjects for Sennett, the comedian's theft of the star-studded picture *International House* (1933) brought a lucrative multiyear deal with Paramount. In contrast, Groucho and company's *Duck Soup* (1933) was so poorly received by both critics and the public that it nearly killed the team's film career. As it was, the failure of the film, now considered a classic, ended their association with Paramount and kept them off movie screens until 1935. (After *Duck Soup* Zeppo left the team and became an agent.)

While Groucho and his brothers took an unwanted break from movies in 1934, their former employer Paramount seemed to want to play catch-up with W. C.'s career, casting the comedian in no fewer than five pictures that year. The best of the bunch were his top-billed appearances in *You're Telling Me, The Old-Fashioned Way,* and *It's a Gift.*

You're Telling Me was the breakthrough film for period critics. *Los Angeles Times* movie reviewer John Scott said it best in an April 6, 1934 article: "W. C. Fields . . . emerges after considerable grooming as a ranking screen comedian." The following day on the East Coast, film critic Thornton Delehanty, writing for the old *New York Evening Post,* stated, "The character which he portrays is droll, sly and pathetic. These ingredients, together with his methods of extolling them inevitably suggest the Chaplin touch."

As a related Chaplin aside, a study of 1930s Fields film reviews demonstrates that W. C.'s highest critical praise invariably utilized the Tramp figure as the measuring device of excellence. For instance, the July 13, 1936, *London Times* review of *Poppy* noted: "Only a Chaplin could steal a scene from Mr. W. C. Fields, and there is no Chaplin in this cast." Quite possibly this "can't escape Chaplin" situation is behind Fields's eventual resentment toward the creator of Charlie.

Fields's productive ways continued in 1935 with three strong films: *David Copperfield, Mississippi,* and *The Man on the Flying Trapeze.* Mistress Monti was cast as the comedian's loyal secretary in *Trapeze*—a tip-off that the film is especially peppered with Fields in-jokes. Besides giving himself another domineering screen wife (an ongoing left-handed tribute to his estranged spouse), Fields's character is saddled with an adult mama's-boy of a stepson named Claude, which was the name of the comedian's own grown son, whom he considered a hopeless mama's-boy. Art further mirrors life when the reel son accuses him of an affair with his secretary (Monti), reflecting a real personal relationship that his own son opposed.

In addition, *Trapeze* showcases several less volatile but still interesting parallels and comic contrasts with his life. The comedian's movie desk looks as if an avalanche of paper has fallen upon it—reflecting his own less than tidy organizational skills. In contrast, Fields casts himself as a memory expert in *Trapeze,* yet his difficulty in memorizing dialogue was well known among his friends and colleagues.

Though Fields sometimes felt that being a screen actor was a silly occupation for an adult, he saw his appearance as Dickens's character Micawber in *David Copperfield* as one of the highlights of his career. Monti described the comedian as "an avid Dickens buff" and portrayed his bedside as "something just this side of a Dickens library" (48). Fields was taken by every aspect of the novelist's work, from his assortment of comic character names and dialogue to "character delineations . . . [which] simply walked off the pages into your life, to live on with you until the end of your days" (Monti, 51).

Of related interest is the fact that Dickens, like his contemporary Barnum, was a publicity-conscious showman whose self-exposure tendencies were well known. Whether or not Fields's own inclination in this direction found encouragement in the similar habit of his favorite author is unclear, but it seems likely.

Fields's view that his childhood was spent largely as an outcast, despite later denials by his family, undoubtedly contributed to his fascination with Dickens—an author obsessed with orphans and outcast children. Such heartfelt connections act as both a reminder of the high cost of art and a persuasion that it is worth the price. And without belaboring the Dickens-on-Fields influence (be it the funny names of the comedian's characters or the flowery comic rhythm of his film dialogue), Micawber was the most fitting of the novelist's characters for the comedian to portray. Fields's film persona constantly "juggled" the language and creditors, two primary occupations of Micawber.

It should be noted at this point that both Fields and Marx were captivated by literature and spent a great deal of time reading. Three shared traits added to this literary inclination. Like many talented people possessing little formal education, they tended to actively pursue the cultural background they had missed as children. Following a natural progression for the avid reader, each man sought success as a writer (which will be examined later in this book). Finally, both men were insomniacs, a condition that became progressively worse with the passing years. Thus, reading was also a way to pass time during what were often very long nights.

Groucho and his brothers staged a major film comeback with the late 1935 release of *A Night at the Opera*. Produced by M-G-M, under the personal guidance of "Boy Genius" producer Irving Thalberg, the team once again found themselves with a critical and commercial smash. This often very funny film gave new impetus to a motion-picture career that, while certainly not over, had been unduly slowed.

Still, there was an artistic cost to be paid. Groucho's and Harpo's characters were homogenized. No longer figures of pure anarchy, there are disturbing attempts to give the two pathos: Harpo is beaten by the singing villain Lassparri (Walter King) and Groucho is booted down three flights of stairs by a minor character. Such actions are not consistent with their aggressively comic personas. In addition, the singing romantic subplot of the film (involving Kitty Carlisle and Allan Jones) at times threatens to supplant Groucho and company.

Of course, period thinking on comedy dictated a fragmented presentation. Morrie Ryskind, co-scripter with George S. Kaufman of *A Night at the Opera*, would later observe, "You have to have a [comedy] break and a change of pace. So the two lovers [enter]. . . . You didn't have ice cream [i.e., comedy] all the way through, you know!" (G. Marx and Nobile, 80). Today's viewers, however, enjoy "ice cream" throughout, which explains why audiences now prefer the nonstop comedy of *Duck Soup* to the intermittent laughter of *A Night at the Opera*.

This M-G-M homogenization of Groucho and company fits humor historian Steve Seidman's theory that personality comedians are ultimately tamed by the movie story—"When the comic figure becomes a responsible socialized being, he becomes someone who, like the spectator, is one of the crowd" (137). But the Seidman position, while provocative and appropriate for some comedians, is not at all applicable to the Paramount Groucho, nor does it work for any of W. C. Fields's huckster roles. At their best, these two personality comedians never threaten to become "one of the crowd."

It was hard, however, arguing with the success of M-G-M's *A Night at the Opera*. Besides Thalberg's masterful reading of the 1930s audience, he had approved a large budget covering everything from the high salary for Broadway's Kaufman (the era's Neil Simon) to authorizing the Marx brothers going on tour to test the material before filming. Thalberg would also be the guiding spirit behind the team's next movie, *A Day at the Races* (1937), which again generated great reviews and a box-office gross that even topped *A Night at the Opera*. Tragically, the producer did not live to see this success, dying in September 1936, after the summertime road-testing of *A Day at the Races* material. With Thalberg's death, Groucho's interest in filmmaking started to die, too, helped along by M-G-M's lessened support of the team without the producer.

Paradoxically, shortly before Thalberg's death from pneumonia, Fields was reported to have nearly died from the same ailment. In poor health both before and during the film production of *Poppy* (released June 19, 1936), he went to Soboba Hot Springs to recover, a health spa near the San Bernardino Mountains. Rushed to a hospital from there, it later came out that he was treated for delirium tremens, not pneumonia.

Fields briefly acknowledged this alcoholic warning and went on the wagon for several months. Too sick to work or even read, the comedian discovered a new medium—radio. Unlike Groucho, W. C. had not taken radio seriously. But between a well-received participation in a January 7, 1937, radio salute to Paramount's longtime leader Adolph Zukor (a microphone was brought to Fields's hospital room) and a convalescence made easier by radio entertainment, Fields's view of the medium changed radically.

This perspective was undoubtedly further sweetened by signing a radio contract in excess of $5,000 a week shortly after leaving the hospital in April 1937. Starting in May he costarred with Edgar Bergen and Charlie McCarthy on NBC's *The Chase & Sanborn Hour*. The phenomenal success of this radio team is all the more unlikely when one considers that the participants were a former juggler, a ventriloquist, and his dummy.

Radio in 1937 revitalized W. C.'s career, but it nearly derailed Groucho's. On November 1 Groucho and Chico were convicted of copyright infringement, using gag material in a radio broadcast from a previously rejected script. Their defense was that the material had been prepared by their late friend and writer Al Boasberg and that they were unaware of any similarities with a previously submitted script. The case was closely followed by the entertainment community, a fact underscored by the large number of period articles on the trial in the Marx brothers files at the Margaret Herrick Library of the Academy of Motion Picture Arts and Sciences (Beverly Hills).

Groucho's authorized biographer Hector Arce claims it was the first time a Hollywood entertainer had been convicted on a charge of criminal plagiarism (258). It was more than a little ironic that someone whose comedy persona was so closely identified with hucksterism should essentially be convicted of theft. But it is fitting to note the connection, since the Academy files suggest that Groucho and Chico initially did not take the trial very seriously, treating it almost as if it were one of their movie-courtroom scenes.

November 1937 found both W. C. and Groucho very thankful comedians. In that month's issue of *Screen Book Magazine* a recovered Fields said, "I feel that this is my second time on earth. I am starting all over again from scratch. It's all borrowed time I am living on . . . [making] me appreciate living, something I never did before" (Darnton, 34).

Groucho and his brother were pleased and considerably more serious when the magnitude of the plagiarism conviction sank in. As the November 2 *Los Angeles Examiner* front-page headline put it: "2 Marx Bros. Fined, Escape Jail Term." Chico, speaking both for himself and for Groucho, observed, "That's a relief. We'll be glad, Groucho and me, to shell out a thousand [dollars] each. But jail—. Say, that's a terrible thought" (1, 4).

As a side note on Fields's long illness, his brother Walter, a former boxing promoter, came out from Philadelphia for several months to stay with W. C. until the comedian's recovery was assured. Years before Walter had very briefly appeared with his famous brother in vaudeville. As is often the case with the families of well-known comedians, the Dukenfields considered the unknown Walter to be the funnier of the two.

Indeed, the same sort of story is true of the Marxes. In terms of public persona, Groucho's comedy character over time would win the funniest Marx Brother title. But privately among the family, the now-little-remembered Zeppo was considered the really funny one. Indeed, Zeppo's confidently breezy real-life personality was sometimes likened to Groucho's screen character.

The Big Broadcast of 1938 was Fields's comeback film. Like earlier "Big Broadcast" pictures, this edition was a variety-show production glued to the thinnest of plot lines. With the comedian's new perspective on "borrowed time," he was even more feisty than usual, feeling strongly about doing things his way.

Not surprisingly, the behind-the-scenes Fields was more interesting than what ended up in the movie. Thanks to young costar Bob Hope, who attached himself to Fields like a comedy groupie during the production, one gets a sense of the independent W. C. Hope wrote in his book *The Road to Hollywood* that while he was sharing time with the comedian in Fields's dressing room, one of Paramount's "top brass" stopped by for a contribution to the studio's

Community Chest drive. W. C.'s response was, "Very nice of you to drop by, my good man. I'd like very much to help you with your highly admirable drive. Unfortunately, there is a very compelling reason why I cannot" (23). When asked what that was, Fields replied he was a member of F.E.B.F. The curious visitor asked what the initials stood for. The comedian replied, "F___ Everybody But Fields."

There is no evidence that this incident had anything to do with Fields being let go by Paramount a few months after the release of *The Big Broadcast of 1938*. His exit was merely a late-1930s economizing move by the studio. Other prominent performers dropped by Paramount during this period included Mae West and Marlene Dietrich. However, his F.E.B.F. attitude made him an ever more challenging actor with whom to work. Difficulties notwithstanding, the comedian was soon welcomed by Universal, where his first feature teamed him with his radio costars, Edgar Bergen and Charley McCarthy. Titled *You Can't Cheat An Honest Man*, this huckster classic (though not fully appreciated at the time) is examined later in the text.

In 1937 Marx brothers agent Zeppo signed the team to a lucrative R.K.O. contract to star in the film adaptation of the big Broadway play *Room Service*. Released the following year, the movie was a major critical and commercial disappointment. (Groucho and company had fulfilled their initial M-G-M contract.) That same year, Groucho and Chico lost their appeal of their plagiarism conviction. Needless to say, the two brothers were very careful about material when they became regulars during the first half of 1939 on the radio program *The Circle* (also known as *The Kellogg Show*).

Later in 1939 Groucho and his brothers returned to M-G-M to make the film *At the Circus*, which was released in the fall of that year. Though an improvement on *Room Service*, it was not up to their earlier high movie standards. At the end of the decade their film future seemed less healthy than that of their older, sickly comedy rival W. C., especially with late 1939 production beginning on an anxiously awaited Fields–Mae West movie. Given their long parallel careers, first in New York and later in Hollywood, there had been surprisingly little contact between the two. Fields was, however, genuinely pleased with the comedy possibilities of being teamed with a one-time sex symbol. Unfortunately, West felt the film something of a comedown. And insiders feared production problems between the two temperamental stars. Possibly because of that, they shared few scenes together. Yet it was a relatively smooth shoot.

In January 1940 Fields turned sixty, and as if to mark this milestone, momentous for one whose drinking habit was so self-destructive, the comedian had an impressive and productively varied artistic year. In February his costarring film with Mae West was released—the parody Western *My Little Chickadee*. Just as the movie sported Fieldsian jargon for a title, W. C. won the comedy battle of the two stars. West was, however, still hindered by the motion-picture censorship code that her earlier provocative humor had helped bring about. The film generated mixed reviews, but Fields was praised, and it would be his top-grossing Universal picture.

While *My Little Chickadee* necessitated splitting screen time with West, Fields's November 1940 film, *The Bank Dick*, was all W. C. A critical and commercial success, many reviewers found this classic antiheroic showcase the Fields tour de force they had long awaited. Pivotal early film critic and longtime Fields champion Otis Ferguson was especially poetic in his *New Republic* review of *The Bank Dick* (900). He capped off his lengthy critique with a moving dream-analogy close that credited Fields with finally having done a movie worthy of his comedy genius. (Though Ferguson was a W. C. fan, his past criticism had not avoided examining perceived weaknesses in the comedian's work.)

Sandwiched between these films was the 1940 publication of the comedian's own book, *Fields for President*. This was a presidential election year, and while there is no record of then-incumbent Franklin D. Roosevelt or Republican challenger Wendell L. Willkie becoming nervous about Fields's candidacy, the comedian certainly offered the public some provocatively funny thinking. For instance, "I shall, my fellow citizens, offer no such empty panaceas as [FDR's] New Deal, or an Old Deal, or even a Re-Deal. No, my friends, the reliable old False Shuffle was good enough for my father and it's good enough for me" (11–12).

Despite this punning political promise, with its huckster overtones (so fitting for the campaigning world), the book is more a comic celebration of the nonpolitical antihero. One such chapter of comic frustration, "How to Beat the Federal Income Tax—And What to See and Do at Alcatraz," might have influenced if not inspired Groucho's book *Many Happy Returns: An Unofficial Guide to Your Income-Tax Problems* (1942), which appeared just two years later. Interestingly, the delightful caricatures that complement both works were drawn by the same artist, Otto Soglow.

Groucho and his brothers' 1940 film release, the Western spoof *Go West*, also seemed to ape Fields; his *My Little Chickadee* was released nine months earlier. In all fairness to the Marxes, however, both parodies were "riding" the 1939 critical and commercial success of John Ford's classic western *Stagecoach* (which revitalized the genre in "A" sound pictures) and George Marshall's celebrated parody of reaffirmation, *Destry Rides Again*, which manages to balance comic spoofing with a genuine genre poignancy not normally associated with parody, such as the death of Marlene Dietrich's dance hall girl.

In April 1941 Marx brothers spokesperson Groucho announced the break up of the team, with that year's December-released *The Big Store* being their alleged swan song. W. C.'s last starring feature film, *Never Give a Sucker an Even Break*, came out in October. Despite generally good reviews for *Sucker*, Universal did not renew the troublesome Fields's contract. Thus, to encourage filmmaking interest by other studios, W. C. proclaimed late in the year that he was on the wagon for life. This was a con, because except for a brief time in the late 1930s, the comedian could not stay away from alcohol.

Paradoxically, while the "retiring" Groucho and company would briefly reteam for the 1946 movie *A Night in Casablanca*, W. C. "I-want-to-work" Fields would never carry another feature. (The 1949 "Marx brothers" *Love Happy* is really a Harpo-Chico film, with Groucho appearing only in a few unrelated framing-device scenes.)

In 1943 Fields's declining health would limit him to guest appearances in movies; there was too much financial risk to build a feature picture around him. But in the early forties he might have squeezed in another starring role or two had it not been for his reputation as difficult.

Writing on Fields seems to have neglected how period critics possibly contributed to this difficulty by puffing up the comedian and/or further alienating Universal. For example, the October 27, 1941, *PM* magazine stated:

> As each new Fields movie comes out . . . it reveals less and less studio control, more and more Fields will. The mighty Universal shrivels, and Mr. Fields expands. At last, with *Never Give a Sucker an Even Break*, Universal Pictures appears to have thrown up its hands or washed them, for the picture is a great bundle of iconoclasm, with Mr. Fields sitting triumphantly, if somewhat pantingly, on top.

And this says nothing of the fact that the film in question is a wonderful satire of studio filmmaking.

There was, in addition, a change taking place in 1940s film comedy. This alteration might best be labeled "Abbott and Costello." In early 1941 Fields's studio, Universal, had released *Buck Privates*, the first feature starring Abbott and Costello, and a major critical and commercial success. Abbott and Costello were representative of a new 1940s breed of personality comedians who could fluctuate between incompetent, comic antiheroes and cool, egotistical wise guys with the fast, smart crack—all in the same scene (something a young Bob Hope would also excel at). But it was a pattern that did not fit W. C. or Groucho.

The power of this Abbott and Costello influence was first brought home to me during my research for a biography of Laurel and Hardy (Gehring, *Laurel & Hardy: A Bio-Bibliography*). That is, the latter team's 1941 service comedy, *Great Guns*, suffered not because it was inspired by Abbott and Costello's *Buck Privates* but rather because it attempted at times to make Laurel and Hardy *into* Abbott and Costello. If as great a team as Laurel and Hardy could be misused along these lines, the threat to artistic integrity for other comedians with diverse styles was clearly serious indeed. Laurel and Hardy's then-poor financial situation made them vulnerable to such artistic compromises. Tightfisted Fields and Marx, however, did not need money. Moreover, W. C. was too independent to change, and Groucho was just generally disenchanted with the movies.

Though Groucho's team's retirement did not come until 1941, the signs were apparent, at least privately, well before this. In an unpublished 1939 letter to Dr. Samuel Salinger, a friend in Chicago, he noted how much he enjoyed working in radio—it did not "require too much work [e.g., no memorizing lines, applying make-up, or running about in costumes] and gives me practice at acting, something I sorely need and rarely get in the movies, where, as you know, I'm constantly playing the same character!" ("April 15, 1939").

In 1940 correspondence with author friend Arthur Sheekman, the comedian observed, "I'm shaping my ambitions in other [nonfilm] directions and discussing a radio show that I might [help create]" ("October 10, 1940").

Writing to Salinger, the most critical of personal friends, in an unpublished letter from 1941, Groucho documents the growing demands for his comic essays: "Despite your sneers at my literary efforts, I'm constantly implored by most of the important national weeklies to contribute to their pages" ("August 14, 1941"). Fittingly, one of the publications Groucho mentions, the Sunday supplement magazine *This Week*, is also one in which W. C.'s short pieces occasionally appeared.

In this same letter Marx speaks of breaking with his film persona: "I've taken the final step and definitely burned my bridges behind me. I'm writing a play with Norman Krasna [what would become *Time for Elizabeth*]. . . .I expect to play in it in New York with none of the former, familiar accoutrements [i.e., no greasepaint mustache and eyebrows, no comic costumes and antics]." Though Groucho would not play the part for some time, this artistic break with his film past was something toward which he was always working after 1940.

Marx managed, however, to keep in perspective his growing disenchantment with film and his natural anxiety about a career in transition. Consequently, in still another unpublished letter to Salinger, from July 13, 1940, the comedian confessed that whenever he started "feeling unhappy or on the verge of complaining about anything, I think of those nice cool [Nazi] concentration camps strung throughout Europe and tap myself on my padded shoulder and say, 'here, here Groucho—just take it easy!'"

After America's late 1941 entry into World War II, Fields and Marx were the most patriotic of citizens. W. C. did a short USO film for the troops, *The Laziest Golfer* (inexplicably never released); and Groucho taped his 1943 radio program, *The Pabst Show*, at various California-area service camps.

In the case of Fields, however, this patriotism could flirt with the surreal. A great student of the war, the comedian maintained a map with colored pins, some of which reflected military actions while others merely indulged his penchant for unusual names. Naturally, the war was a major topic of conversation with his favorite drinking buddies: actor John Barrymore, writer Gene Fowler, and painter John

Decker. After one such "spirited" discussion the group decided it was obvious the Allied effort needed their assistance. Thus, they attempted to enlist in the armed forces, with W. C. requesting duty as a commando!

It must be remembered that these were men both advanced in years and declining in health (largely due to alcoholic excesses). As students of black humor, as the attempt to go soldiering so aptly showed, the inevitable denial of their attempted enlistment was made more palatable for them by the response of the recruiting-center spokesperson: "Who sent you? The enemy?"

In March 1942 the alcoholic Barrymore died. He had suffered from a number of ailments, especially cirrhosis of the liver, but pneumonia was the final cause of death. His alcohol-related death would anticipate that of close friend Fields by four and one-half years. The physical deterioration of the comedian was already apparent in *The Bank Dick* and *Never Give a Sucker an Even Break*, and unretouched studio publicity stills from the period are even more shocking.

Gene Fowler, in his 1954 group biography of these drinking companions (plus painter John Decker and vagabond poet Sadekichi Hartmann), *Minutes of the Last Meeting*, made the apt yet strikingly macabre pronouncement, "They were their own executioners" (104). Yet as Fowler notes, Fields and company "blamed no one but themselves for the outcome of their [alcoholic] follies; self-pity was a stranger to them. They paid all penalties without welshing and lived their last hours without cringing" (31).

The only real friction in the group chronicled by Fowler was between Fields and Hartmann, because the comedian felt the poet was too self-serving. Yet, this rift is very revealing, since literary oddity Hartmann seems the very personification of Fields's dramatic persona—independent to the extreme of contrariness, archetypically cynical, and given to the most comically biting of asides. For example, Hartmann coined such observations as, "Other people talk about dying. I'm doing it," and "If you think vaudeville is dead, look at modern art" (Fowler, 39, 95). Hence it is more than a little possible that Fields feared a rival. Of course, any such anxieties he might have had were unnecessary (as were most of his fears); time has shown that while Hartmann was a self-proclaimed genius, Fields was a real one.

One might go on to say that Fields's ultimate tragedy was inseparable from his triumph. The rebelliousness of the comedian, even when self-destructive, was the same fuel that propelled his anti-establishment comedy personas—the something-for-nothing huckster and the fifth columnist antihero.

"The Man in the Bright Nightgown," Fields's epithet for death, came for him on Christmas Day 1946. Legend has it that those who die on this date go directly to heaven, no questions asked. Interestingly enough, shortly before his death the less-than-religious Fields was caught in the unlikely situation of thumbing through a Bible. When an explanation was requested, he simply replied, "Looking for loopholes." Maybe, he found his loophole in Christmas.

At approximately the same time that Groucho was contemplating a career beyond the Marx brothers, F. Scott Fitzgerald was writing the provocative Hollywood novel *The Last Tycoon*. (Fitzgerald died tragically before its completion, and the work was published posthumously in 1941). The unfinished novel's title character was loosely based on Irving Thalberg, the same producer who had revived the film career of Groucho and his brothers and whose death in 1937 had symbolized the beginning of the end for movies in Groucho's mind. Such disillusionment with Hollywood-the-dream-factory would be at the heart of Fitzgerald's novel, too.

But whereas Thalberg and Fitzgerald would die young, victims in varying degrees of the system, Groucho would win (as if in diddler fashion) by circumventing the movies and moving to radio and television. In doing so, the comedian would also triumph over the most quoted line in *The Last Tycoon*: "There are no second acts in American lives."

Change was the order of the day for Groucho in the early 1940s, from his career focus on radio and freelance writing to a divorce from longtime first wife Ruth. His career difficulties in making a break from his screen persona analogize nicely to the turmoil he was experiencing at home. And though this sense of change was probably a factor, the marriage had been in trouble for some years. A relationship with a comedian is never easy, something Groucho himself had addressed years before in a humorous essay, "My Poor Wife!" (15, 59), which appeared in *Collier's* magazine in 1930.

By the time of their 1942 divorce the occasional anger had moved to a bittersweet acceptance of the need for parting. In a moving letter to son Arthur, serving in the World War II Coast Guard, Groucho documented the initial separation:

Your mother moved out today, and the whole thing was kind of sad. I was sorry to see her go, for I am still fond of her, but obviously this uncomfortable set-up couldn't continue. I said good-bye to her before she drove off in her car. It was one of those awkward, half-serious, half comic moments, and I didn't know quite what to say. I put my hand out and said, "Well, it was nice knowing you, and if you're ever in the neighborhood again, drop in." Your mother seemed to think that was a funny line—so for once in my life I got a laugh when I wasn't trying for one. (A. Marx, *Life with Groucho*, 245–46)

As a later affectionately comic valentine to earlier, happier times, Groucho's writing colleague and family friend Norman Krasna wrote the play *Dear Ruth*. Loosely based on the Marx household, it successfully opened on Broadway in December 1944.

The professional links that so often coincidentally connected Groucho and W. C. seemed to exert one last pull in 1946. Before Fields's end-of-the-year death, Marx made his last sustained return to the old screen Groucho in *A Night in Casablanca*. The film has become most famous for Groucho's hucksterish promotion of it, in the form of a series of letters written to the Warner brothers legal department concerning the studio's supposed contesting of the use of the name *Casablanca* in the title. The issue was whether Warner's, because of its earlier classic film *Casablanca* (1942), had exclusive rights to titular use of the city, a question that generated a great deal of comic interest both in 1945, when the film was in preproduction, and 1967, when some of Groucho's correspondence was published in book form, with the comedian's responses to Warner Brothers opening the volume.

His letters are humorous, fluctuating from comic outrage to outrageous comedy. For example, Groucho asserts that if Warner Brothers has exclusive rights to the word *Casablanca*, then the Marxes have a similar claim to *Brothers*, because "professionally, we were brothers long before you were" (*The Groucho Letters*, 14). But in an obviously unpublished letter to friend Samuel Salinger, dated May 31, 1945, the comedian unloaded a con-man bombshell:

We spread the story that Warners objected to this title purely for publicity reasons. They may eventually actually object to it, although I don't think so. . . . At any rate, the publicity has been wonderful on it and it was a happy idea. I wish they would sue, but, as it is, we've had reams in the papers.

P. T. Barnum would have been proud.

The take-off of Groucho's career as a solo performer is best chart-
ed from the year after *A Night in Casablanca* and his association
with a simple radio show, *You Bet Your Life*, which found equal
success on 1950s television. But hosting a quiz show initially
seemed a comedown for the former chieftain of both Huxley College
(*Horse Feathers*, 1932) and the land of Freedonia (*Duck Soup*,
1933).

"Marx fans mourned that it was like selling Citation to the glue
factory" ("Master Marx," 53). *You Bet Your Life* creator and execu-
tive producer John Guedel said, "Having Groucho as emcee of a quiz
show is like using a Cadillac to haul coal" ("What Comes Naturally," 69). Even Groucho confessed, in another unpublished letter to
Salinger, "It's not too distinguished a set-up [the show], but you
know me; I have no shame" ("October 3, 1947"). What made this
process so provocatively interesting, however, was that this seeming
fall from high comedy grace to mere quizmaster was being undertaken by Groucho with a changed persona in a new medium. It was
not the homogenized misuse of his screen character associated with
the mid-1930s move to M-G-M. Instead, he was an atomic-age
crackerbarrel figure with a real sense of compassion, versus the false
sense of pathos with which M-G-M attempted to saddle the comic
opportunism of his film persona.

Regardless, the quiz show worked. The format proved a perfect
entertainment setting in which a solo Groucho could comically
converse with and kid noncelebrity guests, the quiz itself being of
secondary importance. In 1949 he received radio's greatest tribute—
a Peabody Award as best entertainer. Groucho added television's
highest honor in 1951—an Emmy for most outstanding personality.

First broadcast on October 27, 1947, the radio program started
slowly. Recorded long and then edited down to improve the pacing
and maximize the funniest material, the show eventually caught on,
began obtaining consistently high ratings, and continued its acclaimed run through the 1950s by moving to television. Its last
regular telecast was in September 1961.

In the 1970s, *You Bet Your Life* became a phenomenon in
syndication—successfully entering "nine of the top ten [United
States] markets" as well as going into foreign distribution (Allen,
207). This was an ongoing tribute to Groucho's humor, because
1950s black and white quiz shows were not exactly hot properties in
the 1970s rerun market.

Moreover, Bill Cosby's short-lived 1992 revival of *You Bet Your Life*, with himself as quizmaster, demonstrated just how good Groucho was. Though Cosby's updating of the program was not without comic interest, he brought a somewhat condescending tone to his hosting that Groucho had avoided, despite the eccentric nature of both shows' guests.

In terms of confidence-man humor, an absorbing aspect of *You Bet Your Life* was the hoax of pure ad-libbing. Reminiscent of Chapter 2's examination of the "contract between reader and author," where the reader places confidence in what the storyteller relates, only to be manipulated by that confidence, Groucho made comic hay from the apparent spontaneity of his off-the-cuff remarks.

You Bet Your Life guests were not selected randomly from the audience, despite what was suggested in the show's early years. Instead, they were screened and chosen for their colorful backgrounds and potentially comic personalities. Groucho did not meet them prior to the program, but the contestants were coached on how to tell their stories to the host, including key tagline openings designed for "ad-libs" from the comedian—ad-libs he had time to prepare. Ironically, Groucho was good at legitimate ad-libbing; it was the reason Guedel chose him for the show (Guedel had been impressed with the comedian's impromptu exchanges with Bob Hope on another radio program). Some of Groucho's *You Bet Your Life* ad-libbing was real. But comedy chances were *not* taken.

The quick-witted Groucho had an already long-established gift for making the scripted seem spontaneous. For example, in the unpublished text for the Marx brothers Broadway stage production of *Animal Crackers*, the character of Roscoe W. Chandler makes scripted "mistakes" to comically feed Groucho's Captain Spaulding (Kaufman and Ryskind, I-37). This seemingly impromptu scene, in which Chandler confuses character names, also surfaces (with slight variation) in the 1930 film adaptation. This moment from the movie is priceless, because the scripted comic stumbling over names seems so natural that one cannot believe it also occurs on the printed script page.

This sort of diddle, however, was hardly limited to Groucho. A sense of hoax is at the center of most comedy; for comedy to be effective it needs to be spontaneous *or* at least seem that way. Even that phenomenal fast-forward master of the comic moment, Robin Williams, has occasional soliloquies of absurdity that the student of this gifted comedian recognizes from previous comedy sets. Naturally, there are numerous theories of comedy, from Aristotle's focus on superiority, to Freud's psychoanalytical model. Unfortunately, most of the energy used to study humor misses the point—"It [comedy] is a phenomenon preeminently interactive, immanent, impromptu" (Goodchilds, 176).

It is disappointing to tarnish Groucho's legitimate ad-lib reputation, but *You Bet Your Life* sailed through the 1954 revelation of its manipulative preplanning (*TV Guide* said it most entertainingly, quoting an unnamed source: "That show has all the spontaneity of a Swiss watch" ("For the First time," 5), even maintaining its number-four Nielsen rating from the previous season. This ongoing success goes full-circle back to Barnum's basic precept that the public did not mind being hoodwinked as long as they were entertained. For Groucho, it seemed he could do no wrong.

Weathering of the revelation that discredited the ad-libbing was possibly assisted by Arthur Marx's affectionate 1954 biography of his father, *Life with Groucho*. A critical and commercial success, it is pertinent to mention the book at this point for both its historical timeliness and its huckster slant. The 1954 connection is obvious; the con angle merits an explanation.

The most endearing characteristic of the book is the frequent comic footnotes by Groucho. Fittingly, the biography's first note includes an indirect reference to *You Bet Your Life*. Arthur has stated that his father is a dreamer who likes to pass himself off as a "disillusioned realist." He goes on to add that this attitude is something only his father can answer. Groucho's footnote response: "And I'm not going to [answer]. My racket is asking questions [on the quiz show], not answering them" (3).

The footnotes seem the perfect biographical addition. Besides being funny, they reinforce the image being drawn of the caring father helpfully reading and comically enriching his child's work. But bombshell of bombshells, in Arthur's later book *Son of Groucho* (1972), he reveals himself as author of the footnotes. Like father, like son, as the saying goes, but the "creative" footnotes do reveal much about the son and, indirectly, about the father.

Arthur is a survivor, and that seems to have been a key lesson of late childhood with Groucho. Just as the young Marx brothers had to fend for themselves on the grade-Z vaudeville circuit, Groucho's children were often in a similar position, especially as they neared adulthood. Both of Arthur's books thoroughly document that while Groucho was often wonderful to be around when they were young children, he seemed to feel betrayed as they began to grow up and away from the efforts he had taken to celebrate their childhood. One further *Son of Groucho* diddler bombshell nicely exemplifies Arthur's survivor nature.

Several things bothered Groucho about the book when it was in manuscript form. The most specific was a sentence from a letter (which is quoted earlier at length) that he had written his son concerning Groucho's divorce from Ruth. The line that so offended Groucho when Arthur quoted it—"If you're ever in the neighborhood again, drop in"—was really a classic example of pathos when viewed in the tender context of the complete letter. It revealed a sensitivity Groucho often seemed unwilling to share.

How then does one resolve this and other manuscript conflicts? For Arthur, the confidence man and survivor, the eventual answer proved quite simple. He merely requested two copies of his book's galleys (the typeset text of the book that is proofread before the work is sent to the printer), and gave one copy to his father, telling him to make whatever changes he thought necessary. But the only galley proof Arthur returned to the publisher was his own. Groucho's extensively revised version was simply discarded.

Arthur's actions soon received a double endorsement. The biography was a great success, and Groucho created no further problems concerning it. Arthur hypothesized that his father's initial opposition might have been caused by Groucho's need to remain number one in the family. But an example Arthur provides in support of this stance can also be interpreted quite differently. Nearly paralleling the publication of *Life with Groucho*, the scandal sheet *Confidential Magazine* made disparaging comments about both Groucho's television show and his interest in young women. Where the threat of a lawsuit would certainly be understandable, the comedian merely penned a one-sentence letter of delightful comic surprise: "If you persist in publishing libelous articles about me, I will have to cancel my subscription" (A. Marx, *Son of Groucho*, 291).

Arthur posits that Groucho felt unthreatened by the *Confidential* author, but that the home-grown variety (Arthur) was something else. A certain amount of jealousy is consistent with the elder Marx's competitive nature (especially since he himself was an author). However, Groucho's scandal-sheet letter to the editor also represents the many contradictions about the man and offers additional reinforcement, in part, of a lingering element of the comedian's original comedy persona—a dirty old man who never felt any compulsion to hide the fact. Besides, it was publicity, and as the real story behind the *Night in Casablanca* letters revealed, publicizing "letters" made great newspaper copy.

Disparaging remarks aside, moreover, Groucho *was* interested in younger women. His second marriage (1945), to Kay Marie Gorcey, found the nearly fifty-five-year-old comedian with a bride not much older than his teen-aged daughter Miriam. Indeed, Kay was a friend of Miriam's, trapped in an abusive marriage to "Dead End Kid" actor Leo Gorcey. Miriam had inadvertently played matchmaker by offering her friend sanctuary in the Marx home. Unfortunately for Miriam, when a relationship developed between her father and Kay, followed by marriage and the 1946 birth of a daughter (Melinda), Miriam felt very much displaced. It was a difficult time for a possessive daughter who had been acting as hostess of the Groucho domain since the comedian's divorce three years earlier from her mother.

The comedian and Kay divorced in 1950. Four years later he married Eden Hartford, the sister of model-actress Dee Hartford. Eden, in her mid-twenties, was almost forty years younger than Groucho. Once again there would be a threesome in the Marx home, paralleling the earlier combination of Groucho, daughter Miriam and second wife Kay. This time the grouping was Groucho, eight-year-old Melinda, and Eden. Though custody of Melinda had originally gone to her mother after the divorce, it returned to Groucho in 1952 after Kay had developed a drinking problem.

The stay-at-home Groucho became more socially active with his marriage to Eden. They, too, would eventually divorce (1969), but theirs was, at least for Groucho, a fairly amicable marriage. Moreover, even after a divorce in which Eden received almost a million-dollar settlement, the two frequently appeared together socially. When once asked about this, Groucho gave a much-quoted reply: "I like to be near my money."

In 1971 the comedian met Erin Fleming, whom Groucho's friend and biographer Hector Arce later described as the "ultimate hyphenate," eventually acting as Marx's "girlfriend-mother-actress-adviser-manager" (12). There was a forty-plus-year difference in age. She would later become a figure of controversy, labeled by some a female

Svengali, allegedly manipulating Groucho in his last enfeebled years.

In 1977, the year of his death, there was an ugly conservator fight over Groucho between son Arthur and Erin. Neither he nor Fleming ended up with the position. After Groucho's death August 19, the executor of his estate, the Bank of America, instituted and won an ongoing court battle against Fleming for funds she had received through her association with the comedian, plus punitive damages. There will never be a definitive answer on the Erin factor. But for Groucho's sake, one would like to take the position of the issue-long essay of the Summer 1983 *Freedonia Gazette* (the journal dedicated to the study of the Marx brothers): "Erin Fleming, Who Made His [Groucho's] Life Worth Living" (4–17). Otherwise, there is the irony of a premier reel huckster being taken during the real close to his life.

The sad finale aside, the early 1970s were an ongoing triumph of Groucho and his brothers. In 1970 the tale of the young Marx brothers and their mother, *Minnie's Boys* (coauthored by Arthur Marx), opened on Broadway. In 1972 the French government made Groucho a "Commander dans l'Order des Arts et des Lettres." The award ceremony took place at Cannes, where Groucho was guest of honor during the city's internationally known film festival. Also in 1972 he performed a one-man show at Carnegie Hall.

In 1974 the comedian received a special Oscar for the "brilliant creativity and unequaled achievement of the Marx brothers in the art of motion picture comedy" (Chico and Harpo had both died in the 1960s). That same year *You Bet Your Life* became a hit in syndication, and Groucho attended the New York and Los Angeles premieres of a rescreening of the team's 1930 hit film *Animal Crackers*, which had not been shown for years because of legal questions concerning copyright. In 1975 he was awarded a special Emmy, and Los Angeles Mayor Tom Bradley declared his eighty-fifth birthday "Groucho Marx Day."

Unlike W. C. Fields, Groucho lived long enough to see his work, both as part of the Marx brothers and as a solo artist, rediscovered by a wildly admiring public. He shared with Fields, however, an appreciation by modern audiences that really began to mushroom during the anti-establishment 1960s. In an era when the hypocrisy of the social and political system became apparent as never before, comedy iconoclasts like W. C. and Groucho began to loom large once again.

In a period when the stereotypical establishment good guy was found wanting, Fields/Marx hucksters and antiheroes were figures to be celebrated and admired. To the 1960s battle cry of "Make Love Not War" one might have added "Make Comedy," for the inherent chaos of the comedy of W. C. Fields and Groucho Marx could be reevaluated in a new provocative context.

"Never give a sucker an even break."
    —Professor Eustace P. McGargle
    (W. C. Fields) to his foster daughter
    (Rochelle Hudson) in *Poppy*

*"If you think this country's bad off now, just
wait till I get through with it."*
    —Freedonia dictator Rufus T. Firefly
    (Groucho Marx) to Mrs. Teasdale
    (Margaret Dumont) in *Duck Soup*

CHAPTER 4 **Contrasting Film
Huckster Styles
W. C. versus Groucho**

As examined in Chapter 2, the master of the scam answers to many names: confidence man, con artist, grifter, huckster, diddler, shakedown artist—all terms that are generally used interchangeably, as is the case in this book. For shell-game purists, however, there is an occasional distinction that herein merits noting because of its unique applicability to the difference between the manipulative screen personas of Fields and Marx. The old axiom, which continues to surface (such as in the 1992 comic boxing-scam film *Diggstown*) goes: "A huckster gets out of town as quickly as he can. A con man doesn't have to leave until he wants." Though there are examples of each variety in the filmographies of these two comedians, Fields's type is most often the huckster, whereas Marx's is the con man. And although both men were reared in the waning nineteenth-century heyday of the diddler, Fields's huckster embraces that world, while Marx's con man is more of a twentieth-century hybrid—mixing past tendencies with new developments that will soon be examined.

3. A Fields huckster who does not quite get out of town quickly enough, from *My Little Chickadee* (1940).

(While references will be made to W. C.'s silent films, the focus here is on his sound movies—the body of work upon which his cinema greatness is based as well as the time frame he shared screen comedy acclaim with Groucho.)

P. T. Barnum biographer Neil Harris observed: "Central casting might well have selected W. C. Fields to play the Barnum of popular mythology; in fact it came quite close [historically], for Wallace Beery played Barnum in Gene Fowler's 1934 screenplay" (3). What Harris does not mention was Fowler's close friendship with Fields, which would later result in a 1954 group biography of the comedian's clique, *Minutes of the Last Meeting*. A screening of the Fowler film in question, *The Mighty Barnum*, suggests he was more than a little taken with the Barnum-Fields connection, since the Beery performance is reminiscent of W. C. as huckster.

Regardless, Fields's trickster is in the literary tradition of America's nineteenth-century confidence-man golden age. Like the classic pioneering diddlers, the W. C. manipulator kept on the move. The *London Times* said of his 1936 *Poppy* characterization, "Like all great showmen he knows to a nicety the moment when the prudent man stops talking and makes hurriedly for open country—preferably on his accuser's horse" (July 13, 1936). Movement protected his sneaky character from the law, from creditors, and from the sucker who's wised up to the comedian's "creative" gambling skills. Being forever on the road offered opportunity as well as escape, as Simon Suggs noted long ago: "It is good to be shifty in a new country." Like Suggs's diddler of the Old Southwest, Fields's hucksters engaged in small-time operations that did little if any harm.

As the reviewer for the old *New York Sun* newspaper observed, Fields's comic manipulator in *You Can't Cheat an Honest Man* (1939) trims suckers "with the aplomb that only he can bring to the practice of the gentle art of petty larceny" (Feb. 20, 1939). W. C.'s own axiom on the subject might be drawn from the closing moments of *My Little Chickadee* (1940), when Flower Belle Lee (Mae West) calls him a "cheat" for getting a kiss under false pretenses. His reply, as huckster gambler Cuthbert J. Twillie, is "Anything worth having is worth cheating for."

Fields's shakedown-artist language might be likened to political speech that is said to be full of "verbal parachutes." That is, W. C.'s comments contain wordage he could use for bailing out of anything he had voiced.

A cross-section of Fields's nineteenth-century picaresque diddlers would include his Old West card swindler from *Chickadee* and his pre–Civil War (Mint Julep Belt) riverboat captain Commodore Jackson of *Mississippi* (1935). His signature huckster, Professor Eustace McGargle, the carnival shell-game master of *Poppy* (a role he originally played on Broadway in 1923), is from the 1880s. *The Old-Fashioned Way* (1934) finds "the Great McGargle" (W. C.) leading a less-than-prosperous troupe during the mid-1890s. Fields's card shark, Augustus Winterbottom, in *Tillie and Gus* (1933) again finds himself involved in a riverboat story but closer to the turn of the century. This is also a good approximation of the period setting for *You Can't Cheat an Honest Man* (1939), which has the comedian directing a third-rate circus and wearing the ever-so-fitting name of Larson E. Whipsnade.

Of all these, Fields's riverboat settings, particularly on the Mississippi, especially draw upon a classic nineteenth-century huckster backdrop, as did T. B. Thorpe's pivotal tall-tale-styled diddler in "Big

Bear of Arkansas" and Melville's critical novel of the genre, *The Confidence-Man*. Add to that the centrality of this river to the often-huckster fiction of Twain, and Fields's *Mississippi* becomes the most blatant background connection with an earlier diddler literary tradition.

Newsweek's review of *You Can't Cheat an Honest Man* described Whipsnade as a "bulbous-nosed Barnum" (Feb. 27, 1939). The description is right on the money, for another way in which Fields's hucksters resemble the earlier literary models is that, like Barnum, the comedian's cons are often based in entertainment. The diverting or beguiling scam works on three levels. There is the seemingly upfront sport of gambling, such as the inspired skills the comedian brings to the shell game in *Poppy*, or any number of cinema poker games. In the latter case, W. C. is unusually direct in his philosophy in *My Little Chickadee*. When asked by his dimwitted poker opponent, Cousin Zeb (Fuzzy Knight), "Is this a game of chance?" Twillie replies, "Not the way I play it, no."

An additional entertainment-level scam for the W. C. huckster often involves a show-within-the-film. That is, his manipulative character would have to exercise all manner of deceit to merely put on his stage revue. From its opening moments, *The Old Fashioned Way* is a case study of this any-con-for-the-production. The movie begins with a sheriff at the train depot about to serve Fields's McGonigle with a legal writ to keep him and his troupe in town, for unpaid bills. Luckily for McGonigle, he happens to come up behind the sheriff and wastes no time in lighting the document, which the law officer had been holding behind his back. W. C. allows himself to be seen just as the blazing writ is beyond rescue. The mistakenly confident sheriff then tells him, "I have something for you!" As the surprised constable produces a flaming document from behind him, Fields (with the timing of the comic juggler he was) used this non-conventional blaze to light his cigar. McGonigle then tops the laugh by politely thanking the sheriff. As the reviewer for the old *New York-American* summarized, "McGonigle matches wits with local sheriffs all over the West . . . [and] as the old saying has it, the sheriffs are practically disarmed" (July 14, 1934).

Several other *Old Fashioned Way* scams occur to keep the show going, from Fields's attempt to lift the morale of his underpaid troupe with an upbeat but fake telegram about their next engagement, to his courtship of wealthy widow Cleopatra Pepperday (Jan Duggan), an aging wannabe thespian whose money could keep the McGonigle ship afloat.

W. C.'s romancing of Duggan also showcases how the comedian's hucksters can often, paradoxically, be quite sympathetic. Pepperday, looking "all dressed up like a well-kept grave," is a silly, no-talent singing ninny. But because the comedian has sweetened his money-related romance with a diddler's implication that she could possibly join the troupe, his McGonigle must endure Pepperday's butcheringly endless rendition of the less than memorable "When We Gathered the Shells on the Sea Shore." Amusingly, she then informs Fields, "I can act as well as I can sing." With comic diplomacy befitting his slippery character's nature he answers, "I'm sure of it." Thus, the viewer feels W. C.'s character has more than earned his right to fleece this nincompoop. To paraphrase an old axiom, here is one fool who deserves to be soon parted from her money.

This anticipates the same sort of viewer rationalization Charlie Chaplin later created in his watershed black comedy *Monsieur Verdoux* (1947), where he marries and disposes of several less than sympathetic—frightfully crotchety might be the optimum description—wealthy widows. Had Fields's health not given out in the 1940s, this was a macabre humor path he, too, might have followed. As it was, the comedian's booting of Pepperday's child (Baby LeRoy) demonstrated W. C.'s ongoing appreciation of dark comedy.

Interestingly, the film critic for the old *New World-Telegram* compared Fields's punt of LeRoy to "the famous Charlie Chaplin kick in one of his films years ago [probably *The Pilgrim*, 1923]," an act that "releases the suppressed desires of countless adults, who have nearly been driven crazy by the abuses of some particularly noxious infant" (Boehnel, July 14, 1934). Moreover, Fields's booting of LeRoy ties into a Freudian interpretation of comedy—an offensive infantile demeanor being central to the clown. Thus, "we laugh aggressively at Fields's own aggression insofar as it is a sign, not of his mastery, but of his own infantile lack of control" (Neale and Krutnik, 79).

Fields's *Old Fashioned Way* character generates further empathy by way of the self-parody involved with the first names of McGonigle and Pepperday: Mark Antony and Cleopatra. To be the incongruous namesakes of such celebrated doomed lovers creates (besides the parody), a certain comic fatalism that exonerates

McGonigle's actions as somehow inevitable. There is a certain left-handed logic to Fields being a poor man's Antony, since the student of Shakespeare's *Antony and Cleopatra* knows Antony fumbled nearly everything he did, a trait invariably present in Fields's anti-heroic diddlers (another source of their sympathetic nature which will be expanded upon shortly).

There is even an example of W. C.'s Mark Antony–McGonigle frustration that could be construed as a comic footnote to the classic play's Antony. In the segment of the film devoted to this huckster courtship, the comedian manages to accidentally stab himself by sitting on a basket of knitting needles, a comic wound that might remind the viewer that Shakespeare's Antony bungles his own Roman-style suicide while falling upon his sword.

This comic courtship of Cleopatra, whom McGonigle calls his little "Rocky Mountain Canary" to her face but in an aside his "Rocky Mountain Goat," falls in a long line of "romances" in which confidence men pursue rich widows. As different as W. C. and Groucho screen diddlers are, Marx makes even more of a career pursuing the wealthy romance, generally in the person of Margaret Dumont. She surfaces so often opposite Groucho that for many this perennial mountainous, stuffy dowager has come to represent a "fifth Marx Brother." (There is, however, a key difference between how Fields and Marx woo the rich, which will be addressed later in this chapter.) Dumont would also appear as the object of a Fields monetarily motivated courtship in *Never Give a Sucker an Even Break* (1941). Despite its title, however, the film is more an outgrowth of the comedian's antiheroic world (see Chapter 5).

A further entertainment-level scam to be drawn from *The Old Fashioned Way* involves the comedian's juggling performance for the show-within-the-film. Taken from his much earlier vaudeville routine, this includes balancing twelve cigar boxes, juggling four balls, and holding a stick on one foot and then flipping it to the other foot. The diddler aspect of the act, which differentiates it from so many mere juggling bits, is the comic recoveries he makes from numerous alleged "mistakes"—catching various dropped objects so near the floor.

This final Fieldsian example of the entertainment-level scam did not always depend on the comedian's long vaudeville past, though this experience was a rich mine of material. For instance, in *You Can't Cheat an Honest Man*, his Whipsnade character, which film historian William K. Everson has so nicely described as a "charlatan-at-large" (161) (a delineation that might be used for any number of W. C. hucksters), puts on a fake ventriloquist act. His mouth is hidden behind a false handlebar moustache and some equally fraudulent teeth. Indeed, the choppers of this sneak are so frightfully large the viewer is tempted to call them "crocodile teeth," matching size with the deceitfulness often attached to this beast. (A critic might object, noting Whipsnade's oversized choppers are artificial, whereas a crocodile's are not. But could not the false teeth represent a punning metaphor for the real "bite" all hucksters are after?) Regardless, the obvious obscuring of this charlatan's mouth allows him to comically play at being a ventriloquist.

Besides the inspired humor of faking an act based in deceit, so fitting for a confidence man, W. C.'s routine here also indirectly spoofs his ventriloquist costar Edgar Bergen, whose lips (when providing witty repartee for sidekick Charlie McCarthy) might have used some obscuring, too—a possible outgrowth of the paradox of being a ventriloquist on radio, as Bergen was. For the record, Fields's dummy is called Oliver, and he sports a bulbous W. C. nose.

The third manner in which the W. C. confidence man follows the nineteenth-century huckster tradition is in the seeming joy with which he tells his flimflam stories. Yarn-telling stands for life in these films. Fields's characters are related to Mark Twain's Colonel Sellers, who could be described as "telling his stories as if he believed them—as perhaps he did" (see Chapter 2). The comedian could sometimes use the old tall-tale slant of American humor's Southwest, such as Fields's sale of an alleged talking dog (ventriloquism again) in *Poppy*.

But what more typically starts out as a bit of personal aggrandizement, such as his ongoing *Mississippi* refrain of battling Indians—"Unsheathing my Bowie knife, I carved a path through this wall of human flesh dragging my canoe behind me"—quickly becomes a comic seminar on the pleasure of spinning yarns. And W. C. is at his tall-tale best when a listener questions some detail. After his *Mississippi* Commodore tells of shooting three pistols simultaneously (in each hand and between his teeth) during the early Indian wars, someone notes pistols had not yet been invented. His reply, with all the comic absurdity of a Pecos Bill tale was, "I know that, but the Indians didn't know it."

His pleasure in the telling of tales, as well as the listener's comic enjoyment in the hearing, is further showcased by the fun he has with the language. For instance, in *Poppy* he describes a cottage as a "charming little lean-to. Reminds me of my wickiup on the Limbpoo-poo." Or earlier in the same film, when the bartender to whom he is about to sell the alleged talking dog claims the animal looks like his neighbor's (which it was), Fields's huckster says no, the dog is "a cross between a Manchurian yak and an Australian dingo."

And whatever the entertaining verbal situation, his scam artist is forever capable of a 180-degree switch of supposed values when danger occurs. Thus, shortly after his McGargle starts to operate his shell game booth in *Poppy* the word comes that the mayor is approaching. Before anyone could hide a fifth ace (another occupational hazard he sometimes faced), all evidence of the shell game has disappeared, and McGargle is giving a lecture on the evils of gambling. The comic topper finds the mayor being moved by the talk. One is reminded anew of literary historian Susan Kuhlman's observation (see Chapter 2) that the nomadic American pioneer and huckster were both resourceful and adaptable in their desire to get ahead.

Why is it that the diddler of tall tales, like Fields, continues to be so popular? Beyond entertainment, the appeal is probably rooted in the human condition—who has not told a white lie or a modest embellishment? No less a showman than Ed Sullivan once observed that Fields "gives way to the instinct [to tell a really big lie] that is deep in all of us, brings to the screen something that we can all appreciate. . . . [W]e see ourselves and the sight is funny" (14).

We are all hucksters at some level, however modest . . . or we would like to be. This realistic slant is close to a Fields observation on comedy theory: "I base my comedy on humanness . . . I take the simplest everyday incidents, exaggerate them and turn them into an act and, people seeing themselves, laugh" (Cheatham, 30).

As one might assume, his cinema tall tales were merely an extension of the artist. His longtime last mistress Carlotta Monti observed, "At dinners Wood [Fields] sometimes grew verbose knowing he had a captive audience, and would grossly exaggerate happenings that supposedly occurred to him in far-off places [he enjoyed globehopping during his early juggling years] and generally unheard-of spots in the world" (205).

Fittingly, she added that the "Rattlesnake" story from *You Can't Cheat an Honest Man*, a yarn about the eccentric friendship of

W. C.'s Whipsnade character and a snake, is just the kind of whopper the comedian enjoyed telling to his dinner guests. For the record, Whipsnade met the snake at "Lake Titicaca," and it protected him when a "marauder" broke into his "wickiup"; it bit the burglar and then rattled out the window for a cop. The ongoing comic bonus to Whipsnade's wonderful telling is that the movie's stuffy society matron, Mrs. Bel-Goodie (Mary Borbes) screams and faints each time she hears the word "snake." And she is meant to hear it a lot.

Monti's selection of the "Rattlesnake" yarn is also fortuitous because it is probably the best film example of a Fields character getting lost in the joy of storytelling. After the hostess first faints, his audience-within-the-film desert him to help her; however, he goes right on with his tale. When a latecomer interrupts Whipsnade and asks why everyone is crowded around the unconscious Mrs. Bel-Goodie, he is clearly bored by the question and replies simply, "I don't know." Then Fields's character goes back to the story that he is still spinning when he's later forced to exit the home.

One should remember, however, that for all the amusing pleasure Whipsnade and W. C.'s other screen tricksters draw from the sound of their own voices, much of the comedian's huckster comedy is still based in the effectiveness of a silver tongue. For example, Fields's showboat captain of *Mississippi* manages to make the career of his ship's young entertainer, Tom Grayson (Bing Crosby), by turning him into the notorious Colonel Steele—the "Singing Killer." The captain's verbal skills are all the more diverting when it is noted that Crosby's Grayson is a Quaker. No less a publication than the *London Times* celebrated the captain's "unrivaled powers of rhetoric and invention" in creating the "Singing Killer" (April 22, 1935). As another example, in *Poppy* it could be noted that his McGargle manages to sell bottles of "purple bark sarsaparilla," a potion that allegedly cures warts and grows hair.

Given such praise and the general magic of movies, it should come as no surprise that Fields's yarns proved more problematic in real life. In a 1935 article he admitted to having a lot of tall-tale material, as well as a knack for making it up. But he added:

> I'm not nearly as good at it as I used to be. They [friends and acquaintances] catch me up. Yes, sir, they catch me up. Someone will say, "Bill, tell so-and-so about you and the one-eyed acrobat." and I'll think, "Oh, oh, they got me." For the life of me I can't remember what I made up about that one. (Hamilton 33)

The most fundamental way in which the Fields huckster resembles the nineteenth-century scam artist involves physical, visual comedy. American humor has always placed a high premium on this phenomenon, beginning with the skinny, long-legged caricatures of Jack Downing. But it is especially rich among writers schooled in Southwestern humor, be it George W. Harris's Sut Lovingood putting a lizard down someone's pants or Mark Twain's description of bouncing about in a stagecoach from *Roughing It* (1872).

Fields is the perfect personification of this tradition. His work is peppered with physical and visual material, which varies from the subtle minimalism of his *Mississippi* Commodore as he manipulates in his teeth the up-and-down movement of a cigar caught between the spokes of the ship's wheel he is trying to steer to the broad comedy of Whipsnade's ping-pong match in *You Can't Cheat an Honest Man*. And this says nothing of his ongoing struggles with unmanageable objects like hats and canes.

Consistent with Southwestern humor, the Fields bit often backfired, causing him physical discomfort and/or giving the viewer a mildly earthy shock effect. For example, in *Poppy* he suffers numerous ailments trying to play croquet, while in *You Can't Cheat an Honest Man* he used the circus elephant's trunk as a turn-of-the-century shower—running water with the command, "Give, Queenie!" The latter is a funny sight gag unless one ponders the "running nose" implications, which are still in keeping with the coarseness often evident in Southwestern humor, such as the bug nightmare Tom Sawyer makes Jim suffer through at the close of Twain's *Huckleberry Finn*.

In a *Poppy* review for the old *Brooklyn Daily Eagle*, the comedian explained "that his years of pantomime taught him people laugh more easily at what they see than at what they hear, and laugh harder at things they hear if they see something funny at the same time" (July 19, 1936). By way of a *Poppy* example, Fields stated he had slightly altered the scene where the mayor's appearance is the catalyst for his character's switch from the shell game to a lecture on the evils of gambling. The change: with the mayor's arrival the comedian had put the shell-game pea in his mouth and begun the lecture, only to start choking.

Though there are countless other examples of Fields gags mixing sight and sound, it is hard to neglect the scene where he stumbles over his umbrella in the train coach, bending it into a goofy, contorted state, not unlike the ludicrously crooked sticks that passed for golf clubs in his vaudeville act. Funny in and of itself, Fields straightens the umbrella and adds, "Don't worry, it can't break; it's a genuine Chamberlain!" This political crack satirically skewered the umbrella-toting Neville Chamberlain, who was then the British prime minister engaging in political appeasement (bending) toward the belligerent militancy of Adolf Hitler. The movie was *My Little Chickadee.*

Without trying to belabor this umbrella scene, it also exemplifies a basic comedy rule for Fields. In a 1934 essay on humor, the comedian wrote, "It is funnier to bend things than to break them. . . .In legitimate drama, the hero breaks the sword, and it is dramatic. In comedy, the sword bends, and stays bent" ("Anything for a Laugh," 128–30). This rule has now become such a classic screen-comedy maxim that Woody Allen lampoons the pompous-filmmaker Alan Alda character in *Crimes and Misdemeanors* (1989) by having him excessively going on about comedy theory and bending—overstating the obvious.

Fields's greatest assortment of Southwestern-style physical comedy occurs in *My Little Chickadee,* from a script he coauthored. The film's centerpiece to this school of humor is when W. C.'s Twillie crawls into bed with what he thinks is wife Flower Belle Lee (Mae West) but in actuality is a goat.

Other special visual moments include Fields disguised as the masked bandit, with his sizeable proboscis (the term he preferred over nose) seemingly looming even larger beneath his mask, a comic cross between Zorro and Jimmy "The Schnozzola" Durante; W. C.'s allegedly honored place at a banquet that finds him sitting halfway inside a closet, forced to use his fork to stick a bothersome feathery wrap to the wall out of the way of his soup; and his use of a slingshot against attacking Indians in the film's train battle (a scene further highlighted by the accidental switching of hats with the boy passenger from whom he borrowed the slingshot). Though Fields was never above "borrowing" material from another performer, he generally authored his comedy routines, frequently drawing from his own copyrighted sketches (see Chapter 3). However, two stage productions from the 1920s, *Poppy* and *The Comic Supplement* (see also Chapter 3), were an ongoing influence on his later film work.

It is appropriate in discussing the visual aspects of *My Little Chickadee* to note that the film was influenced by a popular period newspaper cartoon strip. Fields was the inspiration for the Great Gusto, a prominent character in the "Big Chief Wahoo" (1936) strip. Wahoo played the stooge to Gusto, who ran a medicine show—the classic huckster setting for W. C. since essaying a similar role in the 1923 Broadway hit *Poppy*. In fact, Fields starred in the second film adaptation of *Poppy* the same year "Big Chief Wahoo" first appeared—1936. The comedian was a fan of the strip, and its creators Allen Saunders and Elmer Waggon eventually visited him in Hollywood. Thus, in *My Little Chickadee*, Fields's Twillie has the Indian sidekick Clarence (George Moran).

Despite Fields's famous drawling voice, therefore, his humor accent was often on the visual, a philosophy also befitting his long earlier career as a silent comic juggler on stage. When W. C. interviews flirted with comedy theory he invariably gave his preference to physical-visual humor. In an article appropriately titled "W. C. Fields Pleads for Rough Humor," he observed, "Life is slap-stick. I don't care how nice anyone is trying to be, a funny fall can always get a laugh" (Redway, 73).

This visual slant might close (and how it often complements the verbal) with the reminder that Fields's overly flowery scam of a voice was often matched by an equally misleading flamboyant costume, such as his comically oversized stovepipe hat and coat with a similarly large sunflower in the buttonhole in *The Old Fashioned Way*. Indeed, this comic *picture* suggests an individual more likely to be the victim than the instigator of the scam. But just as in the old shell game, things are not always as they appear to be.

An often neglected manner in which Fields's confidence man follows a nineteenth-century diddler model (accent again on Southwestern humor) is in a pattern of comic vulnerability and sympathy. This model is on three levels. The most prevalent involves those frustrations, physical and otherwise, where the diddler's huckster skills have come up lacking, be it his trial for cheating at cards in *Tillie and Gus*, or his near hanging for being mistakenly identified as the masked bandit in *My Little Chickadee*. (His last request in the latter film was, "I'd like to see Paris before I die—Philadelphia will do.") This category would also include crooked dues-paying situations, such as enduring the singing audition of Cleopatra Pepperday in *The Old Fashioned Way*, in order to drain her pocketbook.

The sympathetic level also involves the negative nature of the suckers the W. C. huckster does take. At the start of *You Can't*

Cheat an Honest Man Fields's Larson E. Whipsnade runs the ticket-booth wagon with constant interruptions from his staff. Consequently, as he counts aloud the change to be returned to each customer he is seemingly forever losing track of the figures. After his apparent ongoing math problems, always in the ticket buyer's favor, Whipsnade reminds people to count their change immediately because refunds are not granted after leaving the window. Two of his customers, certain they have made money off this poor distracted booth person, avoid checking and rush away to count their easy extra cash. Only then do they realize Whipsnade has doubled up the bills and cheated them.

Herein lies the title, *You Can't Cheat an Honest Man*. Anxious to diddle, they were diddled. It all could have been prevented had they simply and honestly counted their money at the window—as Fields had reminded them! Fields has nicely updated the real-life axiom of huckster P. T. Barnum: "When people expect to get 'something for nothing' they are sure to be cheated and generally deserve to be" (see Chapter 2).

A last sympathetic slant involves scams that Fields's confidence men pull specifically to benefit a grown cinematic daughter or daughter figure. For instance, in *The Old Fashioned Way*, Betty McGonigle (Judith Allen) has an opportunity to leave her father and his destitute theater troupe and marry a rich, caring suitor. But her loyalty to W. C.'s McGonigle keeps her from departing, until he gets wind of the situation. The huckster father then spins a lie for Betty's benefit. He tells her he has just received a telegram offer to appear on the New York stage. But it is supposedly a solo chance, so he must go it alone, thus providing his daughter with a legitimate, guilt-free exit.

Here and elsewhere, there is an ongoing awareness by the Fields huckster that his daughter or the surrogate character should not be involved with the diddler world. This is showcased early in *The Old Fashioned Way* by a modest W. C. scam attempt. A passenger on the train carrying McGonigle and his troupe drops a sleeping-berth ticket. Fields's character quickly plants a foot on it. (Having borrowed from the early Chaplin before, W. C. might have lifted the move from the famous Tramp film short *The Immigrant*, 1917, where Charlie hastily covers a wayward coin with his foot.) When his daughter asks him what he has, McGonigle claims it is a sleeping-berth ticket he had purchased for her. Betty, however, sees through this and gets him to confess (no small accomplishment) that it probably was lost by a fellow passenger. Moreover, she then has him agreeing to return the ticket. This W. C. "science fiction" has its limits, though, and he goes on to use the berth himself.

In *Tillie and Gus*, Fields and Alison Skipworth, as Aunt Tillie and Uncle Gus, assist a naive young couple who have been bilked out of their inheritance. These long-lost relatives (accent on the *lost*, since the couple think Tillie and Gus are overseas missionaries, when actually they are well-traveled gamblers) use any means to assist their surrogate children. First, they manage to concoct a winner-take-all riverboat race with the crooked lawyer who has defrauded the youngsters. Then Tillie and Gus make an unlikely victory possible by such sneaky maneuvering as Uncle (underwater-diver) Gus hooking the rival boat to the pier and later using old boxes of fireworks to supercharge the engine-room power source.

Fields's *Poppy* finds the huckster attempting to pass off his foster daughter as the missing heir to a large inheritance. But as with *The Old Fashioned Way*, it is established early that the girl wants to settle down and lead a normal existence, like the young people she sees at the film's beginning. Snatching the inheritance would make that possible. Ironically, while the scam of Fields's McGargle fails, it helps precipitate the discovery that the girl actually is the lost heir. This in turn results in W. C.'s character revealing the most fatherly of cons, confessing to Poppy that he is not her biological parent but rather a foster one who has taken care of her since she was three. Thus, the *New York Daily Mirror*'s review of *Poppy* provides a summary that might apply to all of Fields's huckster fathers: "He manages to apply carnival methods to the business of providing happiness and a future for his wistful little girl" (Johaneson, ca. June 1936).

More controversial is the father-daughter relationship of *You Can't Cheat an Honest Man*. Some period critics, such as *The New York Times*'s Frank S. Nugent, found Fields's character here "completely unsympathetic" (Feb. 20, 1939). Thus, it should comes as no surprise that the occasional later Fields critic (such as William K. Everson) defined the comedian's Whipsnade as a less than the perfect father, "an almost total scoundrel . . . so insensitive to his daughter's happiness that he tries to force her into a marriage for money" (163).

Fields himself felt his character had been made too villainous, a complaint he raised in correspondence with producer Universal Studio. For instance, the comedian wanted a scene with his character "apologizing to the children [he has a girl and boy], baring my heart to them and the children deciding in my favor" (R. Fields, 322). In fact, a variation of such a scene occurs in W. C.'s original story outline for *You Can't Cheat an Honest Man* (R. Fields, 313).

But even more to the sentimental father-daughter point is another turn in the outline that borrows directly from the silent film version of *Poppy—Sally of the Sawdust*. Again, a young mother and trapeze artist is dying (only now she is the wife of Fields's character), and he is asked to do right by their children (R. Fields, 307–08). The comedian's real-life diddling of this *Sally* material underscores the importance to him of these sentimental father-daughter relationships. His only addition to this purloined but unfilmed death scene would have made his *You Can't Cheat an Honest Man* father all the more sympathetic—his cinema wife wanted the children out of the circus/carnival life. Thus, getting his daughter married into a rich family would have saved her from this allegedly sordid life.

From a Fields biographical slant, his obsession with this dying-mother motif (he also would attempt to use it in both *My Little Chickadee* and *Never Give a Sucker an Even Break*) has a real-life poignancy to it. The comedian's own long-estranged wife had metaphorically died to him as a young mother, unhappy with the nomadic life of an entertainer when it concerned rearing children. Only in this case, the very much alive Hattie Fields reared their boy apart from show business, forever alienating the youngster from his father in W. C.'s mind (and as previously noted, helping to inspire the comic mama's-boy and male brats that occasionally surface in his work).

By gifting himself with a grown cinema daughter, Fields could modestly play at being a father on his own terms. To paraphrase an old axiom, while things do not always work in life, art is where one gets them right. Along dark-comedy lines, having a Hattie Fields substitute fall from a trapeze was probably one of the nicer scenarios he had envisioned for his estranged wife, just as the inspiration for Chaplin's aforementioned comedy of misogyny, *Monsieur Verdoux*, came during a messy paternity scandal in which the comedian was involved.

Not all Fields fans, however, see his screen father in *You Can't Cheat an Honest Man* as callous. By this late date (1939) in W. C.'s career he had so firmly established the cinematic bond between his dads and grown daughters that many (myself included) still place this relationship in that tradition, "reading" his daughter's near-marriage to the rich comically named Roger Bell-Goodie as a sacrifice *she* is making for a financially pinched father. A period example of this critical position can be found in *Variety*'s review of the film: "Owner's [Fields] daughter, Constance Moore, falls in love with [Edgar] Bergen but decided to marry a rich boy to save her father's show. Fields blows up the wedding plans to clear the road for Bergen and Miss Moore" (Feb. 22, 1939).

An affectionate father-daughter link is not quite in the nine-teenth-century literary-huckster custom. But this idolized father-daughter tie has a rich tradition in western culture's nineteenth-century ideas about women and the male need for females to be innocent and pure. In Bram Dykstra's watershed work on the subject, *Idols of Perversity*, this view of the woman as household nun was often symbolized by Coventry Patmore's period poem, "The Angel in the House" (18–19, 83, 111, 366). With Fields for a subject one is tempted to make a connection with his longtime favorite author Dickens, whose sentimental father-daughter tendency is an outgrowth of "The Angel in the House" phenomenon. Still, one need not search overly hard to find the father-daughter connection in American huckster-period literature. P. T. Barnum's devoted attention to his daughters is a given in his high-visibility nineteenth-century autobiography. And in Mark Twain's writing, of which Fields was also particularly fond, variations of this phenomenon occur, such as Colonel Seller's inclination along these lines with several surrogate daughters in *The Gilded Age*. (One should add that, as will be discussed in the next chapter, Fields's antiheroic film figures never saw an angelic wife in any house, though loving daughter-figures continued to surface.)

A final way in which Fields's screen characters follow the earlier confidence-man tradition is in having a creator (the comedian himself) who indulged in a variety of related deceptions. One might begin with the fact that both *The Old Fashioned Way* and *You Can't Cheat an Honest Man* were based on original stories by one "Charles Bogle"—Fields himself. This same Bogle penned the stories for W. C.'s antiheroic films *It's a Gift* (1934) and *The Man on the Flying Trapeze* (1935).

The comedian's comic-writing aliases became more elaborately absurd with the late antiheroic films *The Bank Dick* (1940) and *Never Give a Sucker an Even Break* (1941). The screenplay for the former movie was by Mahatma Kane Jeeves, while the latter production was from a story by Otis Criblecoblis. As comedy historian and theorist Neil Schmitz noted, "All the important humorists in the nineteenth century write behind assumed names; an alias is their alibi" (28). That is, to break comedy rules they "discount their literary value" (what better example than to become an Otis Criblecoblis?!) and lose themselves in their characters. But it is not that their aliases were some big secret. Period film audiences knew it was Fields behind those zany pen names, just as nineteenth-century readers knew Mark Twain was really Samuel Clemens. It was more that the assumption of a pseudonym gave them a symbolic freedom to be more comically outrageous.

Another Fields-as-creator deception involved his propensity, like many nineteenth-century humorists, to "borrow" material. For instance, one of his most famous alleged ad-libs occurs in *Mississippi*: "Women are like elephants to me. I like to look at 'em but I wouldn't want to own one." Ronald J. Fields even highlights this comic axiom in his generally insightful second volume on his grandfather (*A Life on Film*, 172). Yet, the saying was actually coined by syndicated crackerbarrel humorist Kin Hubbard (creator of "Abe Martin"), who died five years before *Mississippi* appeared (Kelly, 77).

The Fields-Hubbard connection is not without further interest, since both men mixed crackerbarrel and antiheroic traits early in a watershed period in American humor, a transitional era that saw the gradual ascendancy of the antiheroic movement. But the point remains, as was earlier documented when examining Fields's copyrighted sketches, that the comedian occasionally lifted his material. (For an overview of other Fields comedy thefts, see Gerald Weales's chapter on *It's a Gift* in his insightfully entertaining *Canned Goods as Caviar: American Film Comedy of the 1930s*.)

An additional aspect of comic deception in his humor was precipitated by working during the heyday of Hollywood's Hays (censorship) Office. The period strictness might best be suggested by the fact that producer/auteur David O. Selznick had to obtain special permission for Clark Gable to say "damn" at the close of *Gone With the Wind* (1939). In this environment, Fields frequently played fifth columnist in his films (both as huckster and antihero) by slipping in

4. Fields has trouble eating ice cream in *Never Give a Sucker an Even Break* (1941).

provocative names and references, such as his favorite oath, "Godfrey Daniel!" (his euphemism for the forbidden "god damn").

Other examples might range from calling a *Poppy* character Countess Maggie Tubbs De Puizzi (Catherine Doucet) and in a direct-address censorship crack in *Never Give a Sucker an Even Break*. In the latter case, Fields (playing himself) is in a soda fountain that resembles a bar. He turns to the camera (in effect, the viewer) and observes, "This scene's supposed to be a saloon, but the censor cut it out. It'll play just as well." The suppression further

5. Groucho studying his favorite subject—anatomy—in *Horse Feathers* (1932).

accents his appeal: a red-nosed hero to all blue-nosed victims. But even here Fields the artist might be comically conning the audience for support against the general tunnel vision of the Hays Office; a bar had surfaced in the previous year's *The Bank Dick* (part of the "Black Pussy Cafe" establishment). Moreover, the soda-fountain premise gave Fields an excellent opportunity for some visual comedy—trying to eat ice cream with a long, *bent* spoon.

To reiterate the axiom with which the chapter opened, "A huckster gets out of town as quickly as he can. A con man doesn't have to leave until he wants to." There are five ways to differentiate between the Fields-Marx scam artists. Unlike Fields's nineteenth-century huckster, forever on the move with a small-time diddle for small-town America, Groucho's twentieth-century con man frequently operates his more ambitious flimflam from a seeming position of establishment authority. But behind this he is still a comic leech on society; the stakes and subterfuge have just grown larger.

An overview of then-contemporary Groucho gyp artists would include: the hotel owner-manager Mr. Hammer of *The Cocoanuts*

(1929); the famous explorer Captain Spaulding in *Animal Crackers* (1930); Huxley College President and Professor Quincey Adams Wagstaff in *Horse Feathers* (1932); mythical kingdom (Freedonia) Dictator Rufus T. Firefly in *Duck Soup* (1933); press/theatrical agent Otis B. Driftwood of *A Night at the Opera* (1935); and sanitarium physician Dr. Hugo Z. Hackenbush in *A Day at the Races* (1937). While Groucho is neither without nomadic huckster roles (such as being headman in *At the Circus*, 1939) nor exempt from earlier setting (see *Go West*, 1940), the aforementioned roles showcase him at both his best and most typical film occupations.

These key movie parts are not only of the twentieth century but they often draw upon then-topical issues. For instance, *The Cocoanuts* capitalizes on the 1920s Florida land boom ("only 42 hours from Times Square"). *Horse Feathers*'s keying on college football follows another 1920s phenomenon—the establishment of this game as both a major spectator sport and a major distraction from traditional higher-education goals. Moreover, by calling the school Huxley College, one is reminded of controversial period author Aldous Huxley, whose most famous work, *Brave New World* (1932), came out six months *prior* to *Horse Feathers*.

Ironically, the reason Groucho and his brothers' greatest film (*Duck Soup*, the nihilistic satire on the absurdity of government) was a 1933 critical and commercial failure was that it was *too* topical. Sociological film historian (and now screenwriter and director) Andrew Bergman insightfully expands upon this unfortunate timing: "After a year of Roosevelt's energy and activism [e.g., the flurry of New Deal legislation], government, no matter what else it might be, was no absurdity" (37). Interestingly, Dick Cavett and I disagreed about this point on Arts and Entertainment's nationally broadcast cable *Biography* episode on Groucho. Cavett felt that period viewers would not have walked out on *Duck Soup* simply because it satirized the government. But this misses the real thrust of the Bergman position (with which many historians, myself included, concur). The tenor of the times was such—"Give the new President a chance"—that most potential patrons avoided theaters showing *Duck Soup* in the first place.

Second, in contrast to the W. C. huckster basing his swindle in a show of verbal entertainment for a potential comic victim and/or audience within the film, Groucho's con artist is much more abrasively direct in mapping out his fleecing plans. And while the movie viewer is entertained by the genuine exhilaration of his verbal deliveries, the in-film focus of this attack style is often oblivious to his cracks.

For instance, in *Duck Soup* Groucho's Firefly baldly asks Margaret Dumont's Mrs. Teasdale, "Will you marry me? Did he [her late husband] leave you any money? Answer the second question first." Besides such self-serving directness, Firefly is constantly blitzing Teasdale with in-your-face comic insults, such as, "Married! I can see you now bending over a hot stove, but I can't see the stove."

This is typical of the Groucho verbal assaults Dumont characters received throughout her seven Marx brothers films, starting with *The Cocoanuts*, where the mustachioed one, appropriately named Hammer, tells Dumont's Mrs. Potter, "Did anyone ever tell you that you look like the Prince of Wales? I don't mean the present Prince of Wales; one of the old Wales, and believe me when I say Wales, I mean Wales. I know a whale when I see one."

This bluntness is in marked contrast to Fields's courtship, as McGonigle, of wealthy widow Cleopatra Pepperday in *The Old Fashioned Way*, where he must verbally finesse his victim into financial vulnerability. And such an "old-fashioned" finagle means living with liabilities, like Pepperday's awful singing voice. Groucho's con man puts up with very little. When Mrs. Teasdale bursts into unpleasant song at the close of *Duck Soup*, Firefly and his comic cohorts pelt her with fruit.

By factoring the added high-society snobbishness of Dumont's character with her obtuseness (Pepperday seems a rocket scientist by comparison), the viewer is quite prepared to accept the increased harshness Groucho brings to this twentieth-century huckster courtship. But he addresses everyone in this assault manner. In *Horse Feathers* he tells the Huxley College president his character is replacing, "Why don't you go home to your wife? I'll tell you what. I'll go home to your wife and outside of the improvements she'll never know the difference."

Despite the nastiness, it is hard to resist him. I was reminded of this conflict (affection for a comedian whose shtick puts a new emphasis on the cliché "I killed them") when recently reviewing the in-your-face lethal style of Billy Crystal's film character Buddy Young, Jr., in *Mr. Saturday Night* (1992). For example, there is Buddy's historical footnote, "As Mrs. Einstein said to her husband, Albert, 'What the hell do you know?'" Here is brutal humor that also complements the misogynous nature of Groucho's con-man persona. One can imagine him enjoying Crystal's film.

The fact that most Groucho "subjects" just accept his verbal steamrolling, or are oblivious to it, is an interesting commentary on the then-modern citizen, especially when one considers how Firefly's comic dictatorship in *Duck Soup* parallels the rise of Hitler in Germany. Most period reviews were too close to the events to make the connection, though a few critiques did not ignore the foreign ties. For example, *New York Sun* critic John S. Cohen, Jr., found the film's eventual comic war "highly pertinent, looking at the volatile 1930s map of Europe" (Nov. 24, 1933).

This Groucho phenomenon of people loving him regardless of what he does to them is not limited to a single film. Marx brothers authors Paul D. Zimmerman and Burt Goldblatt state the frequency of this occurrence in *Animal Crackers*: "Groucho can be rude with endless variation. . . .The crowd, as always, replies to Groucho's rudeness by extolling him in song and dance" (35). The beauty of this observation is the musical tie-in. First, Zimmerman and Goldblatt posit the classic Groucho song "I Must Be Going" as a study in rudeness, with Captain Spaulding (Groucho's character singing such lines as "I only came to say, I must be going." Then the authors remind the reader how the crowd responds to each Groucho discourtesy—by singing to him, "Hurrah for Captain Spaulding." The significance here is that the Spaulding song, that entertaining tribute to a leader, right or wrong, would eventually become Groucho's *theme* song—a most fitting development.

And one might add, the line "Hello, I Must Be Going," from the aforementioned musical-comedy study in rudeness, has gone on to become a Groucho trademark, too. For example, author Charlotte Chandler would use it as the title of her Groucho biography. But then this is all so fitting for a confidence-man character that even the comedian described his figure as essentially "obnoxious" (*The Groucho Phile*, 86).

Building upon Groucho's more abrasive style, another difference between Fields and Marx shakedown artists is the latter's potential for real danger to both the individual and society. While W. C.'s hucksters merely deal in the "gentle art of petty larceny," Groucho's con men gamble with lives.

Early in *Duck Soup* his Firefly sings that anyone not cutting him in on the graft will be executed. Late in the film he leads Freedonia into a war just for the hell of it. This might best be symbolized by the scene where Groucho's character mistakenly machine guns some of his own soldiers. Fittingly, he covers the error with a bribe, which his Firefly immediately gets back. It is such an apt moment because 1930s critics often noted his "machine gun" verbal patter that, as previously described, metaphorically tore people apart. How appropriate then that he should use the real weapon in his most over-the-top, big-time scamming role.

When Groucho, as Wagstaff, assumes control of Huxley College at the opening of *Horse Feathers*, he anticipates the look and feel of Firefly taking over a country in *Duck Soup*. And after a Huxley student (Zeppo) provides a warning about "dear old Dad [Wagstaff]" being vindictive, Groucho launches into a musical-comedy philosophy as entertainingly despotic as anything in Freedonia: "I soon dispose of all of those who put me on the pan [criticize adversely], like Shakespeare said to Nathan Hale, 'I always get my man.'" Once again Groucho's in-film audience, in this case the educated Huxley faculty and students, eat up this threatening figure, celebrating his every word. In fact, the faculty really get into the spirit of things by also mimicking Groucho's eccentric movements about the stage.

The student of Groucho the Harsh should also note *Horse Feathers*'s tentative script (April 21, 1931, Academy of Motion Picture Arts and Sciences), which finds Marx entering a burning building seemingly to save the leader of a rival college. Instead, he exits with a "hot" diploma for his wayward college-student son Zeppo, leaving the victim behind.

Along more modest yet equally deadly dark-comedy lines, Marx's quack doctor Hackenbush (*A Day at the Races*) says of his future sanitarium clients/victims: "The last job I had [as a questionable horse doctor], I had to take it out in trade and this is no butcher shop—not yet, anyhow."

Groucho's medical harshness can also satirize the stupidity of the milling masses. In *Monkey Business* (1931) non-doctor Groucho attends to an individual who has fainted and around whom a crowd had gathered. Prescribing an ocean voyage—which Groucho and company are currently on—he exits the scene by telling the many onlookers: "Will you all get close so he won't recover? Here, right this way. Step right around here."

In general, however, Groucho charlatans do whatever it takes, whether it is Firefly starting wars or Wagstaff trying to buy athletes and kidnap football opponents. An appropriate Groucho position on morals, or the lack of a need for them, occurs in *Horse Feathers*. When told it is not right to buy players, he observes: "I'll nip that [a belief in ethics] in the bud. How about coming along and having a nip [drink] yourself." Self-centeredness and the con are one and the same for Groucho, or as his character says in *Cocoanuts*, "One for all, and all for me, and me for you, and three for five, and six for a quarter."

Groucho's outrageous behavior is tempered by an equally outrageous appearance, especially the huge greasepaint mustache and eyebrows. And one should quickly add the contorted physique—Marx's bent-over dirty-old-man walk. All Groucho's unusual characteristics suggest the relevance of humor historian/theorist Henry Jenkins's observation that, "like the 'ugly clown' in traditional circus acts or the grotesque figures in Rabelais, the movie clowns' antisocial desires, their physicality and impulsiveness, are marked directly onto their bodies" (227). (Along related lines, Fields's oversized proboscis could be noted.) The shock effect of Groucho's quips is softened by the comic unreality of his looks. One period film critic observed in a review of *A Night at the Opera*, "Groucho would be funny in still photographs" (Ferguson, 130). His eyebrows pack such a comedy wallop that the comedian refused to raise them when doing road tours of potential 1930s movie material because they would win a laugh for any line.

His macabre cracks are also made more palatable by generally deflating worthy targets, whether the puffed-up Margaret Dumonts of the world or genuine dangers like the plotting ambassador of Sylvania (Louis Calhern) in *Duck Soup* and the crooked lawyer (Douglas Dumbrille) in *A Day at the Races*. Part of the fun in these Groucho strikes is that like all things Marx brothers, the action is immediate. Comedy theorist Thomas H. Jordan has pinpointed a Groucho example of this and juxtaposed it with a traditional narrative revelation of a public enemy. Noting that actor Dumbrille plays essentially the same conniving lawyer in both *Races* and director Frank Capra's *Mr. Deeds Goes to Town* (1936), Jordan differentiates between the idealistically honest Deeds taking "most of the film to discover this and decide what to do about him" versus Groucho and company dismantling Dumbrille's character from moment one (99).

A devil's advocate might add, "Yes, and it takes one to know one," since Groucho's character is slippery by nature. Indeed, earlier in the

1930s he had essayed his own sneaky lawyer on radio's *Flywheel, Shyster, and Flywheel*. Author Jordan might have added that there is a certain comic consistency about Groucho bumping into the world of law, since both lawyers and the Marx brothers speak their own surreal languages. The former group just are not intentionally funny. Of course, for more on that one need only review Groucho and Chico's comic interpretation of lawyer double-talk in the contract scene from *A Night at the Opera*.

Unlike the democratic populism of Capra's films, Groucho needs no proof to instantly turn on the villain. And therein lies the dangerous attraction of his con men, for they are forever stuck in the attack mode—often but not always for the good. Thus, one might make another Groucho-Capra comparison to reiterate the sometimes disturbing potential of the mustachioed one. Both *Duck Soup* and *Meet John Doe* (1941), though in decidedly different comedy manners, provide a warning against fascism. But whereas Capra's by now somewhat tarnished populist still plays the hero eventually, in *Duck Soup* Groucho's Firefly *is* the danger (with the ambassador of Sylvania), however entertaining.

For instance, as he leads the cast in "The Country's Going to War," a big production number peppered with several musical styles and an inspired satire of how patriotism can be cranked up among the people to make armed conflict seem like a day in the country, Groucho's mesmerizing comedy presence still has a frightening side. One need only substitute any number of real charismatic despots who have manipulated their citizens into war. His anti-establishment, anti-stuffed-shirt tendencies do not prevent him from comically abusing the power his film character has or to which he aspires. After *Duck Soup*'s concluding Freedonia victory, one would assume it will be back to crooked government business as usual.

It should be remembered that Groucho's "anarchistic comedy" is not limited to Marx brothers films (Jenkins, 23). For instance, one can find common ties between the pivotal *Duck Soup* and the Wheeler and Woolsey take-off on government in *Diplomaniacs* (both 1933 releases). Insightful Jenkins, also a major fan of *Diplomaniacs*, only seems to err in overemphasizing the early 1930s as the key period of "anarchistic comedy." In point of fact, it is hard to find an era when at least some examples do not exist. The most pertinent references for this book would be W. C. Fields's early 1940s films *The Bank Dick* and *Never Give a Sucker an Even Break*.

Of course, Groucho's extreme dark-humor tendencies are also softened through constant victimization by Chico, and sometimes by Harpo. Though this will be expanded on in the discussion of the antihero in the next chapter, it is enough to say here that Groucho's power trip, regardless of the film, is forever pricked by his brothers, just as Chaplin's satirical characterization of Hitler has an inflated globe popping in his *Great Dictator* (1940) face.

This trickiness is especially entertaining because of the contrast in scam-artist types. While Groucho, the new-age huckster, is invariably in a power post, Chico (his primary nemesis) frequently has ties to the simpler nineteenth-century con man, sometimes via the immigrant street vendor. Consequently, in *Duck Soup* Chico sells peanuts from a cart in front of Groucho's government chambers, his affected Italian accent being the obvious immigrant connection here and elsewhere. Chico's *A Day at the Races* entrepreneur hawks tootsie-fruitsie ice cream from another pushcart, while selling worthless betting guides on the side.

Along old-fashioned W. C. Fields–type confidence-man lines is the crooked bridge game Chico and Harpo set up in *Animal Crackers*. Before the first card is dealt Chico asks, "How do you want to play, honest?" But as in a W. C. poker game, honesty is not his policy. Thus, when a player later questions how both Chico and Harpo can have an ace of spades, Chico gestures toward Harpo and innocently replies in a manner Fields probably enjoyed: "Yeah, he's got thousands of them."

Symbolically, one is tempted to add that while President Franklin D. Roosevelt gave 1930s Americans a "New Deal," the Marxes provided a comic false shuffle. In *Animal Crackers*, as in real life, Groucho avoided playing bridge with Chico—an authentic talent with cards. But rare was the movie in which Chico's traditional huckster did not take Groucho's twentieth-century con man. (In contrast, the following chapter will address, in part, the modern manner—comic absurdity—in which Chico and sometimes Harpo get the best of Groucho.)

Taking this Groucho-Chico comparison a step further, the mustachioed one's dastardly amusing acts are often topped by the other's. Groucho's Freedonia leader is crooked, but Chico's character

6. Groucho is always courting wealthy Margaret Dumont (in the center), but his real interests lie elsewhere, from *Animal Crackers* (1930).

(Chicolini) is a spy for the other side, as well as briefly joining Sylvania's army. Fittingly, his character is even capable of verbally zinging Groucho the mouth and getting away with it. For instance, after Chicolini poses the following riddle to Firefly—"What is it got a big black mustache, smokes a big black cigar and is a big pain in the neck?"—Groucho's figure inexplicably (comic surprise, Marx brothers style) offers Chicolini the position of Freedonia's Secretary of War. This is not a bad career advancement for a peanut vendor.

The Fields and Groucho shakedown artists differ in how they pitch the scam. Whereas the W. C. character so loves the yarn it can become an end in itself, the Marx figure has no such old-fashioned notions; time is money. Indeed, Groucho often prefaces his monetarily motivated Dumont encounters with some sort of "stop me if you're not rich" opening. In *Animal Crackers* he tells Mrs. Rittenhouse, "You've got beauty, charm, and money. You have got money, haven't you? 'Cause if you haven't, we can quit right now."

The most obvious difference in the "sales" approaches of the men is showcased in their contrasting speaking patterns. With Fields there is a slow savoring of the words, a comic drawl that will not be hurried. Opponents might momentarily derail it, but there is no rushing his love affair with language.

In contrast, *rushed* does not seem an adequate description of the dialogue that spews out of Groucho faster than the sound from a record turntable pushed beyond yesterday's version of fast forward (78 rpm). This mechanical analogy is not taken randomly. I am reminded of a Firefly comment to Dumont's Mrs. Teasdale which is really much more applicable to Groucho: "You know you haven't stopped talking since I came here? You must have been vaccinated with a phonograph needle."

For a more recent and organic comparison, one might apply *New York Times* film critic Janet Maslin's 1992 description of Robin Williams to Groucho: "More of an energy source than an actor" (Sept. 23, 1992). However the phenomenon is defined, it encourages repeat viewings, since Groucho's cultural allusions go zipping by at warp speed.

At times the words even seem out of Groucho's control, as in his satirical soliloquies (at Eugene O'Neill's expense) in *Animal Crackers*, when "strange interludes" periodically overtake him: "The gods looked down and laughed! This would be a better world for children if the parents had to eat the spinach." To add one further level of contrariness to such Lewis Carroll detours, taken independently of plot (such as it is), Groucho's lines, like his spinach axiom, often hold more common sense than any of his other dialogue.

During the 1930s Groucho's propensity to go into occasional "strange interludes" went under various names. Otis Ferguson, the team's most insightful American critic, titled his *A Night at the Opera* review of Groucho and company: "The Marxian 'Epileptic'" (130). Appropriately, this was also the film that brought the surrealists out of the artistic woodwork. *New York Herald Tribune* critic Joseph Alsop, Jr., was only half kidding when he wrote of the movie, under the title "Surrealism Beaten at Its Own Game," that celebrated surrealist artists "Jean Cocteau, Salvador Dali . . . and their friends . . . may just as well forget about the whole business now" (Dec. 15, 1935). This dream or nightmare art factor is best examined in the following chapter, where the focus moves from the scam-artist accent to the lunatic-humor world of antiheroes.

There is, however, an unusual use of a Groucho surrealistic con that bears noting. In an atypical Marx picture, *Monkey Business*, Groucho finds himself in the uncommon position of being, like his brothers, a lowly shipboard stowaway who gets into trouble with a gun-wielding gangster. But Groucho (who is given no other name in the picture) manages to keep said tough guy off balance by surprising transitions (surrealism at its most fundamental) from one character to another, such as changing through voice and mannerisms into a little boy and a teenage girl.

For instance, when the gangster threatens him—"Do you see this gat [gun]?"—Groucho the fearless youngster replies, "Cute, isn't it? Santy Claus bring it for Christmas? I got a fire engine!" While there is a comic dialogue going on between Groucho and the heavy, the comedian's repeated metamorphoses suggest he had the ability to handle both roles in a dialogue quite nicely all by himself. It is obvious in the evolution of stand-up comedy, from monologuist to comic Sybil (densely populated with numerous personalities), à la Jonathan Winters and Robin Williams, that Groucho remains forever timely. Moreover, such metamorphosing skills represent the ultimate con-man cover, reminiscent of the devilish transformation of Melville's Confidence-Man (see Chapter 2). Such trickster change-overs are, however, most often related to "the frequent presence of animalism in comedian comedy" (Seidman, 65). For instance, late in *Monkey Business* Groucho's comic passion for Thelma Todd has him down on all fours meowing like a cat.

A final manner by which to differentiate the Fields and Marx charlatans concerns screen-audience involvement. W. C.'s characters very rarely entangle themselves in direct address to the viewer, whereas this is a comic given in a Groucho film. Visual address was not uncommon in silent cinema; Charlie Chaplin winked at the audience at the close of his fittingly titled *Behind the Screen* (1916). But Groucho was a pioneer in the *verbal* aside to the screen viewer, an innovation of which he was very proud. Late in his life the comedian observed, speaking in the third person about his film persona: "He was the first one to bring the theatrical convention, the spoken aside, to the film medium" (*The Groucho Phile*, 86).

This direct-address rapport between Groucho and the film viewer puts his scam artists on a more intimate, not-to-be-denied, level and further lowers concern over the victim who is somehow oblivious to these asides. In *A Night at the Opera* Groucho's character has just conned Mrs. Claypool (Dumont) into thinking he only dined with another woman because she reminded him of her. He then tells Claypool:

> That's why I'm here with *you*—because you remind me of you. Your eyes, your throat, your lips—everything reminds me of you. Except you. How do you account for that?

Then in direct address he adds: "If she figures that one out, she's good."

One is further drawn to Groucho's asides because his character is the only one in a Marx film with this ability. Not even the comedian's brothers, who are forever derailing him, have the power. Thus, a Groucho turn to the camera offers him an occasional, all-in-the-family payback. One of the most amusing occurs in *Horse Feathers*, just prior to a Chico piano number. Groucho's Wagstaff gets up from a couch and walks to the camera before saying, "I've got to stay here, but there's no reason why you folks shouldn't go out into the lobby until this thing blows over." Situations like this are reminiscent of Shakespeare's trickster title character from *Richard III*. While most of the play's characters "exist in a single dimension, as distant puppet-like figures . . . Richard exists also in an extra dimension, front of stage, where he shares with the audience his delight in his skills as a puppet-master" (Mellett, 66). When Groucho is victimized by a brother (usually Chico), the direct-address aside can also soften the frustration. For instance, when Groucho's land-auction hustle in *Cocoanuts* is ruined by Chico's nonstop bidding, the mustachioed one tells the viewer: "That was a great success. Yeah, one more success like that and I'll sell my body to a medical institute." In addition, a turn to the camera can deflate a previous Chico action, such as Groucho's *Monkey Business* aside after an especially bad pun from his "Italian" brother: "There's my argument. Restrict immigration." In contrast to Groucho, the direct-address look or aside by other comedians does not always represent superiority. For instance, "The camera looks of . . . [Laurel and Hardy] function to underscore the pair's helplessness in a world in which they are continually victimized" (Seidman, 24).

Direct-address Groucho examples provide both the viewer perk of being an insider (with *the* Marx brother, no less) and the added humor effect of Groucho's awareness he is a character in a fiction. Indeed, Groucho's in-your-face direct address undercuts the complete fictional situation—a one-person spoofing of the film itself.

And his camera asides were not limited to fits of superiority toward Dumont or various responses to Chico. There is Groucho the diddling but discerning comedy critic. When caught in sexy Thelma Todd's apartment by her boyfriend, *Horse Feathers*'s Groucho alibis, "I'm the plumber. I'm just hanging around in case something goes wrong with her pipes." Then in direct address he adds, "That's the first time I've used that joke in twenty years." Like a crossdressing comedy, the fun in direct address comes from seeing characters unaware of the seemingly obvious joke (Groucho commentary) that only the viewer is in on.

If Groucho fan Woody Allen had been directing in the 1930s, the next logical step for the direct-address pioneer would have been stepping off the screen, as Jeff Daniels's character does in Allen's *The Purple Rose of Cairo* (1985). As it is, every example of Groucho-viewer eye contact forever makes it seem imminent.

These, then, have been the modern developments separating the Groucho con man from the W. C. huckster: the establishment front versus the nomadic shakedown artist; a verbal style of hypercomedy speed and abrasive directness contrasted with a casually meandering tempo of flowery language; a threat to society as well as the individual versus the small-time diddle; the preference for spoils over the sheer joy of playing the scam game; and the story-derailing intimacy of the camera asides contrasted with the traditional narrative befitting the old-fashioned world of the nineteenth century huckster.

The last characteristic might be the most threateningly modern of all. As the voyeurism of Hitchcock (the most manipulating of film directors) invariably implicates the viewer in murder, Groucho's direct-address often incriminates us in comedy crimes to come. Moreover, this guilt-by-comic-association can happen with disjointed surprise and speed, given a Groucho wit that makes not linear connections but lateral ones.

Viewer identification with confidence men Fields and Marx, as is the case with most shakedown artists, is an outgrowth of a desire to say and do things that societal norms make taboo. It is an antisocial attractiveness not unlike the fascination of the gangster figure. In fact, the 1930s comedy heyday of W. C. and Groucho was paralleled by a matching audience fascination with the gangster. Both hucksters and gangster heavies, second cousins under a crime umbrella, were nurtured during this period by the discontent of the Depression. The system had broken down, and these were alternatives for survival. The ongoing popularity of Fields and Marx, as well as gangster characters, lifts them above mere period faddishness. But it does isolate a key factor in their success: feeding upon discontent (economic, political, social . . .) over some derailing of the American dream.

As a gangster footnote to this genre's period ties with W. C. and Groucho, *Monkey Business* has the Marxes caught in the middle of a gang war. As originally written (April 21, 1931, p. M-11) but unshot, the ending even more thoroughly plays on stereotypical icons of the gangster genre: "bootleggers' equipment; cases of liquor, bottles, demijohns, barrels, kegs of beer . . . a rum sloop . . . lashed to the dock . . . a bubbling vat of beer."

Indeed, the topper (Harpo swimming in the vat) goes one better than Fields's classic antisocial liquor activities in *International House* (1933), most pointedly the ongoing stream of beer bottles that fall from W. C.'s autogyro (part plane, part helicopter), a wonderful sight gag itself, as he attempts to fly to Kansas City but ends up in China.

And in the tradition of this increased gangster focus (and further evidence of Groucho's dark side), the final *Monkey Business* script also has him snarling with comic menace: "How would you like to be shot, sideways or in a group?" and "Listen, Big Mans [*sic*], there's a certain somebody out to shoot you in your fat little tummy and that certain someone is me" (pp. E-11, E-12). This scripted ending apparently went unfilmed for cost reasons. And while James Cagney and Edward G. Robinson would probably have had nothing to worry about, Groucho as gangster does not seem like that much of a stretch.

In terms of a broader comic heritage, confidence men W. C. and Groucho bring an inspired literalness to that age-old axiom *carpe diem,* "seize the day." That is, they want not only to seize the day but also to sell it at a profit. (Of course, in Groucho's case one can imagine him having to explain to Chico ad infinitum that it is "*seize* the day," not "*see* the day," just as Chico had trouble differentiating between "viaduct" and "Why-a-duck?" in *Cocoanuts.*)

In 1937 Gilbert Seldes, the perceptive popular-culture critic and historian, observed: "The arrival of the Marx brothers and the reappearance of W. C. Fields saved screen comedy" (41). More specifically, W. C. and Groucho brought a real artistry to verbal comedy.

But while Fields is a celebration of the old-fashioned flim-flam tradition, Marx and company represent the confidence man in transition. Groucho is the funny/frightening, big-time future of the shakedown artist, forever tempered by Chico, a sometime throwback to the nineteenth-century huckster. The fact that Chico normally gets the best of the mustachioed one is consistent with the hoary maxim of humor being leery of authority. Yes, we enjoy Groucho because he often pricks the high and the mighty, but when he battles brother Chico it is Groucho who invariably occupies the vulnerable authority position. Moreover, as French film critic Louis Chavance wrote in 1932, Chico is the "smiling accomplice of the public" (175). His is the everyman promise of the small-change nineteenth-century scam artist out to transfer "Manifest Destiny" into the individual profit column.

Humor theorist Neil Schmitz offers an additional slant on the Marxes as con artists with nineteenth-century connections. He notes that writer/producer Herman Mankiewicz once kiddingly described Groucho's brothers as a "mute" (Harpo) and a "guinea" (Chico), a generally derogatory slang term for an Italian (20). Schmitz then observes that three of the alleged identities of the mysterious title character in Melville's watershed *The Confidence-Man* (see Chapter 2) are a fast-talking hustler (a capsule definition of Groucho), a mute, and a guinea (though in this case the term referred to a black person from the West African area of Guinea).

Schmitz's link might seem like a *long shot*, but it translates as another argument for the Marxes to be seen as huckster transition-figures. That is, *The Confidence-Man* showcases the hustler as existing in any number of forms—matching the many scam vulnerabilities of man. The Marxes merely represent modern actualizations of three Melville types: Groucho's machine-gun talker, Harpo's surrealist mute, and Chico's ethnic wise fool.

Moreover, the team as led—or misled—by Groucho personifies the dark-side readings of Melville's novel by twentieth-century critics. Just as the ultimate identity of Melville's Confidence-Man has been seen as the devil, the life-and-death-wielding Groucho of *Duck Soup* and *Horse Feathers* is a fellow three out of four fallen archangels would follow. Punning critics have been seeing it this way since the 1930s, when Groucho and his brothers were periodically labeled "comedemons" (Chavance, 175).

Whether one is discussing good-old-boy huckster Fields or "devilish" con-man Groucho, however, the phenomenon of the shakedown artist is as American as Tom Sawyer's whitewashing scam or the big-game dirty dealings of politics, from the Gilded Age to this century's latest cover-up. And as Huck Finn observes at the beginning of the novel bearing his name, "I never seen anybody but lied, one time or another." Thus, it remains an ethical judgment call as to when a particular lie is acceptable and when it is something questionable. But before becoming too judgmental, let comedy theorist Schmitz remind you that both humor and life are based in lying (*Of Huck and Alice* . . .). It is another way of spelling survival, of coping. So go easy on the flim-flammer, because as *Pogo* comic-strip creator Walt Kelly once observed, "We have met the enemy and he is us."

BOSS *It must be hard to lose your mother-in-law.*

FIELDS *Yes, it is, very hard. Almost impossible.*
                    —*The Man on the Flying Trapeze*

HARPO *[blows a bubble]*
GROUCHO *Say, am I stewed, or did a grapefruit just fly by?*
                    —*A Day at the Races*

CHAPTER 5 **Antiheroes and Absurdity**
As Defined by the Films
of W. C. and Groucho

The previous chapter delineated the confidence-man screen work of Fields and Marx as falling into two distinct camps; another fundamental dichotomy is true of their antiheroic film action. While the cornerstone of the antiheroic world is frustration, the particular derailments of these comedians are decidedly different from one another. The Fields character is invariably a victim of a dominating wife and related circumstances; as the *New York World-Telegram* critic said of *The Man on the Flying Trapeze*, he is "hounded into a succession of catastrophes by malignant forces both in and out of the house" (Delehanty, Aug. 3, 1935). In contrast, Groucho Marx's overbearing figure is often comically neutralized by absurdity . . . absurdity as personified by his brothers, Chico and Harpo, as well as occasions when the mustachioed one jumps the tracks all on his own.

Focusing on the sound era, as in Chapter 4, the pivotal antiheroic W. C. Fields feature films are *You're Telling Me* (1934); *It's a Gift*

(1934); *The Man on the Flying Trapeze* (1935); *The Bank Dick* (1940); and *Never Give a Sucker an Even Break* (1941). Of course, as the last title suggests, hucksterish traits also surfaced in his anti-heroic movies. Still, as this chapter will demonstrate, Fields's tendency was to alternate film roles between flimflam men and weak husbands.

In comparison, the otherwise domineering con artist Groucho played antihero to his brothers in the same films; he could shift back and forth between the two personas from moment to moment. Thus, the key Marx movies are the same as those examined in the last chapter—though the critical filter is now frustration. These films are *The Cocoanuts* (1929); *Animal Crackers* (1930); *Horse Feathers* (1932); *Duck Soup* (1933); *A Night at the Opera* (1935); and *A Day at the Races* (1937). And this new focus, like the one in the previous chapter, can also be addressed through occasional references to other Marx brothers films, especially *Monkey Business* (1931), a quality picture from the team's superior Paramount period (see the Filmography).

Unlike Fields's nineteenth-century nomadic huckster, his anti-hero is a contemporary (for the period), browbeaten family man anchored to a going-nowhere position. Though the image of W. C. is still probably most associated with the confidence man, his anti-heroic film roles better showcase his range as a performer. While no less funny as a figure of frustration, his bumbler is capable of a pathos level not available to his flimflammers. At these times he rivals Chaplin.

Often forgotten today is the fact that period critics appreciated this depth. *New York Sun* reviewer Eileen Creelman was especially articulate along these lines in her comments on Fields in *You're Telling Me*: he is "one of those quietly harassed men whose greatest efforts are met with futility and laughter. It is essentially a character quite as tragic as Chaplin's little tramp, much more credible, and, thus far anyway, much less self-conscious" (April 9, 1934). I find it consistent with the greater-range antiheroic roles provided for Fields that the three reviews of his movies included in critic Stanley Kauffmann's watershed anthology, *American Film Criticism: From the Beginning to Citizen Kane*, were all from this antiheroic camp—*It's a Gift*, *The Man on the Flying Trapeze*, and *The Bank Dick*.

One might best begin an examination of the antiheroic Fields with character surnames. The comedian's figures, whether bumblers or hucksters, invariably have amusing appellations, but the names of his antiheroes, his little men, often invite additional comic ridicule through mispronunciation. For example, in his greatest film of frustration, *It's a Gift*, he is forever reminding people that his wife wants their name pronounced a certain way: "Never call me Mr. Bissonette. It's Bis-o-nay." In *The Bank Dick* Fields is Egbert Sousé, "accent acute over the *e*" and pronounced Su-zay. But as the forever-imbibing (onscreen and off) Fields demonstrates, this is a spelling—souse—he lives up . . . or down . . . to. These descriptively antiheroic surnames also recall the moniker he sometimes gave the focus families in his earlier copyrighted sketches— "Fliverton," after the antiheroic machine of choice, the Model-T Ford, affectionately nicknamed "flivver."

The heart of his bumbler films, or more precisely the broken heart of them, is a marriage made in hell. This situation is patterned after Fields's own estranged marriage (see Chapter 3). His most inspired witch-of-the-week reel wife is played by Kathleen Howard in both *It's a Gift* and *The Man on the Flying Trapeze*. In a 1935 *New York Times* review of the former, film critic André Sennwald was moved to describe this nagging comic nemesis as "so authentic as to make Mr. Fields's suffering seem cosmic and a little sad despite their basic humor" (20).

Of course, wifely comic venom is not limited to Howard. After being called the "luckiest woman" in *You're Telling Me*, his screen mate (Louise Carter) asks: "Is my husband dead?" And as in Thurber's antiheroic battle of the sexes, the Fields husband often finds his wife irrational, or as his character observes after a friend says women are crazy about pets—"They are just crazy; pets have nothing to do with it."

While the Fields huckster fills the air with flowery language, his little man is often all but shut off by the droning monotone of his wife. In *It's a Gift* the comedian answers the phone in the middle of the night. The caller, who's dialed a wrong number, asks if he has reached the maternity hospital. Wicked witch Howard accusingly turns the question around: "Funny thing the maternity hospital should be calling you at this hour."

When W. C.'s Bissonette tries to explain, Howard buries him under a wave of badgering words: "Now you change it. Don't make it any worse. How do you expect anyone to get any sleep around here with you hopping in and out of bed all night, tinkering around the house, waiting up for telephone calls. I have to get up in the morning, make breakfast for you and the children. I have no maid, you know. . . ."

A male fear of matriarchal power in antiheroic American film comedy draws on several sources in addition to the maternal dominance characteristic of immigrant families, which we have discussed earlier. The early twentieth century development of antiheroic humor also paralleled the rise of the women's movement. But the most timely aspect of Fields's later (1930s) comic explorations of matriarchal clout relates to the Depression, a period when it appeared to many Americans that "the husbands' increasing dependence upon their wives to provide additional or even primary income for the family . . . [represented] a rapid deterioration of the father's status" (Jenkins, 255). Moreover, in antiheroic comedy there is seldom a normal way out for the male; Fields's standard film-ending reassertion of manhood is invariably subject to luck. "Fear of matriarchal power is such that it cannot be countered by the strength of the male. Rather it is dissolved by a near-magical occurrence" (Seidman, 153).

Wifely comic abuse is the catalyst for what is possibly Fields's greatest movie sequence, "The Sleeping Porch" routine, originally done on stage in 1925 and first recorded on film in *It's the Old Army Game* (1926), the silent film upon which *It's a Gift* was based. Looking for quiet away from his wife, Fields's character, with his blanket (an over-age 1930s Linus), walks to the back porch on the second level of a three-story apartment complex and beds down in a porch swing. But now it is early morning, and after the obligatory crash of the swing, when one of the support beams to which it is attached gives way, Fields must cope with an awakening neighborhood, from the milkman delivering bottles to a pesky insurance salesman. The latter's pitch is a capsulization of the antihero's ongoing plight: "If you buy a policy now you could retire when you're ninety on a comfortable income." Fields has gone from huckster to potential victim of hucksters. (The insurance-agent bugaboo lives on with later screen antiheroes, such as Woody Allen's observation in *Take the Money and Run* [1969] that there are things worse than death, such as spending an evening with an insurance man.)

Another patented back-porch distraction involves a third-floor neighbor sending her daughter on an errand. Once on the ground floor the girl proceeds to engage the topside parent in a singsong conversation about just what to get and where to purchase it. Like the three-story building, the scene works on as many levels. It is funny as another disruption of Fields's attempt to sleep, and it also precipitates a great example of Fields fifth columnism. When the daughter finally says to her mom, "You tell me where to go," the comedian's floor-below aside is, "I'd like to tell you both where to go." Finally, it showcases the double-whammy penalty antiheroes sometime have to suffer for the most modest of independent actions. That is, though Fields's aside made about as much noise as a mouse peeing on cotton, the loud neighbor above suddenly complains about the "shouting on the floor below." Moreover, W. C.'s wife then appears and insinuates that he is "getting pretty familiar" with their third-floor neighbor.

An additional classic bumbler scene from *It's a Gift* involves the comedian's morning attempt to share the bathroom mirror with a teenage daughter. Though he arrives first to shave, she quickly outflanks him, and he must work behind her. The girl's hair-combing and frequent opening and closing of the mirrored medicine-cabinet door nearly give Fields whiplash. But then again, for this domestic victim, things can only get worse. When his daughter inadvertently combs some hair into his mouth he is reduced to a comic apoplexy— a poor man's imitation of the family cat trying to dislodge a fur ball. Recovered, the comedian turns a different direction and tries to shave from the reflection of a bathroom container. The next surprise attack occurs when the daughter begins gargling without warning. Nearly giving himself a fatal shaving wound, he warns, "You want me to cut my throat, keep it up." Without missing a beat comes another gargle and a frightened jump on Fields's part as he mumbles in an aside, "You evidently do."

Now W. C. ties a hand mirror to the overhead light string and tries to shave as the mirror revolves. Any ritual involving going round and round seems antiheroically appropriate, but he also risks another throat-slitting by waiting until the turning mirror is in front of him and then briefly shaving his neck with reckless abandon. His next careless maneuver has him sitting precariously on the top of a chair . . . from which he immediately falls. His last shaving tactic is to turn the still-revolving hand mirror face down while he lies on the chair underneath it. Naturally, during all these morning contortions Fields does not notice the exit of his daughter. Paralleling this departure is the arrival of his wife, who demands an explanation for his

7. Fields's shaving acrobatics in *It's a Gift* (1934).

gymnastic approach to shaving. He innocently alludes to a daughter now very much gone. Once more he appears the fool to his domineering spouse.

This routine, which Fields had earlier committed to film in the now seemingly lost *The Potters* (1927), makes for a provocative comparison with the memorable mirror scene in Groucho and company's *Duck Soup* (1933). In each case the comedian is driven to anti-heroic distraction. But whereas W. C.'s plight is rooted in a frustrating domestic reality with which innumerable people can identify, Groucho's mirror dilemma is out-of-this-world surrealism.

Groucho's foray behind the looking glass, which Allen Eyles called "Harpo's *tour de force* in outsmarting Groucho" (106), is arguably the greatest of all Marx brothers scenes. Chico and Harpo are on a *Duck Soup* nighttime spying mission dressed to match a ready-for-bed Groucho—white nightshirts, white nightcaps, and mandatory black mustache, eyebrows, and cigar. Harpo separates from Chico and manages to run smack into a wall-size mirror. Though lacking the ability of Lewis Carroll's Alice to go right through a mirror, Harpo's shattering of this looking glass does bizarrely reveal a room beyond it. And when Groucho then happens by (with all the incriminating broken glass now magically gone), Harpo pretends to be Groucho's mirror reflection. Probably, the inspiration for the scene came from the film's director, comedy master Leo "do-it-visually" McCarey, who has captured on film an inspired routine that has Groucho look-alike Harpo wonderfully matching the elaborate tests of his mustachioed brother—ranging from a zany dance to wiggling his backside. This comic jig is not officially over until Chico (still made up as his brother) appears, and suddenly Groucho has two reflections. Needless to say, a surrealistic tone frequently underlies Groucho's antiheroic woes, whereas Fields's problems are more apt to have some basis in reality.

Fields's at-home screen problems are not limited to a nasty spouse and kids. Periodically, there is also a cranky mother-in-law. I am reminded of a popular 1890s (the comedian was born in 1880) children's schoolyard jingle of which W. C.'s friend and colleague Robert Benchley was fond:

> My Mother-in-law has lately died;
> For her my heart doth yearn.
> I know she's with the angels now
> 'Cause she's too tough to burn.
> (Gehring, "Mr. B," 8, 10)

The top candidate for Fields's toughest mother-in-law would be Jessie Ralph—Mrs. Hermosillo Brunch of *The Bank Dick*. She is on his case nearly from film-frame one, even before he makes his initial

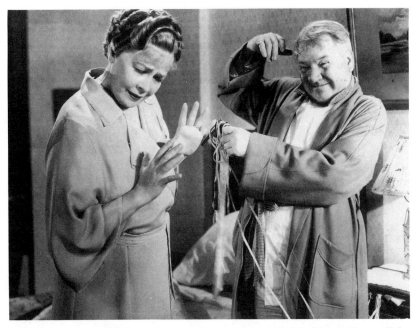

8. Fields with a deadly weapon and a screen wife (Kathleen Howard) he would like to use it on, from *The Man on the Flying Trapeze* (1935).

appearance. As we first meet the family she complains to her daughter about that Sousé of a husband: "Smoking and drinking and reading those infernal detective stories. The house just smells of liquor and smoke. There he goes again [Fields has just appeared] down to the saloon [the Black Pussy Cat Cafe] to read that silly detective magazine." The Fields-authored original script, despite numerous departures from the finished film, is wonderfully consistent and succinct in its description of Mrs. Brunch: "An old nag and a scold" (Jeeves 10).

Though the comedian never actually bumps off one of his screen mothers-in-law, the thought is frequently on his mind. In *The Man on the Flying Trapeze* the first alibi that comes to mind for skipping work is the death of just this live-in albatross—Mrs. Cordelia Neselrode, mother-in-law. While Fields's ruse did not work (antiheroes seldom get away with anything), there is a certain minor victory resulting from commotion surrounding the alleged cause of death for this teetotaling tormentor—bad liquor.

It is a wonder Fields's *Flying Trapeze* character, Ambrose Wolfinger, does not use the pistol he keeps in the nightstand on Cordelia . . . or on himself. As it is, the gun's accidental discharge provides a darkly comic slant on his marriage. The noise causes the overly ornery Mrs. Wolfinger (Kathleen Howard) to faint. The comedian then asks, with little or no regret, "Did I kill you?" After the worst becomes apparent—i.e., she has only fainted—Ambrose displays even less joy in saying, "Oh, good, I didn't kill you."

This is the beginning of Fields's "burglars in the basement" investigation (the fear of intruders having been the reason for the weapon's appearance). But his comic interaction with the two house thieves is further negative commentary on his marriage and mothers-in-law. Instead of calling the police or making some sort of citizen's arrest, he proceeds to join them in the drinking of his own applejack liquor and drunkenly singing Americana songs—though the term *singing* applies only loosely. Here is an antihero who finds more pleasure with crooks in the cellar than with his own family.

Ironically, even when the screen Fields escapes the comic morass known as family, he continues to encounter variations of familial torment in the world outside his domestic disaster. These surrogates include his neighbor's brat Baby LeRoy, who lets molasses run all over the floor in the Bissonette grocery of *It's a Gift*, and the little kid dressed as a cowboy whom W. C. mistakes for an undersized marauder in *The Bank Dick*. But a listing of Fields frustrations covers a broad and still-topical spectrum of comic antihero victimizations, from the parking tickets of *The Man on the Flying Trapeze* to the obnoxious waitress of *Never Give a Sucker an Even Break*, who keeps eliminating items from the menu as Fields attempts to order them. Fields does, however, score a modest point in the latter case when the waitress says he complained too much about a meal. With tongue-in-cheek patience he observes, "I didn't squawk about the steak, dear. I merely said I didn't see that old horse that used to be tethered outside here." The addition of the word "dear" is a well-chosen touch, as it sounds like any number of still-losing conversations he had with screen wives.

Maybe the best demonstration of the banalities we all suffer daily occurs in *The Bank Dick* when he is attempting to see the president of the institution, the appropriately named Mr. Skinner. The previous day Fields had been credited with capturing a bank robber (it was more a case of the crook falling over him), and he now is waiting to

9. Fields subdues a potential criminal in *The Bank Dick* (1940).

see Mr. Skinner about a reward. But even as a hero, he is shunted about, first in one line and then in another. It is reminiscent of Benchley's quip quoted in Chapter 2 about sixty percent of the population spending their entire lives standing in line.

In a more focused antiheroic manner for Fields, bouts with the bottle can also result in comic frustration, beyond the eternal grief he hears about his drinking on the home front. For instance, during one of many alcohol stops at the Black Pussy Cat Cafe (whose name somehow passed the period's motion picture censorship office), Fields, as Egbert Sousé, asks the bartender "Was I in here last night and did I spend a twenty-dollar bill?" When told this was the case Sousé states with relief, "Oh boy, what a load that is off my mind. I thought I'd lost it."

In contrast, the opening of *You're Telling Me* provides an anti-heroic *visual* treat on the excesses of drinking—Fields staggering, but with a certain comic grace, home from a local watering hole. The comedian adds several Fieldsian flourishes, from twice losing his hat to a low-hanging limb (as well as his standard problem of merely placing his hat on his head), to fumbling for his key and dropping said hat, coat, and shoes (which had been removed to avoid awakening his wife). Fittingly, he then has difficulty putting the key in the lock. But the comic topper comes when he produces a keyhole funnel invention that fits over the doorknob. Its wide mouth allows the drunken victim to better target his wayward key into the lock. While the gadget represents a small victory, the need for the device documents an apparent long history of antiheroic staggering.

You're Telling Me also includes Fields's most poignantly funny scene of underdog frustration. Unbeknownst to him, his illegally parked demonstration car with puncture-proof tires has been removed and replaced by a similar-looking *police* vehicle. Naturally, when he then attempts to show the puncture-proof capabilities of his invention to potential backers, its tires go flat and he is humiliated—not to mention being chased by the police.

Returning home by train, he feels a total failure. Consequently, he writes a farewell note, planning to commit suicide by drinking iodine. As he walks to the train's washroom, the movement of the train car gives a comic stagger to his gait that ironically contrasts with his sad mission. Once there he must contend with the good humor of a salesman (comic character-actor Vernon Dent). Fields attempts to take the iodine with another of his inventions, a collapsible spoon. But between a shaky hand and a spoon that continues to, well, collapse, he keeps spilling the iodine. Turning to watch Dent shave, Fields finds the sight of the razor on the salesman's throat most bothersome, given his own plan. The comedian is further distracted by wayward shaving soap that flies off Dent's face and onto his. Trying to just drink the iodine from the bottle, his growing reluctance to kill himself finally wins out when he happens to see a cemetery outside the window of his speeding train. Fittingly, he has been antiheroic (frustrated) at the ultimate antiheroic act—doing away with himself.

This scene of comic pathos is immediately followed by another. Mistakenly entering the private car of a beautiful young woman, he spots another bottle of iodine. Assuming the worst, he asks, "What's this? What are you up to? Don't do it, little lady. It doesn't pay. When you wake up in the morning and find yourself dead, it's too late to regret it." The humor of the last sentence should not belie the quiet yet genuine concern Fields brings to the scene. Like his comedy, the understatedness of his acting here is most effective. And again he has been the conclusive little man, since the viewer knows Fields's character has misread the situation—the person had merely meant to use the iodine for (to borrow from a W. C. alibi for drinking) medicinal purposes.

This encounter, however, allows Fields to unburden himself, for the woman asks what he would know about suicide. Sharing his farewell note, he will later comment, "Suppose I'd sent a telegram. I would have had to go through with it." But he tells her of the failed tire demonstration and then reveals the loss, during his hasty retreat from the police, of his prototype invention, the "nose-lifter-upper," which prevents snoring! More importantly, the scene allows his character to unwind on the general sad plight of his dominated home life, instead of the more typical situation, where the viewer merely sees the wife unloading the proverbial boom. The history his *You're Telling Me* alter ego, Sam Bisbee, then reveals is one of an upper-class-aspiring spouse, a standard antiheroic Fields situation. The example he shares with his train companion involves a recent social gathering at the Bisbee home. The comedian asks his screen wife, "Is it okay if I take my vest off?" She said, "You don't mind keeping your pants on, do you?" "Uncalled-for sarcasm," is Bisbee's view of the crack.

Bittersweet material like this, of attempted and thwarted suicides (at least from Bisbee's perspective) are what had critics praising the comedian's work as "Chaplinesque" (Delehanty, April 7, 1934). But if truth be told, the rank-and-file fan of the antiheroic Fields probably preferred broader, hold-the-handkerchief comedy. *Los Angeles Times* reviewer John Scott said of the *You're Telling Me* screening he attended, "It has been months since I have heard such laughter in a movie theatre as greeted Fields's efforts yesterday. . . . In two scenes particularly the merriment continued for several minutes" (April 6, 1934). Those inspired moments were the aforementioned drunken application of the door-handle invention and the recycling of the comedian's classic frustrated-golfer routine in the movie's closing moments, with Tammy Young playing the exasperating caddy to perfection.

As these various examples of little-man Fields demonstrate, the comedian's work is invariably based in reality, a point he would forever reiterate during interviews. But he was also aware of the need for some "exaggeration" (Cheatham, 30, 31, 62). Such W. C. comic coloring could be broken into two camps: the influence of newspaper cartoon strips and the American dream finale. In the former case, as noted in a previous chapter, Fields was already on record in the 1920s as wanting to play film roles where he would be the sideswiped husband of the funny papers. It was a natural goal for someone whose stage career of the 1910s and early 1920s had already been immersed in frustrated comic-strip-type fathers. One has only to think of his copyrighted sketches (especially the "Fliverton" material) or his work in *The Comic Supplement*.

For instance, *The Comic Supplement* opens with two less-than-pleasant children pestering their father to read them their favorite comic strips. The cartoon settled on itself contains a father reading to more tough children:

> This is the first picture. It shows a father reading a nice story to his children and the little boy says: "Let's hit the old man on the head with a brick." And his sister says, "No, let's hit him on the head with a hammer. It will make more noise." (McEvoy, *The Comic Supplement*)

The Comic Supplement, inspired by the funny papers (as reflected in its title), boasts sketches, such as "The Sleeping Porch," which would later surface in Fields's antiheroic films. But beyond such footnoted scenes is the occasional exaggerated spirit of the comics, such as W. C.'s attempt to brain his bratty *Bank Dick* daughter with an oversized porch planter after she has bounced a catsup bottle off his head.

Another prime candidate for this comic-strip connection is Fields's run-in with miniature hooligans Butch and Buddy (boy comedians Billy Lenhart and Kenneth Brown) in *Never Give a Sucker* an *Even Break*. Butch and Buddy proceed to use the comedian's head for brick-throwing practice. A direct hit from Buddy produces a patented "Godfrey Daniels!" epithet of comic pain from W. C. But when his protective in-film niece Gloria Jean (who, like Fields, is playing herself) attempts to retaliate in kind, W. C. seems to advise her not to throw the brick—"Uh-uh-uh-uh-uh! Hold your temper. Count ten!"—Gloria obeys and the poised brick starts to be lowered. But then Fields, who has just appeared the model of parental wisdom, executes a textbook example of comic surprise by advising, "Now let 'er go. You got a good aim!" With that, Gloria uncorks a brick with eyes on it, because the missile manages to find Buddy's noggin behind some bushes, where he and his sidekick had hidden. Fields, full of dark pleasure at this rare example of antiheroic payback, compliments his niece's aim, "That's a beauty!"

A variation of this brick scene had occurred in Fields's silent film *Sally of the Sawdust* (1925), which was adapted from the comedian's breakthrough Broadway hit *Poppy* (1923–1924). But a link to the funny pages seems a more fruitful tie. For instance, period critic Donald Kirkley labels the troublesome duo as "Katzenjammer Kids," after the pioneering antiheroic newspaper comic strip of the same name (see Chapter 2), which also featured two underaged monsters ("W. C. Fields").

Moreover, brick-throwing in *any* medium of American humor must immediately bring to mind another watershed antiheroic comic strip—"Krazy Kat," whose title character is the perennial victim of the brick-throwing mouse Ignatz (see also Chapter 2). The influential heyday of "Krazy Kat" included the pivotal-to-Fields 1920s and 1930s, but it remains "universally acclaimed as the greatest comic strip" (Horn, 436). And provocatively important comedy theorists like Neil Schmitz continue to use "Krazy Kat" and the brick as a pivotal metaphor (comic absurdity) in the study of American humor (*Of Huck and Alice*).

Fields's cinema frustrations as the little man are probably closest to those of the badgered husband of the strip "Bringing Up Father." Just as the comedian preferred (onscreen and off) male drinking companions to a dominating wife, the strip's Jiggs is always trying to escape the Maggie-controlled home for a night of revelry with the "boys."

But as one goes beyond the domestic battleground that the antiheroic Fields shares with Jiggs, or with the equally browbeaten pioneer American film-comedy star John Bunny, the cartoon-strip influence is grafted to W. C.'s films most thoroughly in his last two features—*The Bank Dick* and *Never Give a Sucker an Even Break*. This is brought about in part by incorporating a movie production into the storyline of each picture. In the former film, a motion-picture company comes on location to W. C. territory—the small town of Lompoc. The latter movie finds Fields pitching a script at Esoteric Studios. The film-within-a-film premise provides even the most outlandish situations with a realistic base, such as the rehearsal area encountered early in *Sucker*, with its eclectic collection of goose-stepping-Nazis, singing dancers, carpenters, assorted technicians . . . not to mention a wind machine going at full capacity. Of course, the ultimate example of the bizarre but explainable comes during the reading of Fields's *Sucker* script. Since the viewer is given a visualization of everything, W. C. gets away with jumping out of an airplane minus a parachute and visiting the fanciful mountaintop preserve of Mrs. Hemoglobin (Margaret Dumont). This "anything goes" flavor is amusingly caught in the *New York Daily Worker*'s review title for *Sucker*—"Maybe It Isn't a Movie But W. C. Fields Is In It" (Meltzer, Oct. 28, 1941).

Along more modestly eccentric lines is Fields's direction of *The Bank Dick*'s film-within-a-film. This would include his impulsive decision to switch what appears to be a drawing-room comedy to a football/circus picture, or his location transportation aboard a covered litter on the shoulders of four stagehands. The latter example also makes for an entertainingly antiheroic contrast with Groucho's *Animal Crackers* (1930) arrival in another covered litter. While Marx's Captain Spaulding seems quite comfortable in his elevated deportment, Fields's Sousé manages to fall over backwards out of his litter (though Fields would probably have preferred the term *bier*). Consistent with the Fieldsian world view, the director whom Sousé replaced in *The Bank Dick*, one A. Pismo Clam, has a drinking problem brought on by trouble with his wife.

In the spirit of a zany film-within-a-film, both *The Bank Dick* and *Sucker*'s closing moments are largely consumed with out-of-control driving sequences. In the first movie Fields is forced to chauffeur a crook at gunpoint while being pursued by the authorities; the second film has the comedian racing what he thinks is an expectant mother to the maternity hospital. All manner of ludicrousness occurs during these automobile misadventures, be it a steering wheel coming off or a passing fire truck inadvertently hoisting Fields's vehicle above the Los Angeles freeway, providing him with a lovely view of southern California.

Such wonderfully ridiculous storylines had many critics labeling these last two Fields films in the tradition of Mack Sennett and his Keystone Kops—film-comedy first cousins to "Krazy Kat" (see Chapter 2). For instance, the *Chicago Daily News* review said of his *Bank Dick* performance that "he is a comic policeman who could have got a job any day on the old Mack Sennett lot" (Bulliet, "Keystone Cop 1940"). *Variety* credited *Sucker* with "resurrecting en route many of the best gags and slapstick situations of the old Sennett Keystone Kop episodes" (rev. of *Sucker*). And the *New York World Telegram*'s critique of *Sucker* was applicable to both pictures: "As funny as anything that ever came out of the Mack Sennett studios, and that's saying something" (Boehnel, "Great Man Goes Back to Sennett").

The second type of comic exaggeration Fields brings to his little-man films, after the influence of newspaper comic strips, involved the American-dream happy ending. The beautiful young woman Fields meets on a train in *You're Telling Me* turns out to be a princess who helps him turn his puncture-proof-tire invention into a fortune. None of his other classics of frustration relies on the appearance of such a metaphorical fairy-tale princess, but most feature some sort of drastic and positive reversal of fortune. In *It's a Gift* his bad land investment suddenly garners a king's ransom when a local businessman needs his property for a nearby grandstand. After being fired from work late in *The Man on the Flying Trapeze*, the ending finds him so indispensable to his company that his character is hired back at twice his old salary, plus a paid vacation. And in *The Bank Dick* a series of events ends up leaving Sousé rolling in money: a bad investment turns good; a royalty check arrives for a zany script; and he receives a reward for capturing a bank crook. Still, as comedy historian Steve Seidman has noted, Fields's protection by "Fate and luck" is more realistic than the later cartoon-like magic of Woody Allen's antihero in *Bananas* (1971), who throws the pin instead of the grenade, yet suffers only a comic injury (128).

Fields's last-minute deus ex machina reversals make for an engrossing contrast with the comedian's huckster films. Unlike W. C.'s manipulative diddler, his antihero is often less than bright (the comedian called his Sam Bisbee character from *You're Telling*

Me "stupid" ["Anything for a Laugh," 130]). The W. C. antihero never seems to be able to correctly "read" a flimflam, good or bad.

For example, when a real princess spins a yarn to Bisbee's credit in *You're Telling Me*, he appreciates her actions but never once believes she is of royal background. But his *Bank Dick* Sousé totally eats up the bogus bond salesman's line about holdings in something with the less than likely title of Beefsteak Mine. Yet when things do pan out (including the now-valuable bonds, to the shock of the crooked seller), it is as if Fields has torn a page from comedy contemporary Harry Langdon, whose character is protected by the grace of God. Still, this Fields figure must wait until the end before his guardian angel (possibly running antiheroically late himself) makes with the miracle. Thus, W. C.'s comic victim has more in common with the total frustration of Laurel and Hardy, despite the general absence for this incompetent duo of any film-closing reprieve.

Because a happy ending is affixed to a story of continued comic frustration, one might interpret the conclusions as an ironic commentary on the less-than-likely availability of the ephemeral American dream. On the other hand, this position ignores the basic pattern of the comedy genre, which moves toward the happy ending after overcoming some initial problems. As literary theorist Northrop Frye suggests in his *Anatomy of Criticism*, the comedy happy ending is not there to impress the audience with truth but rather to give them what is desirable—an upbeat conclusion.

Perhaps with Fields, that cynic with a sentimental streak, one can have it both ways. The central thrust of his antiheroic films is generally a satire of small-town hypocrisy and smug conventions, both on Main Street and in the American Gothic home. The Fields miracle close both allows his buffeted-about character a rare victory *and* continues to demonstrate the duplicity of small minds, since his previous detractors (domestic and otherwise) are now most pleasant to him, given his money and newly acquired status. But to the ongoing praise of his antihero, he remains the same despite the unexpected windfall. Indeed, in the closing film frames of *You're Telling Me*, *It's a Gift*, and *The Bank Dick* he continues to pursue his standard pastime (drinking) while the now ever-loving family bask in his sudden affluence.

The two key thrusts of 1930s antiheroic humor are frustration and absurdity. While Fields more than covers the former, Groucho's world is that of the latter. The Marx brothers donned the mantle of zaniness as a defense, and beat the world gone mad at its own game. As critic and historian Joe Adamson observed, they were cocky enough to "take what order there is in life and impose chaos on it" (156). The later daydream victories of James Thurber's Walter Mitty were business as usual for the Marxes. But within the team, Groucho is often victimized by his brothers, and sometimes by the world in general. In these encounters the mustachioed one becomes the more traditional antiheroic male, while either Chico or Harpo could be labeled a wizard of odd.

The Marxes acknowledged this tie to what is called "lunatic" comedy in a 1939 *Theatre Arts* magazine article, observing that they were "followers" of such literary wits as Stephen Leacock, Donald Ogden Stewart, and Robert Benchley (Seton, 734). (As a historical footnote, the full *Theatre Arts* quotation linking the Marxes to this type of comedy was largely drawn from critic Alva Johnston's detailed analysis of the team in a 1936 article [12].)

During this time antiheroic humor was likely to fall under an absurdist moniker, such as "lunatic comedy" or "crazy fool humor." The latter classification no doubt was drawn from Stewart's popular 1925 novel *The Crazy Fool*, a particularly fitting watershed antiheroic publication, since it is dedicated to Benchley and the central characters are patterned after this humorist and comedy colleague Dorothy Parker. But regardless of the movement's name, this crazy slant is part of what is now considered antiheroic humor, or the frustrations of the little man. The authors noted by the Marxes all belong to this school of comedy, though today a more representative grouping, as noted in Chapter 2, would include Benchley, Thurber, Clarence Day, and S. J. Perelman. (*Monkey Business* and *Horse Feathers* were both scripted, in part, by a very young Perelman. But it was more a job of successfully reflecting the team's style than of molding it.)

Unfortunately, even at this late date discussions of the crazy-fool factor often do not acknowledge either the links to the little man, or Groucho's occasional presence in the antiheroic role. For instance, the example of literary nonsense that film-comedy historian and critic Gerald Weales noted as being most similar to the world of the Marxes comes from Donald Ogden Stewart's novel *Mr. and Mrs. Haddock Abroad* (1924). It finds the zany Groucho-like verbal patter belonging to a supporting character who, to a great extent, is victimizing an antihero—Mr. Haddock (Weales, 58; Stewart, 123–37). This is not meant to take anything away from the wonderful Weales book in which it is found, *Canned Goods as Caviar*, especially since Groucho the con artist can verbally steamroller people. It just does not tell all of the story . . . the Groucho-as-antihero story.

Regardless, period critics provide interesting links between the Marxes and the lunatic school of humor. William Troy's 1933 *Duck Soup* review for *The Nation* is sometimes credited with being the first recognition. In an otherwise less-than-memorable critique (he panned the film), Troy observed in an aside that the team's antics are "like the whole 'crazy-fool' humor of the post-war [after 1918] epoch, it consists in a dissociation of the faculties" (688).

But this is predated by the early-1930s British criticism of John Grierson, who later became a legendary documentary-film producer and theorist. Writing for *The Clarion* and *Everyman* he saw parallels between Groucho and the comedy of Robert Benchley and Donald Ogden Stewart, as well as mentioning the latter's *The Crazy Fool* (52–57).

The Benchley connection is especially appropriate, since this humorist excelled at mixing the antiheroic with lunacy. In the 1930s he was known as the crown prince of the "dementia praecox" process (crazy tendencies and vulnerability, best demonstrated here by language reduced to comic nonsense). His dementia praecox at its most obvious is exemplified by the titles he gave his essay collections, such as *The Treasurer's Report and Other Aspects of Community Singing* (1930) and *From Bed to Worse Or Comforting Thoughts About the Bison* (1934).

Grierson's Groucho-Benchley comment was brief but provocative. One must remember that a central Benchley theme is the satirical skewering of facts. Consequently, his essays and later film short subjects often key on a professorial type who is trying—but comically failing—to impart some information, in quasi-lecture style. It is as if to say: attempting to make sense of this absurd world is an open invitation to ridicule.

Situations like this often befall Groucho. The most obvious instance is the biology classroom of *Horse Feathers*, where Groucho quite literally plays at being a professor but with the hopeless task of trying to teach anything to students Chico and Harpo. Even before the scene disintegrates into the comic chaos of a pea-shooting war between the brothers, one enjoys the mustachioed one's verbal scrambling of a lecture. He observes in part:

We then come to the bloodstream. The blood rushes from the head down to the feet, gets a look at those feet, and rushes back to the head again. This is known as Auction Pinochle. Now, in studying your basic metabolism, we first listen to your heart, and if your heart beats anything but diamonds and clubs, it's because your partner is cheating. . . .

Not every Marx-brothers film has a classroom, but there is invariably a Groucho professorial situation, à la Benchley. Most often this involves a comic tutorial for Chico. For example, in *Monkey Business* the brothers find themselves in the ship captain's office. Groucho picks up a globe and decides to give an impromptu geography and history lesson:

GROUCHO   Well, now, just hop up there, little Johnny [Chico], and I'll show you a few things that you don't know about history. Now, there's Columbus.

CHICO   That's Columbus Circle [the globe].

GROUCHO   Would you mind getting up off that flypaper and giving the flies a chance?

CHICO   Aw, you're crazy. Flies can't read papers.

GROUCHO   Now, Columbus sailed from Spain to India looking for a short cut.

CHICO   Oh, you mean strawberry short cut.

GROUCHO   I don't know. When I woke up, there was the nurse taking care of me.

CHICO   What's the matter? Couldn't the nurse take care of herself?

GROUCHO   You bet she could, but I found her out too late. Well, enough of this. Let's get back to Columbus.

Chico's bad puns and dumb statements constantly derail Groucho's quasi-lecture, as well as encouraging his occasional absurd statement or topic jump, such as from the globe to a nurse.

Still, the professorial Groucho does not require a Chico catalyst. In *The Cocoanuts* another character quite innocently launches Groucho into a dissertation on the nickel:

The nickel today is not worth what it was *fifteen* years ago. Do you know what this country needs today? A seven cent nickel. Yes sirree, we've been using the five cent nickel in this country since 1492 and that's pretty near a hundred years daylight savings. Now why not give the seven cent nickel a chance? If that works out, next year we could have an eight cent nickel. Think what that would mean. You could go to a newsstand, buy a three cent newspaper, and get the same nickel back again. One nickel carefully used would last a family a lifetime!

The political overtones of this zany think-tank lecture also nicely anticipate Groucho's equally eccentric leadership of *Duck Soup's* Freedonia. And while Benchley generally avoided the political scene, demented excursions did occur, like the fanciful "An Interview with Mussolini," from his *The Early Worm* (1927).

As frequently demonstrated earlier in the text, period film reviewers keyed on the dominating Groucho. Unhappily, period critics generally did not focus on the sometimes absurdly antiheroic Groucho. For every one that did, like Grierson, or the anonymous 1933 *New York Evening Post* reviewer with the brilliant aside likening the team to the "four Hawaiians" ("The Marx brothers," Nov. 23, 1933)—a reference to Joe Cook's "nut" stage act of zany comic frustration (see Chapter 2)—there were several critics who simply praised the general nonsense. Before proceeding, however, with the antiheroic undoings of Groucho, two 1930s absurdist-oriented reviews merit attention.

The first is Clifton Fadiman's critique of *A Night at the Opera*. He was particularly taken with the closing moments, when Groucho and company create mayhem to disrupt the New York debut of the film's nasty tenor (Walter King). Fadiman describes it as "resembling Bedlam rearranged by Mr. Thurber" (325). It is a nice analogy, reminiscent to me of the Thurber drawing accompanying his essay "The Day the Dam Broke" in *My Life and Hard Times* (1933), in which a tidal wave of people pours through downtown Columbus, Ohio (the humorist's hometown).

But in general, just as Benchley is an excellent period literary-humorist connection for Groucho, the Thurber tie is closest to the antiheroic W. C. Fields. This is not to take away from Fadiman's comparison. Indeed, earlier in this chapter I drew a parallel between the Marxes and the later time-tripping fantasy of Thurber's Walter Mitty. Still, the real bread and butter of Thurber's little-man legacy is the ongoing comic battle of the sexes . . . the married sexes, with a dominating wife in the driver's seat.

A tragedy of 1930s humor was that Fields never starred in a film adaptation of the henpecked Monroe husband stories in Thurber's *The Owl in the Attic: And Other Perplexities* (1931). But a link of sorts occurred in 1935, when both Thurber's book *The Middle-Aged Man on the Flying Trapeze* and Fields's film *The Man on the Flying Trapeze* appeared. Each work chronicles the antiheroic war games called marriage . . . advantage to the women.

The most celebrated Thurber essay within the collection, "Mr. Preble Gets Rid of His Wife" (a murder that is yet to happen at story's end), has the same on-the-edge comedy as the scene in Fields's *Trapeze* when the comedian thinks he has accidentally killed his spouse. Though the popular-culture historian might attribute both titles to the 1934 hit song *The Man on the Flying Trapeze*, the vulnerable image of the little man on the trapeze is a fitting metaphor for (to borrow from Thurber) "the life and hard times" of an antihero. The humorist's book further begs the question by including a drawing of the husband in mid-air, having let go of his trapeze bar only to find his wife/acrobatic partner pleasantly prepared (with a devilish grin) *not* to catch him.

The other absurdist-directed Marx brothers critique that deserves attention is Joseph Alsop's review of *A Night at the Opera*. Like Fadiman, Alsop was taken with the movie's closing chaos. But the twist here is that Alsop defined the scene as a prime example of surrealism—the movement that originated in 1920s France and attempted to express in art the workings of the unconscious.

Though not the first author even then to draw the Marx-surrealism parallel (see, for instance, Antonin Artaud's 1932 essay "Les Frères Marx au Cinéma do Panthéon"[156–58]), Alsop's article was ambitious for a mid-1930s mainstream American newspaper. I draw attention to the work because it showcased an international high-art link being given to Groucho and company and defined surrealism with a decidedly American comedy slant: "a sort of dream art. There is more than a trace of Freud in it, and more than a grace of a strange lunatic humor" (Alsop, "Surrealism Beaten at Its Own Game"). Alsop's approach to surrealism remains, like that of the Marxes, decidedly topical, as if to suggest that all the weirdness anyone could want is available in everyday life.

The piece is also entertaining for the fun it has celebrating this home-grown crazy comedy while kidding (in Marx brothers tradition) the lofty European surrealism stereotypes. For instance, Alsop contrasts *A Night at the Opera* with two scenes in Luis Buñuel and Salvador Dali's *Un chien andalou* (1928), which is generally considered the beginning of surrealist cinema: "You will not find in it a single slit eyeball, or even one ant crawling out of a hole in a . . . hand, but then, there are the Marx brothers, and they are quite sufficient" (Alsop, "Surrealism Beaten at Its Own Game"). Alsop might have added a further surrealistic connection between Dali and the Groucho gang. The manner in which a Dali figure represents several things at the same time can be equated with a Marx brothers pun—making the viewer cognizant of the multiple purpose of words and their meanings. One is tempted, however, to credit Groucho and company with pushing their often-dark humor beyond surrealism. Because, the main difference between black comedy and surrealism, as defined by humor historian Max F. Schulz, is that surrealism keys on "internal disorder" of the subconscious mind, while black comedy generally suggests that disorder is now the external, real state of things (71). Certainly a pivotal element in the rediscovery of the Marxes during the chaotic 1960s was based on the fact that surrealism was more and more becoming the day-to-day norm.

Regardless of how one characterizes the craziness known as the Marx brothers, master manipulator Groucho (see Chapter 4) is also periodically a comic antihero, confronting several varieties of frustrations. The most eccentric are his run-ins with Harpo. If there ever was a reason for drawing in European surrealism, this would be it. (Harpo was a particular favorite of Dali.) Without using words, Harpo's disruptions are otherworldly, like the inspired mirror sequence noted earlier in the chapter, when Groucho seems to be more than the sum of his reflection.

And to paraphrase an old punchline, the Groucho of *Duck Soup* forever wants to travel in the worst way—the worst way being Harpo's motorcycle sidecar. But the first two times they leave—or more precisely, Harpo leaves—and Groucho and his sidecar are left behind. The topper comes when the mustachioed one makes Harpo get in the sidecar, while he climbs aboard the cycle. Incongruously, this time it is the sidecar that motors Harpo away, leaving Groucho in the dust. In comedy theory this is known as a *triple gag*, a series of actions "linked by a logic of variation"—gag, repetition, reversal (Neale and Krutnik, 53). The unique aspect of this sidecar gag is how it is interspersed through the film. If time had permitted, *Duck Soup's* frustrated leader might have wanted to examine this strange creature. As Dr. Hackenbush of *A Day at the Races* he receives that chance. But medical science is stumped, at least according to Groucho: "I can't do a thing for him. That's a case for Frank Buck [a period hunter/explorer who also produced and starred in adventure films, like the Harpo-sounding *Wild Cargo, 1934*]."

Harpo is also capable of derailing his Benchley-like professorial brother. In the biology classroom of *Horse Feathers* Groucho admonishes Harpo, "Young man, you'll find as you grow older you can't burn the candle at both ends." But the silent one triumphs by instantly producing a candle doing just that—one of the most amusing examples of his trench-coat-pocket wizardry. Groucho is shocked and forced to retract his statement: "I knew there was *something* you couldn't burn at both ends." As Marx brothers author Joe Adamson observed, "The president of a college had been shouted down by a mute" (195).

The relationship between Groucho and his silent nemesis makes for an interesting comparison with comedy contemporary Stan Laurel's reaction to a similar situation. In *Them Thar Hills* (1934) the Laurel and Hardy stock-company professorial-figure Billy Gilbert tells Stan, "You can't burn a candle at both ends." The skinny one replies, "We don't. We burn electric lights." In each case the response is consistent with the viewer's comedy expectations for the character—the inspired stupidity of Stan, and the ephemeral sorcery of Harpo.

This mute also controls Groucho by shock effect. Fittingly, in their first film meeting (from *The Cocoanuts*) an attempted handshake results in Harpo stunning the mustachioed one with a slap to the face. Seconds later, another try at a shake finds Harpo concealing his bulb horn in his hand. The resulting noise when Groucho inadvertently squeezes it sends him scrambling behind the hotel counter in fright. Along related lines, the mute's bizarre appetite for snacking on the strangest things in both this film (he eats a telephone and drinks an ink well dry) and future movies often tends to surprise Groucho into moments of quiet, no small accomplishment for a character famous for his machine-gun patter.

An additional messenger of frustration for Groucho is Chico. He might best be called the ultimate triple threat. As we have already seen, he could out-con a con man, as in the tootsie-fruitsie ice-cream routine of *A Day at the Races*, when he suckers Groucho into buying a mountain of useless betting materials. One might also have added the opening of the otherwise mediocre *Go West* (1940), when Groucho thinks he can easily fleece both Chico and Harpo out of their money in exchange for a complete Western outfit. But these two apparent simpletons turn out to be classic wise fools, ending up with both the money and the clothing.

In contrast to Chico the diddler, however, sometimes his character frustrates Groucho through sheer stupidity. At one point in *Duck Soup* the mustachioed one says of his brother's character, "Chicolini here may look like an idiot, he may speak like an idiot, but don't let that fool you—he really is an idiot." This represents an inconsistency of Chico's figure from film to film; he fluctuates between being a wise fool and simply a fool.

Without detracting from some of his inspired stupidity in encounters with the professorial Groucho, probably Chico's greatest bit of denseness occurs near the close of *Animal Crackers*, when he shares his thoughts on what happened to the stolen painting. After much rambling he hypothesizes the work of art was eaten by "left-handed moths." Groucho's Captain Spaulding is at first speechless, eventually requesting that his brother, "Go away. I'll be alright in a moment." Recovering, he tells Chico, "I'd buy you a parachute if I thought it wouldn't open." But Chico immediately disables him with another stupid statement/bad pun: "I got a pair of shoes [parachute]." This reduces Groucho to jumping up and down while holding his head and moaning.

Then the comic coup de grâce of idiot puns occurs, when the mustachioed one suggests they go to court and request the missing painting. When Chico seems mystified by this, Groucho asks, "Didn't you ever see a habeas corpus?" The leveling answer is, "No, but I see *habeas Irish Rose* [a pun of the theatre play *Abie's Irish Rose*]." This retort pushes Groucho over the brink. He staggers out of the scene moaning, a comically broken man. As Marx author Allen Eyles says of Chico, "his actions suggest that stupidity defeats intelligence every time" (30).

Fittingly, given the earlier Benchley-Groucho connection, there is even a Benchley link to the *Abie's Irish Rose* gag. This Jewish boy–Irish girl romance set box office records by playing more than five years on Broadway. Yet the play was generally panned by critics, with Benchley waging a famous comic war on the unlikely success throughout its long run.

The Benchley barbs came in weekly installments, because as the drama critic for *Life* (a humor magazine, not the later pictorial), he was responsible for the publication's "Confidential Guide," a capsule review of each production. His *Abie's Irish Rose* cracks would include, "Just about as low as good clean fun can get," and "Where do the people come from who keep this going? You don't see them out in the daytime" (Gehring, 50, 224). Thus, period jokes at the expense of the play were synonymous with Benchley. Indeed, the humorist/critic even sponsored a contest for the best one-line slam review/description of the play. Harpo's comment won: "No worse than a bad cold." (Both Groucho and Harpo frequented Benchley's literary circle.)

A final manner in which Chico frustrates Groucho is through direct action. When Chico first visits Groucho's dictator chambers in *Duck Soup* he keeps beating the mustachioed one to the phone, telling the caller Freedonia's commander-in-chief is out. Eventually Groucho's Firefly says, "I wonder whatever became of me." Searching around his desk he adds, "I should have been back here a long time ago." Frequently, this direct frustration has a tie-in with Chico's piano solos, which generally provoke a complaining put-down by Groucho.

But with a put-down or not, he still has to listen. It seems this position was based in fact. His friend Will Rogers observed in a newspaper column, "Groucho can play as good on the guitar as Harpo can on the harp, or Chico on the piano. But he never does. So he is really what I call an ideal musician, he can play, but don't" (84).

Chico's straightforward frustration of Groucho can sometimes have a positive purpose. In *A Day at the Races* he and frequent assistant Harpo manage to destroy the mustachioed one's attempted romantic rendezvous with a blonde. It had been a set-up to discredit Groucho's Dr. Hackenbush before Margaret Dumont's moneybags character. Unfortunately, in the artless Marx brothers films after *A Day at the Races*, Chico's direct frustration of his brother could reach humiliatingly unfunny extremes, such as his almost sadistic prevention of Groucho boarding the train in *At the Circus* (1939). In a 1939 letter Groucho underlines this fall from comedy grace: "The boys at the studio have lined up another turkey for us [*Go West*]. . . . I saw the present one [*At the Circus*] the other day and . . . on leaving the theatre, vowed that I'd never see it again" (Oct. 27, 1939).

While Chico and Harpo are the primary sources of Groucho's frustration, another antiheroic reservoir is the comedian himself. Beyond the professorial illogic addressed earlier, Groucho trips himself up in two additional ways. There is the simple self-deprecating comment. In *Duck Soup* the Minister of Finance gives Groucho the Treasury Department's report and hopes it is clear to the dictator. The mustachioed one replies, "Clear? Huh! Why, a four-year-old child could understand this report. [He then turns to his assistant, Zeppo.] Run out and find me a four-year old child. I can't make head or tail out of it."

A Day at the Races finds his Dr. Hackenbush brought in to run a large sanitarium, a task a supporting character describes as "calling for a man with peculiar talents." Hackenbush, who is really only a horse doctor, observes, "You don't have to look any further. I've got the most peculiar talents of any doctor you've ever met." In *Monkey Business* Groucho's stowaway offers an antiheroic scrambling of Horatio Alger's work ethic: "Oh, I realize it's a penny here and a penny there, but look at me. I've worked myself up from nothing to a state of extreme poverty."

Beyond self-deprecation, Groucho is a periodic victim of runaway paranoia. On a modest level, there is private-secretary Zeppo's correspondence omission in *Animal Crackers* of a Hungerdunger from the law firm of Hungerdunger, Hungerdunger, Hungerdunger, Hungerdunger, and MacCormick. Groucho is bent out of shape by the mistake: "You've left out a Hungerdunger! You left out the main one, too! Thought you could slip one over on me, didn't you, eh?"

Duck Soup finds Groucho's dictator Firefly taking this looniness to black-humor lengths. His paranoia over the intentions of Ambassador Trentino (Louis Calhern) and his nation are the ultimate cause of war between their two countries.

The scene in question is innocently initiated by Margaret Dumont, who as influential Freedonia citizen Mrs. Teasdale, has arranged a meeting between the two men to iron out past differences. Before Trentino arrives Firefly tells Dumont's character:

> Mrs. Teasdale, you did a noble deed! I'd be unworthy of the high trust that's been placed in me if I didn't do everything within my power to keep our beloved Freedonia at peace with the world. I'll be only too happy to meet Ambassador Trentino and offer him, on behalf of my country, the right hand of good fellowship. [*jovially*] And I feel sure that he will accept this gesture in the spirit in which it is offered. . . .[*less than jovially*] But suppose he doesn't? A fine thing that'll be! I hold out my hand and he refuses to accept it! That'll add a

lot to my prestige, won't it? [*shouting indignantly*] Me, the head of a country, snubbed by a foreign ambassador! Who does he think he is that he can come here and make a sap out of me in front of all my people? Think of it! (Sinclair, 160–61)

The scene continues as a comically angry Groucho walks about, waiting on Trentino. His Firefly soon explodes to Teasdale, "I hold out my hand and that hyena refuses to accept it! Why, the cheap, four-flushing swine! He'll never get away with it, I tell you." Naturally, when Trentino does enter, the totally lathered Firefly verbally lambastes the Sylvanian ambassador before the astonished man can say a word: "So! You refuse to shake hands with me, eh?" And Firefly slaps him with his gloves. Not surprisingly, this leads to war. Marx brothers scholar Martin A. Gardner, in an unpublished dissertation on the team, has insightfully connected Groucho's paranoia here to American historian Richard Hofstader's suggestion that this country's foreign policy has often been based in a psychotic preconception that an evil foreign conspiracy is out to do dastardly deeds (Gardner, "The Marx Brothers"; Hofstader, *The Paranoid Style*).

Groucho's mercurial disposition to irrational violence is obviously best showcased in *Duck Soup*. Besides the aforementioned hand-shake paranoia, there is irrational militancy when another overture to peace is made. Groucho's response: "But there must be a war—I've paid a month's rent on the battlefield!" Yet, it is less than startling that a scaled-down version of this comment had already occurred in *Horse Feathers*. When a character attempts to avoid a fight with Groucho's college president, the mustachioed one cracks, "You've gotta fight, I've already taken my coat off." And just as fittingly, the comedian finds time to echo a variation of his *Duck Soup* refrain, "Then it's war!" in *A Day at the Races*—"So it's war!"

In terms of film history, Groucho's comic interpretation of a persecution complex anticipates the even darker paranoia of General Jack Ripper in *Dr. Strangelove; or, How I learned to Stop Worrying and Love the Bomb* (1964). Played by Sterling Hayden, Ripper starts an apocalyptic atomic war because he believes the fluoridation of America's post–World War II water supply to be an evil plot hatched by the Soviet Union to communize this country. Though *Strangelove* does not offer the viewer a case history of Ripper's paranoia, one need not be Dr. Freud to suggest this is the action of a sexually frustrated individual. It seems that Hayden's character links his im-

10. Chico comes between Groucho and the sexy Thelma Todd, in *Horse Feathers.*

potence to fluoridation and the violation of his precious bodily fluids. He becomes the ultimate antihero; in attempting to exert his manhood he extinguishes mankind.

The General Ripper sexual-frustration scenario makes for a provocative analogy with Groucho, especially in terms of an additional antiheroic perspective on the comedian's screen image. Given the mustachioed one's dirty-old-man image, a regular "King Leer," this might at first seem comic blasphemy. But when teamed with Thelma Todd in *Monkey Business* and *Horse Feathers*, there is the suggestion that Groucho's sexual bravado is mere show. Unlike Margaret Dumont, who is neither physically attractive nor frequently mentally attuned to Groucho's amorous innuendo, Todd is both inviting and *inviting*. During their cabin scene from *Monkey Business* she seems to be on the same steamy wavelength as Groucho. She even quotes from an earlier delightful bit of his dialogue, a comic anthem to hot-bloodedness: "I want excitement. I want to ha-cha-cha-cha." She then breaks into dance, as Groucho did after uttering these lines. That he does not take her up on the "ha-cha-cha-cha" (period censorship for film not withstanding), is an interesting calling of Groucho's sexual bluff. Moreover, as a 1930s studio publicist for the team later observed, "Todd always gave the appearance of being far too worldly and conniving a woman ever to be taken in by Groucho's wooing" (Carle, 145). Appropriately, the wedding that closes *Horse Feathers* has Todd marrying Groucho *plus* Chico and Harpo.

Though given little screen time, a variation of the Thelma Todd character also surfaces in *Duck Soup*. The sexy Vera Marcal (Raquel Torres), accomplice to Trentino, catches Groucho's attention by suggestively murmuring that maybe they could dance some time. But he seems intimidated by the possibilities. Thus, after initially telling her "I could dance with you 'till the cows come home," her affirmative response brings an inexplicable recanting, "On second thought, I'd rather dance with the cows 'till you came home." Groucho later reconsiders, after she places a hand on his chest and risqué ly asks, "Oh, your Excellency, isn't there something I can do?" He provocatively replies, "Yes, but I'll talk to you about that later." Yet nothing comes of this. Maybe Groucho's sexual bravado is a search for a metaphorical mirror—someone who would simply reflect back how fascinating he attempts to be. Yet each success, the open invitation of a sexy Todd or Marcal, breeds antiheroic frustration: he cannot perform. No wonder he seems more secure around Dumont.

And like the later General Jack Ripper, the rest of Groucho's activity as *Duck Soup*'s dictator has him waging war. His Rufus T. Firefly leaves no sexually frustrated notes pertaining to fluoridation at his battlefield post, but even here there are references to such antiheroic moments. For instance, in one scene he gets a huge vase stuck on his head and observes, "The last time this happened to me I was crawling under a bed." Marx critic Allen Eyles calls this scene "another glimpse of the thwarted Casanova" (109). Regardless of how you read it, the antiheroic side of Groucho's persona has a certain sexual vulnerability to it, despite (and possibly better explaining) the showy swagger. In addition, it provides a fresh slant to other scenes, such as the dialogue between Groucho and Dumont as they board the ship in *A Night at the Opera*. Her Mrs. Claypool (no sexual threat there) innocently asks, "Are you sure you have everything, Otis?" In a much too defensive manner he replies, "I've never had any complaints yet."

This overview of the antiheroic dimensions of Groucho's more-famous-for aggression screen character has pointed to the many derailing techniques of Chico and Harpo and the comic cracks in his own normally formative armor. This discussion must not be taken for an attempt to explain everything about his character's more fragile side, but it at least begins to address a comic complexity that is often neglected.

W. C. Fields's antihero, like his huckster, is totally likeable but for entirely different reasons. His diddler does what the viewer would like to do (but on a scale modest enough to hurt no one), and the comedian's little man helps diffuse our shared vulnerabilities.

Fields's compartmentalization of these two types in separate sets of films says several things. His huckster is a romanticized survivor from an earlier age, who first surfaced at a time (the Great Depression) when surviving was the most topical of concerns. In contrast, his antihero is a pivotal early blueprint for a comic character that, while not entirely new (few things are), was then fashionably fresh when placed at American humor's center stage. If his dominated husband sometimes seems too victimized, chalk it up to a pioneering showcase of domestic frustration, a comic foundation to darker disappointments (disguised as entertainment) to come. Moreover, there are the moments of pathos his little man somehow wrestles from what is essentially a live-action twist on the funny papers' underdog husband/father. Yet the portly body and bulbous nose did suggest some fifth-columnist success at overindulging in booze and food. This modest antiheroic success also helps entertainingly diffuse guilt in the non-achiever portion of most viewers, even if that only applies to overeating, or cheating on the latest diet.

When character types are not compartmentalized, as Groucho's are not, they are harder to read and fully appreciate. In the scores of film reviews I studied to prepare this text, period critics were generally more articulate in critiquing Fields's work. Though most of them unquestionably enjoyed Groucho and company, the team's comedy chaos often seemed to overwhelm them, as in the following, quite typical, review of *Duck Soup:* "Many screen fans call them the world's funniest comedians. Others claim they are the worst. All, however, agree on one point—that the Marxes cop the palm for sheer insanity" ("Marxian Insanity").

Naturally, with time has come a better understanding. The Marx brothers are celebrated today for, among other things, pioneering saturation comedy—breaking ground for such diverse later talents as Ernie Kovacs, Robin Williams, and Monty Python's Flying Circus. They took comic iconoclasm to new heights (as well as sideswiping the general goofiness of modern life), and they pushed the absurdity element into new black-comedy territory—all things in which Groucho was at the center. However, his mix of con man and anti-heroic vulnerability has not been fully appreciated. The latter trait gives his character a built-in sympathy that people like Irving Thalberg, M-G-M's architect of a later artificial team pathos, never fully recognized.

The combination of confidence man and antihero is also what gives Groucho's character its ongoing modern complexity—making him less predictable and potentially more dangerous (despite all that anti-establishment fun) than the W. C. Fields alternatives, as wonderful as they are.

For many viewers today, particularly younger ones, the comically methodical Fields appears to be an acquired taste, while Groucho still resonates as an *on-the-edge* contemporary. His rapid mood changes, comic paranoia, fast-forward monologues, petty selfishness, self-deprecating cracks, and sexual frustrations more readily speak to a modern audience. And Groucho's antiheroic inadequacies lend his screen persona a link to reality, despite the patently false greasepaint mustache and eyebrows, or the occasional flights of certifiable absurdity—whether generated by his character, or by Harpo and Chico.

*When the "Esoteric Studio" cleaning lady
bumps Fields's (playing himself) face with a
push broom, he says, "Take that Groucho
Marx out of here!"*
      —Never Give a Sucker an Even Break

*Groucho, at a society party, is surrounded
by pretty girls, to whom he observes, "No,
you're wrong, girls. You're wrong. In the first
place, Gary Cooper is much taller than I
am."*
                          —Monkey Business

CHAPTER 6 Epilogue

Just as the above quotations are movie-to-movie allusions, dependent upon the film for their success, American screen comedy is
more than a little indebted to W. C. Fields and Groucho Marx for its
success. During the 1930s, the golden age of sound comedy, these
pioneering sound comedians were huckster bookends in an antiheroic age. Their confidence-men personas gave a Depression age
two perspectives on tough-times survival. One paid comic homage
to a shell-game past; the other gave a dark-humor salute to future
ambivalently funny/frightening charlatans—wheeling and dealing
from within an established power base, be it the halls of government
or academe. Yet, like all great artists, their diverse diddlers succeed
on several levels, beyond the inspired comedy. Most significant for
Fields was his shakedown artist's embrace of the nineteenth century's "individualization of manifest destiny," turning his grifter toward the sympathetically provocative pursuit of the American success story.

And Groucho, despite the scary overtones of his big-scale manipulators, still manages to so entertainingly prick the high and the mighty that he is frequently celebrated as an anti-establishment hero. The praise is earned, as long as one does not forget the question posited by comedy historian Gerald Weales: "Where are these Pied Pipers [Groucho and company] leading us?" (80). That is, with the mustachioed one there is forever the danger, as best showcased in the war setting of *Duck Soup*, for him to take us over the precipice . . . the ultimate accenting of "to die laughing."

Coupled to these complex characterizations are Fields's and Marx's forays into the antiheroic world, a development often minimized in Groucho literature. But whereas their confidence men could build upon a long nineteenth-century American literary tradition, the twentieth-century world of the antihero was still evolving as Fields and Marx entered its comedy fray. Part disciples of Benchley and Thurber, newspaper comic strips, vaudeville—and a host of possible popular-culture influences, their lunatic/little-man humor occurs early enough (be it their joint vaudeville roots, or Fields's copyrighted sketches), that one can argue that W. C. and Groucho also merit pioneering status in the antiheroic world.

Regardless of how the comedy credentials are stamped, there is no denying their ongoing impact on this school of comedy, with Marx again pushing the dark side of the envelope (as he did in the huckster realm). That is, Groucho's screen character is capable of a comically paranoid, over-the-top response to even the *thought* of a provocation. Another comedian might be tempted to say, "Groucho reacts with all the calm moderation of the French revolution!" Marx remains as much a product of overstatement as the antiheroic Fields is of understatement (the flowery flamboyance of W. C. the huckster is something else again). Of course, Groucho's more typical antiheroic behavior comes at the zany hands of Chico and Harpo. Groucho is derailed by them so much that one might call him self-destructive; as the old joke goes, "It's one thing to see the train coming and another to get out of the way."

Just as the richly varied careers of W. C. and Groucho had so many parallels, their early difficult years gave them a shared foundation (for survival) in real-life hucksterism and antiheroic victimization. Thus, as we commemorate their comic resiliency (both physical and spiritual) in the arts, their triumphs over personal adversity ("life's funny sadness" [Yanni, 124]) provoke additional admiration, à la the stuff of comic legend—creating laughter despite personal sadness. And as with all great clowns, this resiliency, whether on the screen or behind it, gifts the viewer with entertainment and hope. . . .

Near the close of Fields's *It's a Gift*, a businessman calls the comedian's character, Harold Bissonette, a drunk. Fields answers, "I'm drunk and you're crazy. But I'll be sober tomorrow and you'll be crazy for the rest of your life." I conclude with this anecdote only as a reminder that my text is meant to be as much a celebration of humor as an exploration of its analysis. Both humor and intellectual exploration help us learn more about ourselves—because, as comedy author Michael Grayn suggests, we all have some funny arrangement in our lives. We all live in a comic way (*Now You Know*). And that comic way is a personal outpost of freedom and sanity in a world too often controlled by intimidation. Long live irreverent stances.

FILMOGRAPHY

This study focuses largely on selected films starring W. C. and Groucho, drawn primarily from the 1930s. Although for convenient reference this filmography lists all their movie appearances, additional detail is presented for the works on which this volume keys. Both comedians' films are listed together to better facilitate the Fields-Marx comparison that was the catalyst for the book.

The pre-1929 silent-film listings are all Fields's, with the exception of the Marx brothers' privately funded and never released *Humorisk* (now lost). Though there are numerous silent titles, Fields's movie career did not take off until screen audiences could hear him. The silent work, while representing a foundation for several of his late sound classics, should not detract from the unique golden age of sound-comedy juxtapositioning of W. C. and Groucho that prompted this study. Along darker lines, the mediocre all-star productions in which both comedians sometimes surfaced late in their careers merit inclusion for the sake of history, though not artistry; like athletes playing past their prime, the stars could not add to their artistic record.

Silent Films

Sept. 1915   *Pool Sharks* (1 reel, approximately 10 minutes). Produced by Gaumont Co.; Mutual distributes. Director: Edwin Middleton. Story inspired by W. C. Fields's pool act. Fields stars

Oct. 1915 *His Lordship's Dilemma* (1 reel). Produced by Gaumont Co.; Mutual distributes. Director: William Haddock. Story inspired by Fields's golf act. Fields stars

1920 *Humorisk* (1 reel, now lost). Produced privately; never distributed. Marx Brothers star. (Sometimes listed as 1926.)

Oct. 1924 *Janice Meredith* (153 minutes). Also known as *The Beautiful Rebel*. Produced by Cosmopolitan; M-G-M distributes. Director: E. Mason Hooper. Based on Paul Leicester Ford novel. Marion Davies stars; Fields has a modest supporting role

Aug. 1925 *Sally of the Sawdust* (104 minutes). Produced by D. W. Griffith, Inc.; United Artist distributes. Director: D. W. Griffith. Based on the Dorothy Donnelly stage play *Poppy*. Screenplay: Forrest Haley. Carol Dempster has title role, with Fields costarring as Professor Eustace McGargle

Dec. 1925 *That Royle Girl* (114 minutes). Produced by Famous Players–Lasky Corp.; Paramount distributes. Director: D. W. Griffith. Based upon Edwin Balmer novel. Screenplay: Paul Scholfield. Dempster and Fields star

May 1926 *It's the Old Army Game* (70 minutes). Produced by Famous Players–Lasky Corp.; Adolph Zukor and Jesse L. Lasky distribute. Director: Edward Sutherland. Draws heavily upon J. P. McEvoy's musical comedy revue *The Comic Supplement*, to which Fields contributed. Screenplay: Thomas J. Geraghty. Fields stars, with Louise Brooks in support

Oct. 1926 *So's Your Old Man* (67 minutes). Produced by Famous Players–Lasky Corp.; Paramount distributes. Director: Gregory LaCava. Based upon Julian Street's award-winning short story "Mr. Bisbee's Princess." Adapted by Howard Emmett Rogers and Thomas J. Geraghty. Screenplay: J. Clarkson Miller. Fields stars

Jan. 1927 *The Potters* (71 minutes). Produced by Famous Players–Lasky Corp.; Paramount distributes. Director: Fred Newmeyer. Adapted by Sam Mintz and Ray Harris from the J. P. McEvoy play. Screenplay: J. Clarkson Miller. Fields stars

Aug. 1927 *Running Wild* (68 minutes). Paramount. Director: Gregory LaCava. Adaptation and screenplay by Roy Briant, from a LaCava story. Fields stars

Dec. 1927   *Two Flaming Youths* (55 minutes). Paramount. Director: John Waters. Screenplay: Percy Heath and Donald Davis, from a Heath story. Fields stars

Mar. 1928   *Tillie's Punctured Romance* (57 minutes). Produced by Christie Studio; Paramount distributes. Director: Edward Sutherland. Screenplay: Monte Brice and Keene Thompson, from the Edgar Smith play *Tillie's Nightmare*. Fields stars, with support from Chester Conklin and Mack Swain

May 1928   *Fools for Luck* (60 minutes). Paramount. Director: Charles F. Reisner. Screenplay: Sam Mintz and J. Walter Ruben, from a Harry Fried story. Fields stars, with Chester Conklin.

Sound Films

Aug. 1929   The Cocoanuts (96 minutes). Paramount. Directors: Robert Florey and Joseph Santley. Screenplay Adaptation: Morrie Ryskind. Based on stage production *The Cocoanuts*: George S. Kaufman and Morrie Ryskind; music and lyrics: Irving Berlin. Cast: Groucho (Mr. Hammer), Harpo (himself), Chico (himself), Zeppo (Jamison), Mary Eaton (Polly Potter), Oscar Shaw (Bob Adams), Katherine Francis (Penelope), Margaret Dumont (Mrs. Potter)

Aug. 1930   *The Golf Specialist* (2 reels). RKO. Director: Monte Brice. Story drawn from Fields's copyrighted routine "An Episode on the Links." Fields stars

Sept. 1930   *Animal Crackers* (98) minutes). Paramount. Director: Victor Heerman. Screenplay: Morrie Ryskind. Based on stage production *Animal Crackers*: George S. Kaufman and Morrie Ryskind; music and lyrics: Bert Kalmar and Harry Ruby (including "Hooray for Captain Spaulding"). Cast: Groucho (Capt. Jeffrey T. Spaulding), Harpo (the Professor), Chico (Signor Emanuel Ravelli), Zeppo (Horatio Jamison), Lilian Roth (Arabella Rittenhouse), Margaret Dumont (Mrs. Rittenhouse), Louis Sorin (Roscoe W. Chandler)

Sept. 1931   *Monkey Business* (77 minutes). Paramount. Director: Norman McLeod. Screenplay: S. J. Perelman and Will B. Johnstone. Additional dialogue: Arthur Sheekman. Cast: Groucho, Harpo, Chico, Zeppo (playing themselves as stowaways), Thelma Todd (Lucille)

Dec. 1931   *Her Majesty Love* (75 minutes). Warner Brothers. Director: William Dieterle. Screenplay: Robert Lord and Arthur Caesar, from the R. Bernauer and R. Oesterreicher play. Fields in a supporting role

1931   *The House That Shadows Built* (feature). Paramount. The Marx brothers do a sketch from their stage production, *I'll Say She Is!* in this tribute to Paramount

July 1932   *Million Dollar Legs* (64 minutes). Paramount. Director: Edward Cline. Screenplay: Henry Myers and Nick Barrows, from a Joseph L. Mankiewicz story. Fields stars with top-billed Jack Oakie in a spoof of the 1932 Olympics (held in L.A.)

Aug. 1932   *Horse Feathers* (68 minutes). Paramount. Director: Norman McLeod. Screenplay: Bert Kalmar, Harry Ruby, S. J. Perelman, and Will B. Johnstone. Music: Bert Kalmar and Harry Ruby (including "I'm Against It"). Cast: Groucho (Prof. Quincey Adams Wagstaff), Harpo (Pinky), Chico (Barovelli), Zeppo (Frank Wagstaff), Thelma Todd (Connie Bailey)

Dec. 1932   *If I Had a Million* (88 minutes, many segmented feature). Paramount. Director (Fields episode): Norman Taurog. Screenplay (Fields episode): Joseph L. Mankiewicz. W. C. segment also stars Allison Skipworth

Dec. 1932   *The Dentist* (2 reels). Produced by Mack Sennett; Paramount distributes. Director: Leslie Pearce. Screenplay: W. C. Fields, from his multi-copyrighted "An Episode at the Dentist." W. C. stars

1932   *Hollywood on Parade* (1 reel). Paramount. Brief footage of Groucho, Harpo, and Chico, off the set with their families

Mar. 1933   *The Fatal Glass of Beer* (2 reels). Produced by Mack Sennett; Paramount distributes. Director: Clyde Bruckman. Screenplay: Fields, adapted from his copyrighted sketch "Stolen Bonds." Fields stars

Apr. 1933   *The Pharmacist* (2 reels). Produced by Mack Sennett; Paramount distributes. Director: Arthur Ripley. Screenplay: Fields, adapted from his stage sketch "The Druggist." Fields stars

June 1933   *International House* (70 minutes). Paramount. Director: Edward Sutherland. Screenplay: Francis Martin and Walter DeLeon, from a Lou Heifetz and Neil Brant story. Small-car material draws from Fields's copyrighted *Midget Car*. W. C. appears with an all-star cast, including Burns and Allen and Franklin Pangborn

June 1933   *Hip Action* (1 reel). Paramount. Director: George Marshall. Fields supports golfing great Bobby Jones in a lesson

July 1933   *The Barber Shop* (2 reels). Produced by Mack Sennett; Paramount distributes. Director: Arthur Ripley. Screenplay: Fields, adapted from his stage sketch "The Barber Shop." Fields stars

Sept. 1933   *Hollywood on Parade B-2* (1 reel). Paramount. Director Louis Lewyn. Studio PR short includes W. C. and Groucho, though the latter is not featured

Oct. 1933   *Tillie and Gus* (58 minutes). Paramount. Director: Francis Martin. Screenplay: Walter DeLeon and Francis Martin, from a Rupert Hughes story. Cast: Fields (Augustus Winterbottom), Alison Skipworth (Tillie Winterbottom), Bobby LeRoy (the "king"), Jacqueline Wells (Mary Sheridan), Clifford Jones (Tom Sheridan), Clarence Wilson (Phineas Pratt).

Nov. 1933   *Duck Soup* (70 minutes). Paramount. Director: Leo McCarey. Screenplay: Bert Kalmar and Harry Ruby. Additional Dialogue: Arthur Sheekman and Nat Perrin. Music and Lyrics: Bert Kalmar and Harry Ruby (including "This Country's Going to War"). Cast: Groucho (Rufus T. Firefly), Chico (Chicolini), Harpo (Pinkie), Zeppo (Bob Rolland), Raquel Torres (Vera Marcal), Louis Calhern (Ambassador Trentino), Margaret Dumont (Mrs. Teasdale), Edgar Kennedy (Lemonade Peddler)

Dec. 1933   *Alice in Wonderland* (90 minutes). Paramount. Director: Norman McLeod. Fields appears as Humpty Dumpty in an all-star cast production of Lewis Carroll

Feb. 1934   *Six of a Kind* (65 minutes). Paramount. Director: Leo McCarey. Screenplay: Walter DeLeon and Harry Ruskin, from a Keene Thompson and Douglas MacLeon story. Fields adds a variation of his pool sketch. W. C. is in a supporting role

Apr. 1934   *You're Telling Me* (66 minutes; remake of *So's Your Old Man*). Paramount. Director: Erle Kenton. Based upon a Julian Street story. Screenplay: Walter De Leon and Paul M. Jones. Dialogue: J. P. McEvoy. Cast: W. C. Fields (Sam Bisbee), Joan Marsh (Pauline Bisbee), Larry "Buster" Crabbe (Bob Murchison), Adrienne Ames (Princess Lescaboura), Louise Carter (Mrs. Bessie Bisbee), Kathleen Howard (Mrs. Murchison)

Apr. 1934   *Hollywood on Parade B-10* (1 reel). Paramount. Director:

Louis Lewyn. Studio PR short includes W. C. and Groucho

July 1934 *The Old Fashioned Way* (66 minutes; loose remake of *Two Flaming Youths*). Paramount. Director: William Beaudine. Screenplay: Garnett Weston and Jack Cunningham, from a story by Charles Bogle (Fields). Cast: W. C. Fields (The Great McGonigle), Jan Duggan (Cleopatra Pepperday), Nora Cecil (Mrs. Wendelschaffer), Baby LeRoy (Albert Wendelschaffer)

Oct. 1934 *Mrs. Wiggs of the Cabbage Patch* (80 minutes). Paramount. Director: Norman Taurog. From the frequently adapted story by Alice Hegan Rice and Anne Crawford Alexander. Fields in comedy support

Nov. 1934 *It's a Gift* (73 minutes; remake of *It's the Old Army Game*). Paramount. Director: Norman McLeod. Screenplay: Jack Cunningham, from a story by Charles Bogle [W. C. Fields; see esp. his copyrighted stage routine "The Sleeping Porch" and the multi-copyrighted "The Family Ford"] and adapted from J. P. McEvoy's musical comedy revue *The Comic Supplement*. Cast: W. C. Fields (Harold Bissonette), Kathleen Howard (Amelia Bissonette), Jean Rouverol (Mildred Bissonette), Julian Madison (John Durston), Tom Bupp (Norman Bissonette), Baby LeRoy (Baby Dunk), Tammany Young (Everett Ricks)

Jan. 1935 *David Copperfield* (133 minutes). M-G-M. Director: George Cukor. Screenplay: Howard Estabrook; adapted from Dickens' novel by Hugh Walpole. Fields appears as Micawber in an all-star cast

Mar. 1935 *Mississippi* (80 minutes). Paramount. Director: Edward Sutherland. Screenplay: Francis Martin and Jack Cunningham, adapted from the Booth Tarkington play *The Magnolia* by Herbert Fields and Claude Binyon. Cast: Bing Crosby (Tom Grayson), W. C. Fields (Commodore Jackson), Joan Bennett (Lucy Rumford), Gail Patrick (Elvira Rumford), Queenie Smith (Alabam')

July 1935 *The Man on the Flying Trapeze* (65 minutes; loose remake of *Running Wild*). Paramount. Director: Clyde Bruckman. Screenplay: Ray Harris and Sam Hardy, from a story by Charles Bogle [Fields] and Sam Hardy. Cast: W. C. Fields (Ambrose Wolfinger), Mary Brian (Hope Wolfinger), Kathleen Howard (Leona Wolfinger), Grady Sutton (Claude Bensinger), Vera Lewis (Mrs. Cordelia

Neselrode), Tammy Young (Burglar), Walter Brennan (Burglar), Carlotta Monti (Ambrose's Secretary)

Nov. 1935   *A Night at the Opera* (92 minutes). M-G-M. Director: Sam Wood. Screenplay: George S. Kaufman and Morris Ryskind. Additional material: Al Boasberg. Story: James Kevin McGuinness. Cast: Groucho (Otis B. Driftwood), Chico (Fiorella), Harpo (Tomasso), Kitty Carlisle (Rosa), Alan Jones (Richardo), Walter King (Lassparri), Siegfried Rumann (Herman Gottlieg), Margaret Dumont (Mrs. Claypool)

June 1936   *Poppy* (75 minutes; loose remake of *Sally of the Sawdust*, but much closer to original Dorothy Donnelly play). Paramount. Director: A. Edward Sutherland. Screenplay: Waldemar Young and Virginia Van Upp. Cast: W. C. Fields (Prof. Eustace McGargle), Rochelle Hudson (Poppy), Richard Cromwell (Billy Farnsworth), Catherine Doucet (Countess Maggie Tubbs DePuizzi), Lynne Overman (Attorney Whiffen), Granville Bates (Mayor Farnsworth); others include Bill Wolfe and Tammany Young

June 1937   *A Day at the Races* (109 minutes). M-G-M Director: Sam Wood. Screenplay: George Seaton, Robert Pirosh, George Oppenheimer; from a Seaton and Oppenheimer story. Cast: Groucho (Dr. Hugo Z. Hackenbush), Chico (Tony), Harpo (Stuffy), Allan Jones (Gil), Maureen O'Sullivan (Judy Standish), Margaret Dumont (Mrs. Emily Upjohn), Leonard Ceeley (Whitmore), Douglas Dumbrille (Morgan), Siegfried Rumann (Dr. Leopold X. Steinberg)

Feb. 1938   *The Big Broadcast of 1938* (97 minutes). Paramount. Director: Mitchell Leisen. Screenplay: Walter DeLeon, Francis Martin and Ken Englund. This Paramount variety show features Fields in two roles (the brothers T. Frothingell and S. B. Bellows). All-star cast includes Bob Hope

Sept. 1938   *Room Service* (78 minutes). RKO-Radio. Director: William A. Seiter. Screenplay: Morrie Ryskind, from the John Murray and Allen Boretz play. Marx Brothers star

Feb. 1939   *You Can't Cheat an Honest Man* (76 minutes). Universal. Director: George Marshall (though an uncredited Edward Cline worked with Fields). Screenplay: George Marion, Jr., Richard Mack, and Everett Freeman, from a Charles Bogle [Fields] story. Cast: W. C. Fields (Larsen E. Whipsnade), Edgar Bergen (himself), Charlie McCarthy (himself), Constance Moore (Vicky Whipsnade), John Arledge (Phineas Whipsnade), James Bush (Roger Bel-Goodie), Thurston Hall (Mr. Bel-Goodie), Mary Forbes (Mrs. Bel-Goodie)

Oct. 1939   *At the Circus* (87 minutes). M-G-M. Director: Edward Bussell. Screenplay: Irving Brecher. Marx Brothers star, with support from Margaret Dumont

Feb. 1940   *My Little Chickadee* (83 minutes). Universal. Director: Edward Cline. Screenplay: Mae West and W. C. Fields. Cast: W. C. Fields (Cuthbert J. Twillie), Mae West (Flower Belle Lee), Joseph Calleia (Jeff Badger/Masked Bandit), Dick Foran (Wayne Carter), Ruth Donnelly (Aunt Lou), Margaret Hamilton (Mrs. Gideo), Donald Meek (Amos Budget), Fuzzy Knight (Cousin Zeb)

Nov. 1940   *The Bank Dick* (74 minutes). Universal. Director: Edward Cline. Screenplay: Mahatma Kane Jeeves [W. C. Fields]. Cast: W. C. Fields (Egbert Sousé), Cora Witherspoon (Agatha Sousé), Una Merkel (Myrtle Sousé), Evelyn Del Rio (Elsie Mae Adele Brunch Sousé), Jessie Ralph (Mrs. Hermisillo Brunch), Franklin Pangborn (J. Pinkerton Snoopington), Shemp Howard (Joe Guelpe), Richard Purcell (Mackley Q. Greene), Grady Sutton (Og Oggilby), Russell Hicks (J. Frothingham Waterbury), Pierre Watkins (Mr. Skinner)

Dec. 1940   *Go West* (80 minutes). M-G-M. Director: Edward Buzzell. Screenplay: Irving Brecher. Marx Brothers star

June 1941   *The Big Store* (83 minutes). M-G-M. Director: Charles Reisner. Screenplay: Sid Kuller, Hal Fimberg, and Ray Golden. Marx Brothers star, with support from Margaret Dumont

Oct. 1941   *Never Give a Sucker an Even Break* (70 minutes). Universal. Director: Edward Cline. Screenplay: John T. Neville and Prescott Chaplin, from an Otis Criblecoblis (W. C. Fields) story. Cast: W. C. Fields (The Great Man), Gloria Jean (his niece), Leon Errol (His rival), Billy Lenhart(Butch), Kenneth Brown (Buddy), Margaret Dumont (Mrs. Hemogloben), Susan Miller (Ouliotta Hemogloben), Franklin Pangborn (the producer), Mona Barrie (the producer's wife), Jody Gilbert (Tiny, waitress), Minerva Urecal (Mrs. Pastrome), Carlotta Monti (producer's receptionist)

Oct. 1942   *Tales of Manhattan* (118 minutes). Twentieth Century-

Fox. Many segmented feature. In order to reduce running time, the W. C. Fields episode was cut before release

1942   *The Laziest Golfer* (unfinished, never released USO short subject). W. C. Fields golfing at home

1943   *Screen Snapshots No. 2* (1 reel). Columbia. Groucho doing a radio broadcast

1943   *Screen Snapshots No. 8* (1 reel). Columbia. Stars include Groucho, Harpo and Chico

May 1944   *Follow the Boys* (118 minutes). Universal. Director: Eddie Sutherland. Screenplay: Lou Breslow and Gertrude Purcell. Fields does his pool routine in this all-star patriotic feature

June 1944   *Song of the Open Road* (93) minutes). United Artists. Director: Albert Mannheimer. W. C. Fields is one of several guest stars, rekindling feud with Edgar Bergen's Charlie McCarthy

June 1944   *Sensations of 1945* (87 minutes). United Artists. Director: Andrew L. Stone. Screenplay: Dorothy Bennett. W. C. Fields does a variation of his copyrighted sketch "The Caledonian Express." Once again, it is merely another all-star variety show, with Fields describing it as "high class vaudeville."

May 1946   *A Night in Casablanca* (85 minutes). United Artists. Director: Archie L. Mayo. Screenplay: Joseph Fields and Roland Kibbee. Additional material: Frank Tashlin. Groucho, Harpo, and Chico star, with support from Siegfried Rumann

Mar. 1950   *Copacabana* (92 minutes). United Artists. Director: Alfred E. Green. Screenplay: Laslo Vadnay, Allen Boretz, and Howard Harris. Groucho Marx stars with Carmen Miranda

Mar. 1950   *Love Happy* (85 minutes). United Artists. Director: David Miller. Screenplay: Frank Tashlin and Mac Benoff, from a Harpo story. Minor support by Groucho

Dec. 1950   *Mr. Music* (113 minutes). Paramount. Director: Richard Haydn. Screenplay: Arthur Sheekman, based on Samson Raphaelson play *Accent on Youth*. Groucho Marx makes guest appearance, probably for friend Sheekman

Dec. 1951   *Double Dynamite* (80 minutes). RKO. Director: Irving Cummings, Jr. Screenplay: Melville Shavelson. Stars Jane Russell, Frank Sinatra, and Groucho Marx

Feb. 1952   *A Girl in Every Port* (86 minutes). RKO. Director: Chester Erskine. Groucho stars with Marie Wilson and William Bendix

Sept. 1957 *Will Success Spoil Rock Hunter?* (94 minutes). Twentieth Century–Fox. Director Tashlin. Screenplay: Frank Tashlin; based on George Axelrod play. Groucho Marx makes an unbilled cameo at the close—the secret love of Jayne Mansfield's character

Nov. 1957 *The Story of Mankind* (100 minutes). Warner Brothers. Director: Irwin Allen. Screenplay: Irwin Allen and Charles Bennett. Sketches with all-star cast include Groucho, Harpo and Chico—but not together! Groucho's third wife, Eden, and youngest child, Melinda, also appear

Dec. 1968 *Skidoo* (98 minutes). Paramount. Director: Otto Preminger. Screenplay: Doran William Cannon. Another all-star cast with Groucho appearing briefly as the mobster "God."

BIBLIOGRAPHY

Adamson, Joe. *Groucho, Harpo, and Chico and Sometimes Zeppo.* New York: Simon and Schuster, 1973.

Allen, Steve. *Funny People.* New York: Stein and Day, 1981.

Alsop, Joseph, Jr. "Surrealism Beaten at Its Own Game." Rev. of *A Night at the Opera. New York Herald Tribune,* 15 Dec. 1935. In *A Night at the Opera* file, Billy Rose Theatre Collection, New York Public Library at Lincoln Center.

Animal Crackers Rev. *Variety,* 3 Sept. 1930.

Arce, Hector, *Groucho.* New York: G. P. Putnam's Sons, 1979.

Arkinson, J. Brooks. Rev. of *Ballyhoo. New York Times,* 23 Dec. 1930.

"Arrest of the Confidence Man." *New York Herald* 8 July 1849. In Hershel Parker, ed., text and study of Melville's *The Confidence-Man* (1857). New York: W. W. Norton & Co., 1971.

Artaud, Antonin. "Les Frères Marx au Cinéma du Panthéon." *Nouvelle Revue Francaise,* 1 Jan. 1932.

Astruc, Alexandre. "The birth of a new avant-garde: La caméra-stylo" (1948). In Peter Graham, ed., *The New Wave.* Garden City, N.Y.: Doubleday & Co., 1968.

Barnum, P. T. *Struggles and Triumphs; Or, Forty Years' Recollections of P. T. Barnum* (1855). Carl Bode, ed. New York: Penguin Classics, 1987.

Bazin, André. "Charlie Chaplin" (1958). In Hugh Gray, ed. and trans.,

What is Cinema?, vol. 1. Berkeley and Los Angeles: University of California Press, 1967.

Benchley, Robert. "A Few Words About Joe Cook." *Life*, 2 Aug. 1923.

———. "Back in Line." In Benchley, *No Poems; Or, Around the World Backwards and Sideways*. New York: Harper & Brothers, 1932.

———. "The Follies." *Life*, 14 July 1921.

———. "How Do You Like Hollywood?" *Hollywood Reporter*, 29 Sept. 1934.

———. "How to Break 90 in Croquet." In Benchley, *From Bed to Worse; Or, Comforting Thoughts About the Bison*. New York: Harper & Bros., 1934.

———. *Inside Benchley*. New York: Harper & Bros., 1942.

———. "Kiddie-Kar Travel." In Benchley, *Pluck and Luck*. New York: Henry Holt and Co., 1925.

———. "Overture." *Life*, 20 Sept. 1923.

———. "The Personal Service of Mr. Ed Wynn." *Life*, 6 May 1920.

———. "Rapping the Wrapper!" In *Benchley—Or Else!*. New York: Harper & Bros., 1947.

———. "Three Men in the Dog House." In Benchley, *After 1903— What?*. New York: Harper & Bros., 1938.

———. Letter of Dec. 7, 1928. In Box 5, Robert Benchley Collection, Mugar Memorial Library, Boston University.

———. Diary entry of June 5, 1913. In Box 5, Robert Benchley Collection, Mugar Memorial Library, Boston University.

Berger, Arthur Asa. *The Comic-Stripped American*. Baltimore: Penguin, 1973.

Bergman, Andrew. "Some Anarcho-Nihilist: Laff Riots." In Bergman, *We're in the Money: Depression America and Its Films*. New York: Harper and Row, 1972.

Bernstein, Burton. *Thurber: A Biography*. New York: Ballantine, 1976.

Billington, Sandra. *A Social History of the Fool*. New York: St. Martin's, 1984.

Blackbeard, Bill. Introduction to Bud Fisher, *A. Mutt: A Complete Compilation: 1907–1908*. Westport, Conn.: Hyperion Press, 1977.

———. Introduction to George McManus, *Bringing Up Father: 1913– 1914*. Westport, Conn.: Hyperion Press, 1977.

Blair, Walter. Introduction to Blair, *Horse Sense in American Humor*. Chicago: University of Chicago Press, 1942.

———, ed. *Native American Humor* (1937). San Francisco: Chandler, 1960.

Boehnel, William. "Great Man Goes Back to Sennett." Rev. of *Never Give a Sucker an Even Break*. *New York World-Telegram*, 27 Oct.

1941. In *Never Give A Sucker an Even Break* file, Billy Rose Theatre Collection, New York Public Library at Lincoln Center.

———. "Horseplay's the Thing in New Fields Picture." *New York World-Telegram*, 14 July 1934. In *The Old-Fashioned Way* file, Billy Rose Theatre Collection, New York Public Library at Lincoln Center.

Broun, Heywood. "W. C. Fields and the Cosmos." *The Nation*, 7 Jan. 1931.

Bulliet, C. J. "Keystone Cop, 1940: W. C. Fields in *The Bank Dick*." Rev. of *The Bank Dick*. *Chicago Daily News*, 19 Dec. 1940. In *The Bank Dick* file, Billy Rose Theatre Collection, New York Public Library at Lincoln Center.

Carle, Teet. "'Fun' Working with the Marx Brothers? Horsefeathers!" *Los Angeles Magazine*, Oct. 1978.

Cawelti, John G. *Apostles of the Self-Made Man*. Chicago: University of Chicago Press, 1965.

Chaplin, Lita Grey, with Morton Cooper. *My Life with Chaplin*. New York: Barnard Geis Associates, 1966.

Chavance, Louis. "The Four Marx Brothers As Seen by a Frenchman." *The Canadian Forum*, Feb. 1933.

Cheatham, Maude. "Juggler of Laughs." *Silver Screen*, Apr. 1935.

Cohen, Hennig. Introduction to Herman Melville, *The Confidence-Man* (1857). New York: Holt, Rinehart and Winston, 1964.

Cohen, John S., Jr. "*Duck Soup*, a Marxian (Brothers) Burlesque That Is Below Their Standard." *New York Sun*, 24 Nov. 1933. In *Duck Soup* file, Billy Rose Theatre Collection, New York Public Library at Lincoln Center.

Cooper, Arthur. "His Last Chickadee." *Newsweek*, 21 June 1971.

Creelman, Eileen. "W. C. Fields Clicks Again as a Movie Star, This Time in *You're Telling Me*." Rev. of *You're Telling Me*. *New York Sun*, 9 Apr. 1934. In *You're Telling Me* file, Billy Rose Theatre Collection, New York Public Library at Lincoln Center.

Crichton, Kyle. *The Marx Brothers*. Garden City, N.Y.: Doubleday & Co., 1950.

Darnton, Charles. "Mr. Fields Wins by a Nose!." *Screen Book Magazine*, Nov. 1937.

Delehanty, Thornton. Rev. of *The Man on the Flying Trapeze*. *New York Evening Post*, 3 Aug. 1935. In *The Man on the Flying Trapeze* file, Billy Rose Theatre Collection, New York Public Library at Lincoln Center.

———. Rev. of *You're Telling Me*. *New York Evening Post*, 7 Apr. 1934. In *You're Telling Me* file, Billy Rose Theatre Collection, New York Public Library at Lincoln Center.

Dijkstra, Bram. *Idols of Perversity*. New York: Oxford University Press, 1986.

Duyckinck, Evert A. ["The New Species of the Jeremy Diddler"]. 18 Aug. 1849. In Hershel Parker, ed., text and study of Melville's *The Confidence-Man* (1857). New York: W. W. Norton & Co., 1971.

"Erin Fleming, Who Made His Life Worth Living." *The Freedonia Gazette*, Summer 1983.

Everson, William K. *The Art of W. C. Fields*. New York: Bonanza Books, 1967.

Eyles, Allen. *The Marx Brothers: Their World of Comedy*. New York: Paperback Library, 1971.

Fadiman, Clifton. Rev. of *A Night at the Opera*. *Stage*, Jan. 1936. In S. Kaufman and B. Henstell, eds., *American Film Criticism: From the Beginning to Citizen Kane*. Westport, Conn.: Greenwood Press, 1979.

Ferguson, Otis. "The Marxian Epileptic." *New Republic*, 11 Dec. 1935.

———. "The Old Fashioned Way." *New Republic*, 30 Dec. 1940.

Fields, Ronald J., ed. *W. C. Fields: A Life On Film*. New York: St. Martin's Press, 1984.

———. *W. C. Fields By Himself: His Intended Autobiography*. Englewood Cliffs, N.J.: Prentice-Hall, 1973.

Fields, W. C. "Anything for a Laugh." *American Magazine*, Sept. 1934.

———. *Fields for President*. 1940. New York: Dodd, Mead and Co., 1971.

———. "The Great Cigar-Box Trick." In Percy Thomas Tibbles, ed., *The Magician's Handbook: A Complete Encyclopedia of the Magic Art for Professional and Amateur Entertainers*. London: Dawburn and Ward, 1901.

Ford, Corey. "The One and Only." *Harpers*, Oct. 1967.

"For the First Time: The Truth about Groucho's Ad Libs." *TV Guide*, 19–25 Mar. 1954.

Fowler, Gene. *Minutes of the Last Meeting*. New York: Viking, 1954.

Frayn, Michael. *Now You Know*. New York: Viking, 1992.

Franklin, Benjamin. *Autobiography and Other Writing*. Edited by Russel B. Nye. Boston: Houghton Mifflin, 1958.

Gardner, Martin A. "The Marx Brothers: An Investigation of Their Films as Social Criticism." Ph.D. diss., New York University, 1970.

Gehring, Wes D. *Charlie Chaplin: A Bio-Bibliography*. Westport, Conn.: Greenwood Press, 1983.

———. "Fields and Falstaff." *Thalia: Studies in Literary Humor*, Fall/Winter 1985.

———. "Kin Hubbard's Abe Martin: A Figure of Transition in American Humor." *Indiana Magazine of History*, March 1982.

_____. *Laurel & Hardy: A Bio-Bibliography*. Westport, Conn.: Greenwood Press, 1990.

_____. *The Marx Brothers: A Bio-Bibliography*. Westport, Conn.: Greenwood Press, 1987.

_____. "The Marx of Time." *Thalia: Studies in Literary Humor*, Spring/Summer 1989.

_____. "Mr. B"; Or, Comforting Thoughts About the Bison: A Critical Biography of Robert Benchley. Westport, Conn.: Greenwood Press, 1992.

_____. *W. C. Fields: A Bio-Bibliography*. Westport, Conn.: Greenwood Press, 1984.

_____. "W. C. Fields: The Copyrighted Sketches." *Journal of Popular Film & Television*, Summer 1986.

_____. "Television's Other Groucho." *Humor: International Journal of Humor Research* 5:3 (1992).

_____. "Groucho Lost & Found: His *Other* Letters." *Studies in American Humor*, Summer/Fall 1986.

Goodchilds, Jacqueline D. "On Being Witty: Causes, Correlates, and Consequences." In Jeffrey H. Goldstein and Paul E. McGhee, eds., *The Psychology of Humor: Theoretical Perspectives and Empirical Issues*. New York: Academic Press, 1972.

Grierson, John. "The Logic of Comedy." In Forsyth Hardy, ed., *Grierson on Documentary*. London: Faber and Faber. Berkeley and Los Angeles: University of California Press, 1966.

Haliburton, Thomas Chandler. "The Clockmaker: Opinion of Halifax." In Eyre Waters, ed., *The Sam Slick Anthology*. Toronto: Clark, Irwin & Co., 1976.

Hamilton, Sara. "A Red-Nosed Romeo." *Photoplay*, Dec. 1934.

Hanemann, Helen. "He Hated Alarm-Clocks." *Motion Picture*, Aug. 1926.

Harris, Neil. *Humbug: The Art of P. T. Barnum*. Boston: Little, Brown and Co., 1973.

Hayford, Harrison. "Poe in *The Confidence-Man*." In Hershel Parker, ed., text and study of Melville's *The Confidence-Man* (1857). New York: W. W. Norton & Co., 971.

Hermann, Dorothy. *S. J. Perelman: A Life*. New York: Simon & Schuster, 1986.

Hill, Hamlin. "Modern American Humor: The Janus Laugh." *College English*, Dec. 1963.

Hoffman, Daniel. *Poe Poe Poe Poe Poe Poe Poe*. 1972. Garden City, N.Y.: Anchor Press, 1973.

Hofstader, Richard. *The Paranoid Style in American Politics*. New York: Alfred A. Knopf, Inc., 1965.

Home Again Rev. *Variety,* 12 Feb. 1915.

Hooper, Johnson J. *Simon Suggs' Adventures* (1867). Americus, Ga.: Americus Book Co., 1928.

Hope, Bob, and Bob Thomas. *The Road to Hollywood.* Garden City, N.Y.: Doubleday & Co., 1977.

Horn, Maurice, ed. *The World Encyclopedia of Comics.* New York: Avon Books, 1977.

Hubbard, Kin. *Abe Martin: Hoss Sense and Nonsense.* Indianapolis: Bobbs-Merrill, 1926.

Jeeves, Mahatma Kane [W. C. Fields]. *W. C. Fields in The Bank Dick.* Script, 1940. New York: Simon and Schuster, 1973.

Jenkins, Henry. *What Made Pistachio Nuts! Early Sound Comedy and the Vaudeville Aesthetic.* New York: Columbia University Press. 1992.

Johaneson, Bland. Rev. of *Poppy. New York Daily Mirror,* ca. June 1936. In *Poppy* film file, Billy Rose Theatre Collection, New York Public Library at Lincoln Center.

Johnston, Alva. "Profiles: Legitimate Nonchalance—I." *The New Yorker,* 2 Feb. 1935.

_____. "Profiles: Legitimate Nonchalance—II." *The New Yorker,* 9 Feb. 1935.

_____. "The Scientific Side of Lunacy." *Woman's Home Companion,* Sept. 1936.

Jordan, Thomas H. "The Marx Brothers." In Jordan, *The Anatomy of Cinematic Humor.* New York: Revisionist Press, 1975.

Kaplin, Justin. *Mr. Clemens and Mark Twain* (1966). New York: Simon & Schuster, 1970.

Kaufman, George, and Morrie Ryskind. *Animal Crackers.* 1928. Script in Box 1, script section, Groucho Marx Papers, State Historical Society of Wisconsin Archives, Madison.

Kelly, Fred C. *The Life and Times of Kin Hubbard: Creator of Abe Martin.* New York: Farrar, Straus and Young, 1952.

Kirkley, Donald. "W. C. Fields." *Dallas Morning News,* 20 Dec. 1941. In *Never Give a Sucker an Even Break* file, Billy Rose Theatre Collection, New York Public Library at Lincoln Center.

Kuhlmann, Susan. *Knave, Fool, and Genius: The Confidence Man as He Appears in Nineteenth Century American Fiction.* Chapel Hill: University of North Carolina Press, 1973.

Lindberg, Gary. *The Confidence Man in American Literature.* New York: Oxford University Press, 1982.

Mallett, Phillip. "Shakespeare's Trickster-Kings: Richard III and Henry V." In Paul V. A. Williams, ed., *The Fool and the Trickster.* Oxford, Engl.: D. S. Brewer, 1979.

Marx, Arthur. *Life With Groucho: A Son's-Eye View.* New York: Simon and Schuster, 1954.

———. *Son of Groucho.* New York: David McKay Co., 1972.

"The Marx Brothers." Rev. of *Duck Soup. New York Evening Post,* 23 Nov. 1933. In *Duck Soup* file, Billy Rose Theatre Collection, New York Public Library at Lincoln Center.

Marx, Groucho. *Groucho and Me* (1959). New York: Manor Books, 1974.

———. *The Groucho Letters: Letters from and to Groucho Marx.* New York: Simon and Schuster, 1967.

———. The Groucho Marx Papers. Includes unpublished letters dated 1930 [?], 1931 April [?], 1932 [?], and 1932 April (all in Box 1, Folder 1); 15 April 1939, 14 July 1940, and 14 August 1949 (all in Box 1, Folder 2); and 31 May 1945 and 3 October 1947 (both in Box 1, Folder 3). In State Historical Society of Wisconsin Archives, Madison.

———. *The Groucho Phile.* New York: Pocket Books, 1977.

———, and Richard J. Anobile. *The Marx Bros. Scrapbook.* New York: Gossett & Dunlap, 1974.

———. "My Poor Wife!" *Colliers,* 20 Dec. 1930.

Marx, Harpo, with Rowland Barber. *Harpo Speaks!* (1961). New York: Freeway Press, 1974.

Marx, Maxine. *Growing Up with Chico.* Englewood Cliffs, N.J.: Prentice-Hall, 1980.

"Marxian Insanity: The Mad Brothers Coming in *Duck Soup* to the Rivoli." Rev. of *Duck Soup,* 1933. In *Duck Soup* file, Billy Rose Theatre Collection, New York Public Library at Lincoln Center.

Maslin, Janet. "Nothing Stands in the Way of a Laugh." *New York Times,* 23 Sept. 1992.

"Master Marx." *Newsweek,* 2 May 1949.

Mast, Gerald. *Film/Cinema/Movie: A Theory of Experience.* New York: Harper & Row, 1977.

Matterson, Stephen. Introduction to Herman Melville, *The Confidence-Man* (1857). New York: Penguin Classics, 1990.

Matthiessen, F. O. *American Renaissance: Art and Expression in the Age of Emerson and Whitman* (1941). New York: Oxford University Press, 1954.

McEvoy, J. P. *The Comic Supplement.* Script (1924), avail. only at Library of Congress Copyright Dept., Madison Building, Washington, D.C.; dress rehearsal version (1925), avail. only at Billy Rose Theatre Collection, New York Public Library at Lincoln Center.

McGee, Paul E. *Humor: Its Origins and Development.* San Francisco: W. H. Freeman and Co., 1978.

McLean, Albert F., Jr. *American Vaudeville as Ritual.* Lexington: University of Kentucky Press, 1965.

Melville, Herman. *The Confidence-Man* (1857). New York: Penguin Classics, 1990.

Melzter, Milton. "Maybe It Isn't a Movie but W. C. Fields Is in It." Rev. of *Never Give A Sucker an Even Break. New York Daily Worker*, 28 Oct. 1941. In *Never Give a Sucker an Even Break* file, Billy Rose Theatre Collection, New York Public Library at Lincoln Center.

Mississippi Rev. *London Times*, 22 Apr. 1935. In *Mississippi* film file, Billy Rose Theatre Collection, New York Public Library at Lincoln Center.

Monkey Business. Script (21 Apr. 1931) in Box 1, Folder 6, State Historical Society of Wisconsin Archives, Madison.

Monti, Carlotta, with Cy Rice. *W. C. Fields & Me.* New York: Warner Books, 1973.

Mullett, Mary B. "Bill Fields Disliked His Label, So He Laughed It Off." *American Magazine*, Jan. 1926.

Murphy, Kathleen. "Sam Peckinpah: No Bleeding Heart." *Film Comment*, April 1985.

Neale, Steve, and Frank Krutnik. *Popular Film and Television Comedy.* New York: Routledge, 1990.

Never Give a Sucker an Even Break Rev. *Variety*, 8 Oct. 1941. In *Never Give a Sucker an Even Break* file, Billy Rose Theatre Collection, New York Public Library at Lincoln Center.

Nugent, Frank. Rev. of *You Can't Cheat an Honest Man. The New York Times*, 20 Feb. 1939.

Perelman, S. J. "Week End with Groucho Marx." *Holiday*, April 1952.

Poe, Edgar Allan. "Diddling." In *The Complete Tales and Poems of Edgar Allan Poe.* New York: Random House, 1938.

Pollio, Howard R., and John W. Edgerly. "Comedians and Comic Style." In A. J. Chapman and H. C. Foot, eds., *Humour and Laughter: Theory, Research and Applications.* London: John Wiley & Sons, 1976.

Poppy Rev. *London Times*, 13 July 1936. In *Poppy* file, Billy Rose Theatre Collection, New York Public Library at Lincoln Center.

Poppy Rev. *Brooklyn Daily Eagle*, 19 July 1936. In *Poppy* file, Billy Rose Theatre Collection, New York Public Library at Lincoln Center.

Redway, Sara. "W. C. Fields Pleads for Rough Humor." *Motion Picture Classic*, Sept. 1925.

"Refineries 'Five-Star Theatre' For Every Type of Radio Listener." *Variety*, 6 Dec. 1932.

Rogers, Will. "The Singing Don't Hurt" (24 Dec. 1933). In S. K. Gragert, ed., *Will Rogers' Weekly Articles.* Stillwater: Oklahoma State University Press, 1982.

Rourke, Constance. *American Humor: A Study of the National Character* (1931). New York: Harcourt Brace Jovanovich, 1959.

Schmitz, Neil. *Of Huck and Alice: Humorous Writing in American Literature.* Minneapolis: University of Minnesota Press, 1983.

Schultz, Max F. *Black Humor Fiction of the Sixties.* Athens: Ohio University Press, 1973.

Scott, John. "Response to Comic Hilarious." *Los Angeles Times,* 6 Apr. 1934. In *You're Telling Me* file, Billy Rose Theatre Collection, New York Public Library at Lincoln Center.

Seidman, Steve. *Comedian Comedy: A Tradition in Hollywood.* Ann Arbor: University of Michigan Research Press, 1981.

Seldes, Gilbert. *The Movies Come from America.* New York: Charles Scribner's Sons, 1937.

Sennett, Mack, with Cameron Ship. *King of Comedy* (1954). New York: Pinnacle Books, 1975.

Sennwald, André. Rev. of *It's a Gift. New York Times,* 5 Jan. 1935.

Seton, Marie. "S. Dali + 3 Marxes = ." *Theatre Arts,* Oct. 1939.

Sinclair, Andrew. *Monkey Business and Duck Soup.* Scripts ed. by Sinclair (1972). Letchwood, Engl.: Lorrimerr Publishing, 1981.

Stewart, Donald Ogden. *Mr. and Mrs. Haddock.* New York: George H. Doran Co., 1924.

Sullivan, Ed. "The Lovable Liar." *Silver Screen,* Sept. 1935.

Tandy, Jennette. *Crackerbarrel Philosophers in American Humor and Satire.* New York: Columbia University Press, 1925.

Taylor, Robert Lewis. *W. C. Fields: His Follies and Fortunes.* Garden City, N.Y.: Doubleday & Co., 1949.

Thurber, James. "The Car We Had to Push" (1933). In Thurber, *My Life and Hard Times.* New York: Bantam Books, 1947.

———. "Destructive Forces in Life" (1937). In Thurber, *Let Your Mind Alone! And Other More or Less Inspirational Pieces.* New York: Universal Library, 1973.

———. "Mr. Monroe and the Moving Man" (1931). In Thurber, *The Owl in the Attic.* New York: Harper & Row, 1965.

Troy, Williams. Rev. of *Duck Soup. The Nation,* 13 Dec. 1933.

Tully, Jim. "The Clown Who Juggled Apples." *Photoplay,* Jan. 1934.

Twain, Mark. *A Connecticut Yankee in King Arthur's Court* (1889). New York: New American Library, 1963.

———. *The Adventures of Tom Sawyer* (1876). New York: Saalfield Publishing Co., n.d.

———, and Charles Dudley Warner. *The Gilded Age: A Tale of Today* (1873). New York: New American Library, 1969.

"2 Marx Bros. Fined; Escape Jail Term." *Los Angeles Examiner,* 2 Nov. 1937.

Ward, J. A. "The Hollywood Metaphor: The Marx Brothers, S. J. Perelman, and Nathanael West." *The Southern Review,* Summer 1976.

Waterbury, Ruth. "The Old Army Game." *Photoplay*, Oct. 1925.

Waters, Eyre. Introduction to Waters, ed., *The Sam Slick Anthology*. Toronto: Clark, Irwin & Co., 1976.

"W. C. Fields Stars in Hilarious Film at the Paramount." *New York American*, 14 July 1934. In *The Old-Fashioned Way* film file, Billy Rose Theatre Collection, New York Public Library at Lincoln Center.

Weales, Gerald. "Duck Soup." *Canned Goods as Caviar: American Film Comedy of the 1930s*. Chicago: University of Chicago Press, 1985.

Welsford, Enid. *The Fool: His Social and Literary History*. New York: Farrar & Rinehart, 1935.

"What Comes Naturally." *Time*, 7 Nov. 1949.

Wilson, B. F. "The Mad Marxes Make for the Movies." *Motion Picture Classic*, Feb. 1928.

Woollcott, Alexander. "Shouts and Murmurs: Obituary [of Minnie Marx]." *The New Yorker*, 28 Sept. 1929.

Yates, Norris. *The American Humorists: Conscience of the Twentieth Century*. Ames: Iowa State Press, 1964.

Yanni, Nicholas. *W. C. Fields*. New York: Pyramid Publications, 1974.

You Can't Cheat an Honest Man Rev. *New York Sun*, 20 Feb. 1939. In *You Can't Cheat an Honest Man* file, Billy Rose Theatre Collection, New York Public Library at Lincoln Center.

You Can't Cheat an Honest Man Rev. *Variety*, 22 Feb. 1939.

You Can't Cheat an Honest Man Rev. *Newsweek*, 27 Feb. 1939.

Zimmerman, Paul D., and Burt Goldblatt. *The Marx Brothers at The Movies*. New York: Berkley Publishing Co., 1975.

INDEX